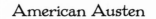

American Austen

American Austen

The Forgotten Writing of Agnes Repplier

Editor

John Lukacs

*For my dear Pamela,
con amore,
John
Dec 2011*

ISI
BOOKS

Wilmington, Delaware

Repplier, Agnes, 1855–1950.

    American Austen : the forgotten writings of Agnes Repplier / Agnes Repplier ; editor, John Lukacs. —1st ed. —Wilmington, Del. : ISI Books, c2009.

      p. ; cm.
      ISBN: 978-1-933859-86-6
      Includes bibliographical references.

      1. American literature—19th century. 2. American literature—20th century. I. Lukacs, John, 1924–. II. Title.

PS2696 .A 4 2009   2008939114
814/.4—dc22   0905

Jacket design by Sam Torode
Cover image: Agnes Repplier, Rare Book & Manuscript Library, University of Pennsylvania

ISI Books
Intercollegiate Studies Institute
3901 Centerville Road
Wilmington, DE 19807-0431
www.isibooks.org

Manufactured in the United States of America

Contents

Books & Education

On Storytelling, Writing, and the Literary Way of Life

BIOGRAPHICAL SKETCHES

Editor's Introduction*

Agnes Repplier, or the Writer in Solitude

Among the surviving photographs of Agnes Repplier there is one in which she sits, not very comfortably, fidgeting with her cup, with the looks of a retired schoolmarm, dowdy, thick-ankled, her humorless countenance topped by a black pot of a hat, or one resembling a caricature thereof. The picture is a period piece. It shows a library of a late-Victorian or an early-Edwardian kind: an entire wall constructed of ornate shelves and books, the latter mostly Collected Editions in fine bindings, a heavily sumptuous collection. Tightly framed by the shelves, a portrait of Samuel Johnson hovers over the assembly. A. Edward Newton, the host and noted book collector, is holding Miss Repplier's recently published volume (a collection of essays in praise of tea) in his left hand and a cup of tea in his other hand; he is sporting a large checked tweed suit and the expression of a large and benevolent retriever. His wife and another gentleman complete the human components of the picture. Between them stands a delicate galleried tea table, top-heavy with a very elaborate silver tea set, the entire assembly resting on a correspondingly ornate, rich Oriental carpet. By contemplating the atmosphere I can *smell* the fine dust of that carpet. And when was this picture taken? My friends look at the furnishings, the clothes, the library; they say, without much hesitation: "Nineteen-twelve." "Nineteen-oh-nine." "Nineteen-nineteen."

---

* A part of the Editor's Introduction is from *Philadelphia: Patricians and Philistines, 1900–1950* (New York: Farrar, Straus and Giroux, 85–146).

1

They are wrong. The picture was taken in November 1932. It is a period piece of a certain kind—which tells us something about Philadelphia, but not about the then celebrated author for whom this depressingly genteel tea party was given. Photographs, like phonographs, can blatantly lie. Agnes Repplier did not teach school, she was not retired, she had a great sense of humor, she was extremely witty, she was tall and long-legged. What is more important, she was not a period piece. The few literati (very few) who remember her name may think so. They are wrong.

She came into this world in the year of the Charge of the Light Brigade, and she left it the year after the hydrogen bomb; she preceded Theodore Roosevelt by four years and she survived Franklin Roosevelt by another five. When she was a child steel pens were beginning to replace quill pens, and she lived to see (if that is the word) television beginning to replace what was left of reading; the last of the Brontë sisters died the year she was born, and she outlasted James Joyce by nearly ten years. Her life was solitary, vexatious, and long.

For ninety-five years she lived in Philadelphia, this woman whose tastes and whose learning were as cosmopolitan as anything. She was utterly honest, and assertive without pretense, a rare combination. There were only three instances when she chose to alter her record. In the supreme court of her feminine conscience she decided that she was born a few years after her arrival in this world. That was her own dread decision: she liked the years 1857 and 1858 so much that they occasionally became the years of her birth. She loved France so much that France eventually became the land of her ancestry.[1] Since she was not merely a Francophile but her mind was in ways thoroughly Gallicized, was this not what counted, after all? She was not *une française malgré soi*; she was that vastly preferable kind of person, *une française à cause de soi*. In the third place (in order, though probably first in importance), she spun a veil over her unhappy childhood. She wrote about it as if it had been sufficiently sunny and reasonably secure: it wasn't so.

1. Her Repplier grandfather was Alsatian. She preferred to think of him as having come from Lorraine. Yet she refused to Frenchify the pronunciation of the family name, which was (and remains) Repplier, not Repplié.

Her father was handsome and weak; her mother was plain, strong, and intelligent. Her own qualities were compromised fatally by the fact that Mrs. Repplier, born Agnes Mathias in 1832, was a Thoroughly Modern Woman in more than one way. She hated domestic duties, and she disapproved of children, including her own. Such inclinations, widely current a century later, were luxuries then. The Reppliers were not rich. Rich parents could afford to be uninterested in their children, since they could deputize nannies and governesses and tutors and domestic servants of all kinds for the discharge of those domestic and educational responsibilities for which they themselves had no particular taste. Other children would be permanently maimed by the deliberate withholding of parental affection. Agnes was not.

She got a Spartan taste of life from the start. "My mother," Agnes told her niece many decades later, "was perfectly just, but her justice was untempered by mercy. No one loved or tried to understand me, and I think I was an interesting child, if anyone had cared enough to find out."[2] Her mother tried to force her to read, for a long time in vain. Agnes taught herself how to read at the age of ten. Before her opened a world of unexpected delights. Her reading capacity was extraordinary; it was wedded auspiciously to an astonishing memory. Well before she knew how to read she could recite alarmingly lengthy poems by heart.[3] Throughout her life she could draw on her astonishing memory with astonishing ease. She seemed to have read everything, and forgotten nothing. She would instinctively react to the resonance of words—an unusual inclination, since she was otherwise tone deaf, and her interest in music nonexistent.

When she was twelve her mother enrolled her in Eden Hall, the Convent of the Sacred Heart, in Torresdale. Liquidated exactly one hundred years later because of the temporary insanity of worldli-

---

2. Emma Repplier Witmer (Mrs. Lightner Witmer), *Agnes Repplier, a Memoir* (1957) (hereafter Witmer), 17.

3. "Until I had mastered print, my memory was abnormally retentive. There was nothing to disturb its hold. My mother taught me viva voce a quantity of English verse, sometimes simple as befitted my intelligence, sometimes meaningless, but none the less pleasant to the ear. I regret to say that I was permitted and encouraged to repeat these poems to visitors. Why they ever returned to the house I cannot imagine. Perhaps they never did." Agnes Repplier, *Eight Decades* (New York, 1937), 6.

ness that infected the nuns in charge, Eden Hall was then a singular institution: a Catholic school in America attempting to maintain the traditions of the Sacré Coeur of the Old World. From Eden Hall—a pile of a building in the middle of what was then a country estate—issued generations of unusual American women, not all of them Catholics.[4] Eden Hall was *très Sacré-Coeur*: strictly pious and hierarchical, aristocratic in aspirations and slightly brushed with snobbery, French with touches of the Second Empire, sentimental and disciplinarian, Victorian as well as classical, the regimentation of its days and the corridors of its building decorated by a statuary that was marble-cold. Wealthy parents drove out in their carriages to visit their daughters. "Energetic parents made the trip by street car and train. Mrs. Repplier, who was neither wealthy nor energetic, stayed home."[5]

Agnes Repplier, often called "Minnie" (she despised the name), occasionally "April Fool" (she was born on April 1), was not a popular child. She was a self-conscious little girl, independent, and occasionally rebellious. At the end of her second year her parents were told not to bring her back.[6] Her convent days were over. *In Our Convent Days* is the title of the memoir of those two years that she wrote more than thirty years later, dedicated to her closest friend from Eden Hall, the difficult Elizabeth Robins Pennell. It is a small hand-wrought piece, one of the finest of her writings, shot through with silver threads of delicacy and proportion: light and serious, shimmering and somber, a recollection of pieties and impieties, of young girlhood and enduring childishness, this *bonbonnière* of a book is more than a precious trinket of period recollections; it is a minor masterpiece that ought to rank with that other *fin de siècle* book of a similar milieu, Valéry Larbaud's *Fermina Marquez*. Agnes Repplier had at least as much, if not more, cause for bitterness about

---

4. "Possibly because of the recent anti-Catholic riots, it had been constructed mainly after sundown by candlelight, and the pointing wavered in perpetual sympathy with what had been the workmen's unsteady illumination." George Stewart Stokes, *Agnes Repplier* (Philadelphia, 1949) (hereafter Stokes), 20.

5. Witmer, 23.

6. She was supposed to have been caught smoking, but we cannot be sure. She was, in any event, a smoking addict during the next eighty years.

her school as the well-known English writers of the succeeding generation; she had a healthy talent for irony, and a reserve capacity of sarcasm; moreover, she had been expelled from school, an achievement of which Maugham, Greene, Orwell, Waugh, et al., could not boast. Nonetheless, she elected to spin the tale of her convent days into a fine lacy book, unweighted by sentimentality and not at all genteel. She simply chose to come to the best possible terms with her memories. She decided that her childhood had not been unhappy; and that was that.

Perhaps she knew that it is more difficult to be happy than to be unhappy, and she must have realized the silliness of Tolstoy's famous first sentence in *Anna Karenina*: "Happy families are all alike; every unhappy family is unhappy in its own way." (She never liked Tolstoy very much.)

She would have, I am certain, agreed rather with La Rochefoucauld, whom she admired: "We are seldom as happy or as unhappy as we imagine."

In that year, 1869, Miss Agnes Irwin took over the school of Miss Tazewell, victim of a properly Philadelphian nautical tragedy. (She had drowned on a boating excursion off Mount Desert Island in Maine.) Mrs. Repplier and Miss Irwin were friends. In the latter's West Penn Square Seminary for Young Ladies, Agnes Repplier was now enrolled. There, too, she was not a success. Most of the girls, less interesting than her friends in Eden Hall, snubbed her.[7] Miss Irwin appreciated her intellectual talents.[8] She also considered the consequences of Agnes's rebellious nature, concluding that they were considerable. One afternoon, Agnes, confronted with the task of reading a disagreeable book, looked straight at Miss Irwin and threw the book on the floor. That evening she met Miss Irwin on the steps of their house. She had come to visit her friend Mrs. Repplier,

---

7. Her niece: "Judging from my own later experience, a new pupil was practically certain to be asked three questions by her classmates, 'Where do you live?' 'What does your father do?' 'What church do you go to?' Depending on the answers, you were apt to be graded socially." Witmer, 28–29. Agnes's grades were low.

8. One day Miss Irwin asked her something in class. "I'm sorry," Agnes replied, "I forget."

"You have a tenacious memory," Miss Irwin said, "and you have no business forgetting anything." Stokes, 35.

a not unusual occurrence. Nothing was said. Agnes retired in peace. As she put on her coat and scarf and cap next morning, her mother stopped her. Where was she going, she asked, with an asymmetrical smile on her dark face. To school, Agnes answered—wide-eyed, serious, a little frightened perhaps. Her mother told her that she was not going to school that morning, or ever again.

There and then began the most difficult years of her life, stunted and scarred and poor. Her mother would scratch her own bitterness with diamond-hard lines on the interior window-pane of her daughter's eye. "Your daughter has strong opinions," said a guest to Mrs. Repplier. "Yes, indeed," replied the mother, "in spite of their being worthless." "One morning at the breakfast table, when Agnes was about fifteen, her mother regarded her critically and observed, 'You look like a leper who has had smallpox.' Agnes burst into tears. Her mother went on to say that it was silly to behave this way because one had a bad complexion. 'Mirabeau was ugly and pockmarked, yet he grew up to become one of the great writers of France.'"⁹ This was not the voice of the Modern Woman. It was the voice of a hard Victorian eccentric who knew talent wherever she saw it, including in her children. She turned Agnes to a career of writing, while she nearly crushed her spirit. Mrs. Repplier was not strong enough to avoid the temptations of self-pity, an indulgence the results of which can be more disastrous to those close to us than to ourselves. When she was "beaten down by life and knew she was dying, she asked Agnes' forgiveness for bringing her into so undesirable a world."¹⁰

It was an undesirable world. Agnes's adversities were oppressive. Her gentle and taciturn father lost most of his money in his business: added to the social handicaps of being German and Catholic, the Reppliers were now impecunious as well. Agnes had to live through that saddest of young experiences, moving away from a house in which many things were close and familiar. From Twentieth and Chestnut, a mildly fashionable and genteel portion of the swelling city, the Reppliers moved to Fortieth and Locust in West Philadel-

---

9. "My aunt was over eighty when she told me of this incident, but there was no emotion in her voice, neither anger nor resentment. The years had erased all passion, but the words remained fresh and indestructible." Witmer, 35.
10. Ibid.

phia.[11] She was no longer a child, but she was deeply affected by the move to this somber portion of the city, with its dusty trees, hardwood porches, Methodist respectabilities, and the waiting in the rain for the horsecars, ramshackle and crowded, nearly an hour away from the lights of central Philadelphia, with its theaters, stores, and badly lit library. What kind of life was this, composed of tiresome duties of the day, the dullness and dampness of the house, even when the sun was shining, when the depressing heat lay on West Philadelphia like a beached and breathless whale; with the vulgar decorativeness of the hydrangeas, with the dark green weediness of it all.

When the financial catastrophe overcame John George Repplier, his wife, quite reasonably, decided that her daughters would con-tribute to keeping the Repplier household afloat.[12] She was an intel-ligent woman, after all. The younger daughter (Mary) would teach. Mrs. Repplier dismissed the idea, bruited about the family earlier, that Agnes should enter a convent. Agnes should write. Agnes was barely past sixteen, but "from that very moment she was fired with both desire and need, the best of all possible goads for the artist."[13] The best of all possible goads, perhaps; but the worst of all pos-sible circumstances. The chances for an untutored and ungainly girl, plunked down in the dullest portion of dullest Philadelphia, to earn a respectable living by becoming a writer were not minimal; they were virtually nonexistent. Compared to such circumstances, the lives of Agnes's English contemporaries, of Gissing's writers in New Grub Street, struggling at the feet of the moloch of Commerce, were melodrama. Here is this gawky girl, this early caricature of a bluestocking, scratching away with her pen on the second floor of a West Philadelphia house, weighed down by the dreariest conditions of enforced domesticity, without friends, without a swain, without

11. She was born on North 11th Street. They moved to 2005 Chestnut Street when she was seven or eight, and to 4015 Locust Street when she was twenty-one.
12. The youngest son, John (for whom his mother seemed to have cherished a, for her, unusual affection), a handsome and preternaturally clever child, perished of the croup at the age of four. Another son, Louis, afflicted by partial paralysis, would remain the burdensome responsibility of his sisters until his death at the age of seventy-five.
13. Stokes, 47.

any knowledge of the world. During the most formative years of her life, her imagination is not nourished by any kind of experience. It is no less powerful for that. It is nourished by books, by the best of books.

The American newspaper, then even more than now, had some of the characteristics of a magazine. It needed "fillers": sketches, odd pieces of information, stories of all kinds. Thousands of now forgotten scribblers, housewives and clerks, filled these gaps for a few dollars. Few of them aspired to much more. Agnes did. As her niece wrote eighty years afterward: "She had abandoned many early hopes, only to cling with increasing tenacity to one dominant ambition—to become a writer of distinction."[14] In 1937, when she was more than eighty years old, she wrote about herself in this autobiographical fragment:

> *1877.* I am twenty years old, and I have begun to write. It is the only thing in the world that I can do, and the urge is strong. Naturally I have nothing to say, but I have spent ten years in learning to say that nothing tolerably well. Every sentence is a matter of supreme importance to me. I need hardly confess that I am writing stories—stories for children, stories for adults. They get themselves published somewhere, somehow, and bring in a little money. Otherwise they would have no excuse for being; a depressing circumstance of which I am well aware.[15]

For seven years more she wrote and wrote, for seven years that were as lean as any. Her mother died. She had to take care of her old and sick father and her paralytic brother. She struggled on in the night. She was getting closer and closer to the summit of her talent, though she did not know this. In July 1884 a very important thing happened. She met Father Isaac Hecker, a German-American priest of some renown, a compassionate and cultured man who was the founder of the Paulist order and of the *Catholic World* magazine. He had been publishing some of Agnes Repplier's stories.

---

14. Witmer, 7.
15. *Eight Decades*, 9.

Father Hecker told me that my stories were mechanical, and gave no indication of being transcripts from life. "I fancy," he said, "that you know more about books than you do about life, that you are more a reader than an observer. What author do you read the most?"

I told him "Ruskin," an answer which nine out of ten studious girls would have given at that date.

"Then," said he, "write me something about Ruskin, and make it brief."

That essay turned my feet into the path which I have trodden laboriously ever since.[16]

This was that rare thing of perfect advice perfectly accepted and carried out. Less than two years later Agnes Repplier reached the summit of her ambitions. The *Atlantic Monthly* would publish her essay.[17] Its editor, Thomas Bailey Aldrich, saw that he was in the presence of a writer of talent.

She was invited to Boston to meet the Aereopagus of American intellect, the circle of Lowell, Holmes, et al. Against all odds (and what odds!) Agnes Repplier achieved what she wanted. Her talent was now public. The pattern of her future was set.

She was thirty-one years old, tall, with a serious mien, no longer very young. How acutely, how permanently, she was aware of that! In 1937, when she was eighty-two, she recounted her crucial conversation with Father Hecker, an account every word of which rings true. There is, however, one white lie. She wrote that this meeting had taken place in 1877. It occurred in 1884. Add to this the two years that she customarily deducted from her age, as in this account in *Eight Decades,* when she writes about herself as "a girl of twenty" in 1877. The crucial interview with this good Father Hecker happened not when she was twenty but when she was rising thirty, past the twenty-ninth birthday of her life. Even at the age of eighty-two she wanted to direct minds away from the stunting sadness of those struggling solitary years. She wanted to give the impression of a

16. Quoted by Stokes, 59.
17. April 1886: "Children, Past and Present."

young girl, succeeding in literature not merely through her gifts but with the help of great good luck. She dreaded giving the impression that her eventual success was the result of her perseverance: the world might think that she was married to books because no man had wanted her when she was marriageable and young. She had been in love with her half-brother, and perhaps also with a cousin.[18] She liked the company of men, she knew how to flirt, she was sensitive to male flattery; while she was not beautiful, she was not in the least unattractive; but the pattern was set; she would remain a maiden woman for the rest of her long life.

The pattern was set: her first publication in the *Atlantic* brought her a kind of renown that would not cease for the next fifty years. Every man and woman of letters in the English-speaking world learned her name. Within four years of her first publication in the *Atlantic*, Gosse and Saintsbury wrote her complimentary letters. Awards, medals, honorary doctorates came to her in succession. She was the dean of American essayists.[19] Even in her own "dull, tepid" Philadelphia she was discovered. She became a cherished friend and the pride of some of the best patrician houses. She was eighty-one when Ellery Sedgwick, then editor of the *Atlantic*, wrote:

> For two full generations Miss Agnes Repplier has not ceased to be a bright and finished ornament of American letters. Who matches her in craftsmanship? Who excels her in discipline, in the honest withholding of praise, or in its just bestowal? She is the inheritor

18. Agnes's father had two sons from his first marriage. At the age of sixteen George Repplier ran away from home, where his stepmother had been cold and hostile to him. He fled to South America. Fifteen years later he returned to Philadelphia. He asked his father to come to his wedding in Savannah, where he was about to marry a divorced woman in a civil ceremony. The plan was torpedoed by his stepmother, and the link between the two families was broken. Thirteen years later Agnes, "immediately after her mother's death, and while still in deep mourning . . . appeared suddenly and without warning in my parents' home in New York. Her purpose was to make peace and offer amity, and the success of her mission brought to me, a little girl of five, the rarest of gifts, her life-long friendship and love." Witmer, 35.

19. "The chair of the American Essay is in Philadelphia, on Clinton Street in the old city. It has been gloriously occupied for forty years by Agnes Repplier who is at present denied the title of professor emeritus, even though she were ready for it, since there is no worthy successor." Mary Ellen Chase, "The Dean of American Essayists," *Commonweal*, August 18, 1933.

of a more ancient excellence than ours, and among Americans she has become a sort of contemporary ancestor, a summation of the best that has gone before. . . .[20]

Few American writers received, or deserved, this kind of encomium.

The pattern was set, by her talent and by her sense of duty. She was compelled to live with her older sister and with her half-paralyzed brother, in modest circumstances, without domestic help.[21] They took their meals in a small residential hotel in the neighborhood, including breakfast: perhaps the most depressing of their meals, as the three of them sat hardly saying a word. Wilde, whose work she admired, said that he put all his art into his life. Agnes Repplier, whose wit and learning and whose appreciation for the finer things in life were comparable to Wilde's, subordinated her life to her art. Returning from those silent breakfasts through the dreary emptiness of city streets (the streets of American cities do not shine in the morning), she would hasten toward her room. When she was younger she took refuge in books. Now she would escape to her work. Her cat would perch on the chair, or on the far edge of her writing table. She would take up her pen; and in her large, curious, stilted handwriting the words were beginning to form.[22]

She kept up her work for sixty-five years: more than two dozen books, perhaps as many as four hundred essays. The books are now difficult to find, not very attractive in their looks: dun little Quakerish books in gray covers.[23] (A handsome exception is *Eight Decades,*

---

20. Stokes, 217–18.

21. "In different ways, though proud of her achievements, the sister and brother resented her constant engagements and growing fame. These three ill-assorted characters . . ." Witmer, 118. Agnes to Harrison Morris: "'The Reppliers,' like the Jameses or the Robinsons, sets my teeth on edge."

22. To Harrison Morris: "I can only work in the morning and for three or four hours. Then I grow tired and stupid. The pleasure is gone, and I have to stop. So I don't accomplish a great deal, try as I may. Neither do I work with ease, but with infinite painstaking." Stokes, 116.

23. Houghton Mifflin, her first publisher, was uninspired and niggardly with her first collection of essays (Books and Men: a singularly dull title) in 1888; Miss Repplier had to pay some of the costs of the first printing. In October 1888 she wrote: "My copies of the essays have just arrived: neat quakerish little books with an air of deprecating modesty

printed in 1937, her own selection of her best, and probably the best introduction to her prose.)

She was a superb craftsman. "Every misused word," she wrote, "revenges itself forever upon a writer's reputation."[24] She knew the value of words: "For every sentence that may be penned or spoken the right words exist."[25] She rose above the not inconsiderable accomplishments of a linguistic precisionist; she was sufficiently strong-minded to improve upon Shelley. ("For the mind in creation is as a fading coal, which some invisible influence, like an inconstant wind, awakens to transitory brightness.") Agnes Repplier: "The substitution of the word 'glow' for 'brightness' would, I think, make this sentence extremely beautiful."[26]

Words are not mere instruments of precision. They ought to convey delight. "'The race of delight is short, and pleasures have mutable faces.' Such sentences, woven with curious skill from the rich fabric of seventeenth-century English, defy the wreckage of time."[27] The history of mankind is the history of mind; and the history of mind is the history of speech: "How is it that, while Dr. Johnson's sledgehammer repartees sound like the sonorous echoes of a past age, Voltaire's remarks always appear to have been spoken the day before yesterday?"[28] She was one of those writers who have a special affinity for the mysterious evocative power of names: "It took a great genius to enliven the hideous picture of Dotheboys Hall with the appropriate and immortal Fanny, whom we could never have borne to lose. It took a great genius to evolve from nothingness the name 'Morleena Kenwigs.' So perfect a result, achieved from a mere combination of letters, confers distinction on the English alphabet."[29]

---

about them that forcibly suggests the most remote corner of the bookseller's shelf. I can see them already shrinking bashfully into their appointed nooks and powdering their little gray heads with the dust of the undisturbed." Reprintings followed swiftly. Her diffidence was unwarranted.

24. Agnes Repplier, *Points of Friction* (1920), 93.
25. Agnes Repplier, *Essays in Idleness* (1893), 115.
26. Ibid., 117.
27. Ibid., 116.
28. Ibid., 94–95. "Dr Johnson," she wrote elsewhere, "whose name is a tonic for the morally debilitated . . ." *Points of Friction*, 217.
29. *Points of Friction*, 154–55.

Her own descriptions were no mere combinations of adjectives. Besides her *mots justes* there was, often unexpected, evidence of her own preferences. She was Catholic; she loved Spain; but she was no Hispanomaniac. Here is a great phrase: "The Escorial," she writes, "is Philip, it is stamped with his somber, repellent, kingly personality."[30] Three perfect words: compressed and jeweled expressions of a lifetime of historical thinking.

She read everything; indeed, what she reread would be sufficient unto a department of English in our colleges now.[31] One of the most attractive features of her writing is its unpredictability: neither frivolous nor impulsive, it sprang from the independence of her spacious mind. Of the fifty years in English letters that preceded the death of Byron she knew just about everything that is worth knowing. She sometimes regretted that she had not lived during that "happy half-century"[32] of "sunlit mediocrity"; yet writing about it, she remained as clear-eyed as ever: she took great pleasure in pointing a descriptive, a definite finger on the inane writings and opinions of that period—indeed, of any period.[33] Accepted opin-

---

30. Witmer, 88.

31. "But of what earthly good or pleasure is a book which is read only once? It is like an acquaintance whom one never meets again, or a picture never seen a second time." *Eight Decades*, 5.

32. "For myself, I confess that the last twenty-five years of the eighteenth century and the first twenty-five years of the nineteenth make up my chosen period, and that my motive for so choosing is contemptible. It was not a time distinguished—in England at least—for wit and wisdom, for public virtues or for private charm; but it was a time when literary reputations were so cheaply gained that nobody needed to despair of one." Agnes Repplier, *A Happy Half-Century, and Other Essays* (Boston, 1908), 1–2. "Like the fabled Caliph who stood by the Sultan's throne, translating the flowers of Persian speech into comprehensible and unflattering truths, so Dr. Johnson stands undeceived in this pleasant half-century of pretence, translating its ornate nonsense into language we can too readily understand. "But how comfortable and how comforting the pretence must have been, and how kindly tolerant all the pretenders were to one another! If, in those happy days, you wrote an essay on 'The Harmony of Numbers and Versification,' you unhesitatingly asked your friends to come and have it read aloud to them: and your friends—instead of leaving town next day—came, and listened, and called it a 'Miltonic evening.'" Ibid., 11–12.

33. Writing about the inane Mrs. Chapone, an English educationist during the "happy half-century": "A firm insistence upon admitted truths, a loving presentation of the obvious, a generous championship of those sweet commonplaces we all deem dignified and safe . . ." Ibid., 122. Elsewhere: "Alas for those who succeed, as Montaigne observed,

ions! *Idées reçues!* They got what they deserved: an impatient but precise sweep of her verbal broom, leaving an elegant pattern on the museum floor, with an upward swirl in accord with the very tone of English speech. In a private letter about Alma-Tadema, whom she met in London: "a kind, self-satisfied man, who told venerable stories all wrong."[34] When in Boston James Russell Lowell descended from upstairs to take her coat, the ladies oohed and aahed. She did not. Why, oh why, Lowell asked her, did people in Philadelphia call Whitman the good gray poet. "I dare say," the great Boston panjandrum growled, "nobody calls me the good, gray poet, though I am as gray as Whitman and quite as good—perhaps a trifle better." "He paused," Agnes adds to a friend, "and I was on the point of saying, 'Then there is only the poet to consider,' but I forbore."[35] Yet she was not an indiscriminate admirer of Whitman: "The medium employed by Walt Whitman, at times rhythmic and cadenced, at times ungirt and sagging loosely, enabled him to write passages of sustained beauty, passages grandly conceived and felicitously rendered. It also permitted him a riotous and somewhat monotonous excess."[36] A bearded sage whom she profoundly disliked was Tolstoy, who, perhaps "with the noblest intentions, made many a light step heavy, and many a gay heart sad." She greatly preferred Wilde, at a time when such preference was not fashionable, especially in America. About Lytton Strachey's principal shortcoming she was unerring: "the amazing and unconcerned inaccuracies of the modern biographer" (and perhaps about Virginia Woolf, too: "thin" and "self-conscious").[37]

She was Catholic: in England she found Canterbury Cathedral "an empty shell inside. The shrine of the Saint has vanished, and his very bones were burned by that brute, Henry VIII. A chattering

---

in giving to their harmless opinions a false air of importance." Agnes Repplier, *Points of View* (Boston, 1891), 99.

34. Witmer, 77.

35. Ibid., 49.

36. *Points of Friction*, 93. She had gone to Camden with her friend Harrison Morris. Whitman was rather dirty and offered his guests whiskey in a tooth mug. His own diary does not improve upon this impression: "My friend, Harrison Morris, brought Agnes Repplier, a nice young critter, to see me." Ibid., 101.

37. Ibid., 252, 248.

verger leads scores of scattering tourists over the level marble floor, once the holiest spot in England."[38] Yet she had none of the sentimentalities of the Chesterbelloc type: when she spent a Holy Week in Rome, "the processions were scrubby little affairs."[39]

She saw it her duty to point out the shortcomings of popular idols as well as of popular ideas. "The fact that Miss [Helen] Keller has overcome the heavy disabilities which nature placed in her path, lends interest to her person, but no weight to her opinions, which give evidence of having been adopted wholesale, and of having never filtered through any reasoning process of her own."[40] She saw through the superficialities of Victorian as well as of post-Victorian sentimentalities. "When we permit ourselves to sneer at Victorian hypocrisies," she wrote, "we allude, as a rule, to the superficial observance of religious practices, and to the artificial reticence concerning illicit sexual relations. The former affected life more than it did literature; the latter affected literature more than it did life."[41] She admired Thackeray: "The world is not nearly so simple a place as the sexualists seem to consider it. To the author of *Vanity Fair* it was not simple at all." Yet her ire rose when "Trollope unhesitatingly and proudly claimed for himself the quality of harmlessness. 'I do believe,' he said, 'that no girl has risen from the reading of my pages less modest than she was before, and that some girls may have learned from that that modesty is a charm worth possessing.'"

"This," Agnes adds, "is one of the admirable sentiments which should have been left unspoken. It is a true word as far as it goes, but more suggestive of *Little Women*, or *A Summer in Leslie Goldthwaite's Life*, than of those virile, varied, and animated novels which make no appeal to immaturity."[42] She had a great admiration for

---

38. Ibid., 146.

39. *Eight Decades*, 861. Still, on another occasion she wrote that "the Englishman who complained that he could not look out of his window in Rome without seeing the sun, had a legitimate grievance (we all know what it is to sigh for grey skies, and for the unutterable rest they bring); but if we want Rome, we must take her sunshine, along with her fleas and her Church. Accepted philosophically, they need not mar our infinite content."

40. Agnes Repplier, *Counter-Currents* (1916), 281.

41. *Points of Friction*, 150.

42. Ibid., 158–59. She may have meant Dickens: "Readers of Dickens (which ought to

male virtues, including martial ones; she took a romantic delight in beholding certain warriors. She quoted Ruskin: "All healthy men like fighting and like the sense of danger; all brave women like to hear of their fighting and of their facing danger": *but* then she flew at Ruskin, "who has taken upon himself the defense of war in his own irresistibly unconvincing manner."[43] She spared not Carlyle, "whose misdeeds, like those of Browning, are matters of pure volition," and who is "pleased, for our sharper discipline, to write 'like a comet inscribing with his tail.' No man uses words more admirably, or abuses them more shamefully, than Carlyle."[44] Like Carlyle, Meredith could be tiresome. When "he is pleased to tell us that one of his characters 'neighed a laugh,' that another 'tolled her naughty head,' that a third 'stamped: her aspect spat,' and that a fourth was discovered 'pluming a smile upon his succulent mouth,' we cannot smother a dawning suspicion that he is diverting himself at our expense, and pluming a smile of his own, more sapless than succulent, over the naïve simplicity of the public."[45] Her admirations were never undiscriminating: Sir Walter Scott "always shook hands with his young couples on their wedding-day, and left them to pull through as best they could. Their courtships and their marriages interested him less than other things he wanted to write about—sieges and tournaments, criminal trials, and sour Scottish saints."

The sour Scottish saints of Scott!

"When we read, for instance, of Lady Cathcart being kept a close prisoner by her husband for over twenty years, we look with some complacency on the roving wives of the nineteenth century. When we reflect on the dismal fate of Uriel Freudenberger, condemned by the Canton of Uri to be burnt alive in 1760, for rashly proclaiming his disbelief in the legend of William Tell's apple, we realize the inconveniences attendant on a too early development of the critical faculty." This kind of wit, taken from the first paragraph of her first book, was her hallmark: polished and dry, it has none of the upstag-

---

mean all men and women who mastered the English alphabet) . . ." *Happy Half-Century*, 217.

43. *Essays in Idleness*, 85.

44. Ibid., 120.

45. Agnes Repplier, *Compromises* (Boston and New York, 1904), 50.

ing one-liner characteristics of much of American humor. How many pearly sentences rolled off her pen, to vanish unremarked! They were too fine for many of her readers, as was often the wittiness of her conversation. In Philadelphia, perhaps especially among her fellow Catholics, she suffered often from the reputation of being a "cynic," from the age-old habit of people finding themselves ill at ease in the presence of unaccustomed opinions, dubbing them "cynical" even when, in reality, the speaker is far more of an idealist than are her unwitting listeners. "We can with tranquility forgive in ourselves the sins of which no one accuses us," she once wrote.[46] This is emphatically not the voice of a cynic—rather the contrary.

"Wit," she said, "is the salt of conversation, not the food, and few things in the world are more wearying than a sarcastic attitude towards life."[47] A man should live within his wits as well as within his income: she liked this Chesterfieldian maxim. Her wit was never forced. Since it came to her naturally, it had none of the marks of effect-writing, none of the absurd, surrealistic, oxymoronic verbal juxtapositions so typical of present-day American humor. Her wit was all intertwined with her learning. Madame de Montolieu was a, now justly forgotten, French sentimentalist novel writer, the author of *Caroline de Litchfield*. Her equally witless English admirer, a Miss Seward, wrote that "the merits of graces" of Madame de Montolieu's volumes were due to their author's "transition from incompetence to the comforts of wealth; from the unprotected dependence of waning virginity to the social pleasures of wedded friendship." "In plain words," Agnes Repplier adds:

> we are given to understand that a rich and elderly German widower read the book, sought an acquaintance with the writer, and married her. "Hymen," exclaims Miss Seward, "passed by the fane of Cytherea and the shrine of Plutus, to light his torch at the altar of genius"—which beautiful burst of eloquence makes it painful to add the chilling truth, and say that *Caroline de Litchfield* was written six years after its author's marriage with M. de Montolieu, who was a Swiss, and her second husband. She espoused the

---

46. *Happy Half-Century*, 176.
47. *Essays in Idleness*, 181.

first, M. de Crousaz, when she was eighteen, and still comfortably remote from the terrors of waning virginity. Accurate information was not, however, a distinguishing characteristic of the day. Sir Walter Scott, writing some years later of Madame de Montolieu, ignores both marriages altogether, and calls her Mademoiselle.[48]

She carried her learning as lightly as her wit. "Erudition," she said, "like a bloodhound, is a charming thing when held firmly in leash, but it is not so attractive when turned loose upon a defenseless and unerudite public."[49] What she (like Wilde) held principally against the Victorians was their deadening seriousness. She asked herself, in 1890, "whether the dismal seriousness of the present day was going to last forever."[50] "Humor would at all times have been the poorest excuse to offer to Miss Brontë for any form of moral dereliction, for it was the one quality she lacked herself, and failed to tolerate in others."[51] She could not stomach the Brownings. "It is hard to tell what people really prize. Heine begged for a button from George Sand's trousers, and who shall say whether enthusiasm or malice prompted the request."[52] She admired the essentially aristocratic virtue of gaiety: "Cheerfulness and melancholy can be, and usually are, equally odious; but a sad heart and a gay temper hold us in thrall."[53] She could achieve a felicitous alliance of common sense with wit: "Poetry weds King Cophetua to a beggar maid, and smilingly retires from any further contemplation of the catastrophe."[54]

48. *Happy Half-Century*, 79–80. I know but one example (a not altogether incontestable one) in which Miss Agnes allowed herself a touch of earthly humor. She was writing about the monumentally silly Mrs. Barbauld, another female educationist of the eighteenth century. "This pregnant sentence . . . occurs in a chapter of advice to young girls: 'An ass is much better adapted than a horse to show off a young lady.'" Ibid., 5.
49. In the superb essay "Books That Have Hindered Me," *Points of View*, 71. Also: ". . . if the experience of mankind teaches anything, it is that vital convictions are not at the mercy of eloquence." *Eight Decades*, 267.
50. *Points of View*, 1.
51. Ibid., 8.
52. Agnes Repplier, *Americans and Others* (Boston and New York, 1912), 245–46.
53. *Eight Decades*, 62–63.
54. *Compromises*, 55. "The Cardinal de Rohan had all his kitchen utensils of solid sliver, which must have given as much satisfaction to his cooks as did Nero's golden fishing-hooks to the fish he caught with them," Agnes Repplier, *In the Dozy Hours, and Other*

She once "saw a small black-and-white kitten playing with a judge who, not unnaturally, conceived that he was playing with the kitten."[55]

Humor is a mark of maturity: it "is seldom, to the childish mind, a desirable element of poetry."[56] In national life it "illuminates those crowded corners which history leaves obscure."[57] This view of humor accorded entirely with her *persona,* and with her style of expression. She was a prose writer, steeped in the French tradition of letters, and thoroughly urban.

She was urban, urbane, cosmopolitan in the literal sense of these words. Philadelphia was not much like Dr. Johnson's London; but, like Dr. Johnson—and probably even more like all true Parisians of her own time—she found little of life that was worth living outside a city. In one of her acutest essays, "Town and Suburb," written during the 1920s, she saw clearly what the abandonment of the city meant: the abandonment of civilizational, even more than civic, responsibilities by the very class of citizens upon whose support, and cultivation, urbane life in America had to depend. "Suburbanites are traitors to the city." As in many of her essays, sixty years of distance has not dimmed the acuity of her insights, often prophetic ones. "The present quarrel is not even between Nature and man, between the town and the country. It is between the town and the suburb, that midway habitation which fringes every American city, and which is imposing or squalid according to the incomes of the suburbanites."[58] Much of this was the result of the adolescent national mania for automobiles, and of their sanctimonious spokesman, Henry Ford, for example, whom she could never stand and who has "added the trying role of prophet to his other avocations." Her preferences for city life were not merely those of practical convenience, and she had little time for the pious preachings of nature lovers: ". . . it is hardly worth while to speak of city life as entail-

---

Papers (Boston and New York, 1894), 117.
55. *Eight Decades,* 302.
56. *Essays in Idleness,* 42.
57. *In the Dozy Hours,* 95.
58. *Eight Decades,* 106.

ing 'spiritual loss,' because it is out of touch with Nature.[59] It is in touch with humanity, and humanity is Nature's heaviest asset."[60] She cited Santayana, her favorite American philosopher, who also prized "civilization, being bred in towns, and liking to hear and see what new things people are up to."[61]

Her independence of mind, her love of conversation, were as French as they were English. ("It is not what we learn in conversation that enriches us. It is the elation that comes of swift contact with tingling currents of thought. It is the opening of our mental pores, and the stimulus of marshaling our ideas in words, of setting them forth as gallantly and as graciously as we can.")[62] Yet the often endless volubility of Parisian talk was not for her; her love for the English temper of speech defined her prosody as well as her rhetoric: "If everybody floated with the tide of talk, placidity would soon end in stagnation. It is the strong backward stroke which stirs the ripples, and gives animation and variety."[63] She minded not a certain kind of restraint: "a habit of sparing speech, not the muffled stillness of genuine and hopeless incapacity."[64] When Henry James came to Philadelphia in 1904, Agnes Repplier was asked to introduce him. The lecture was a muffled disaster, James mumbling for an hour and shuffling his papers. The introduction was a small triumph: perfectly minted, witty, engaging, modest, and short.[65]

---

59. Even so, these lines penned more than fifty years ago ring ever more true: "Professional men, doctors and dentists especially, delight in living in the suburbs, so that those who need their services cannot reach them. The doctor escapes from his patients, who may fall ill on Saturday, and die on Sunday, without troubling him. The dentist is happy in that he can play golf all Saturday and Sunday while his patients agonize in town. Only the undertaker, man's final servitor, stands staunchly by his guns." *Eight Decades*, 118.

60. Ibid., 105. "They talk with serious fervour about Nature, when the whole of their landed estate is less than one of the back yards in which the town dwellers of my youth grew giant rosebushes that bloomed brilliantly in the mild city air." Ibid.,109.

61. Ibid., 103. But William Penn said: "The country life is to be preferred, for there we see the works of God, but in cities little else than the works of men." (*Reflexions and Maxims*, no. 220).

62. *Compromises*, 5.

63. Ibid., 7.

64. Ibid., 6.

65. James wrote to Gosse that he liked Agnes Repplier for her "bravery and (almost) brilliancy." Around that time she wrote in her essay on conversation: "We realize how far the spirit of lecture had intruded upon the spirit of conversation forty years ago, when Mr.

Delighted as she was with the music of words, immense as was her mnemonic genius for verse, she was essentially a prose writer. Her one collection of verse, including her introduction to it,[66] belongs to that very small minority of her writings that has a musty and dated touch, and which is rather late-Victorian in its limitations. Her inclination for the fine-turned phrase was at least as French as it was English; she liked paradox, and expression that was elegant and sharp, rather than blunt or muted by suggestiveness. "When Voltaire sighed, 'Nothing is so disagreeable as to be obscurely hanged,' he gave utterance to a national sentiment, which is not in the least witty, but profoundly humorous, revealing with charming distinctness a Frenchman's innate aversion to all dull and commonplace surroundings."[67] "It is bad enough to be bad, but to be bad in bad taste is unpardonable."[68] She preferred the qualities of French lyric expression: "The delicacy of the sentiment is unmatched in English song. The Saxon can be profoundly sad, and he can—or at least he could—be ringingly and recklessly gay; but the mood which is neither sad nor gay, which is fed by refined emotions, and tranquilized by time's subduing touch, has been expressed oftener and better in France."[69]

She was a *moraliste* in the French tradition—something different from what "moralist" in English means. She liked Sainte-Beuve ("I always tremble when I see a philosophical idea attached to a novel"); and Sainte-Beuve "was spared by the kindly hand of death from the sight of countless novels attached to philosophical ideas."[70] Philosophical ideas were one thing, the need for discrimination quite another. "There is no measure to the credulity of the average semi-educated man when confronted by a printed page (print carries such authority in his eyes), and with rows of figures, all showing conclusively that two and two make three, and that with

---

Bagehot admitted that, with good modern talkers, 'the effect seems to be produced by that which is stated, and not by the manner in which it is stated'—a reversal of ancient rules." *Compromises*, 4.

66. *A Book of Famous Verse* (Boston, 1892), edited by Agnes Repplier.

67. *Essays in Idleness*, 186.

68. Points of Friction, 73–74.

69. *Compromises*, 166.

70. *Points of View*, 117.

economy and good management they can be reduced to one and a half. He has never mastered, and apparently will never master, the exact shade of difference between a statement and a fact."[71] Sentimentalist nonsense, whether in literature or in education, made her angry. "The assumption that children should never be coerced into self-control, and never confronted with difficulties, makes for failure of nerve. . . . The assumption that young people should never be burdened with responsibilities, and never, under any stress of circumstances, be deprived of the pleasures which are no longer a privilege, but their sacred and inalienable right, makes for failure of nerve. The assumption that married women are justified in abandoning their domestic duties, because they cannot stand the strain of home life and housekeeping, makes for failure of nerve. . . . The assumption that religion should content itself with persuasiveness, and that morality should be sparing in its demands, makes for failure of nerve."[72]

She was intellectual; but she knew the limitations of the intellect. "The clear-sighted do not rule the world, but they sustain and console it. It is not in human nature to be led by intelligence. An intelligent world would not be what it is today: it would never have been what it has been in every epoch of which we have any knowledge."[73] She—a rarity among women writers, this—had a very strong, a deep knowledge of history. Her *Philadelphia: The Place and the People* (which she wrote in 1898 upon a publisher's suggestion) remains to this day the most readable history of her native city. Her often superbly detached and witty style of writing; her strong, and instinctively intelligent, judgments are complemented by her talented evocation of atmosphere, and by her interest in all kinds of details of social and of everyday life: the *petits faits* dear to Taine and to some of the best historians of the twentieth century. (In this respect, too, Agnes Repplier proved herself to be a "threshold" writer: standing firm on what was best in the standards of the nineteenth as well as of the twentieth century.) The book suffers from a certain lack of proportion: three-fourths of it deals with the

71. *Americans and Others*, 160.
72. *Compromises*, 39–40.
73. Ibid., 145.

eighteenth century, and hardly more than one-eighth of it with the nineteenth; she may have become somewhat bored with her task, even though the writing of the last chapters surely matches that of the earlier ones.[74] Agnes Repplier belonged to the tradition that considered history to be the narrated past, a form of high literature, and her histories are none the worse for it, to say the least; but she understood history well enough to know in her bones that history was more than that, too: not only a form of literature, but also a form of thought.

> The mediæval chroniclers listened rapturously to the clamor of battle, and found all else but war too trivial for their pens. The modern scholar produces that pitiless array of facts known as constitutional history; and labors under the strange delusion that acts of Parliament, or acts of Congress, reform bills, and political pamphlets represent his country's life. If this sordid devotion to the concrete suffers no abatement, the intelligent reader of the future will be compelled to reconstruct the nineteenth century from the pages of *Punch* and *Life,* from faded playbills, the records of the race-track, and the inextinguishable echo of dead laughter.[75]

She wrote this in 1893. Eighty-seven years later this historian, after a lifetime of studying the character of modern history and the requisites of modern history writing, can but lift his imaginary plumed hat and shout: "Brava!"

---

74. Example: "Judge Peters enjoyed an enviable reputation as a wit, and some of his pleasantries have come floating down to us in cold unsympathetic print, illustrating, as a captious biographer expresses it, 'the great difference between hearing a joke and reading one.' The Indians, whose councils he occasionally attended, and who are not a humorous race, christened him the Talking Bird. It is a pity ever to waste wit upon Indians." Agnes Repplier, *Philadelphia: The Place and the People* (New York, 1898), 163. She could write with wit and detachment about the saddest of events in her native city, the anti-Catholic Know-Nothing riots of the 1840s: "They stretched ropes across the darkening streets to obstruct the passage of the cavalry. It was picturesque, and exceedingly like Perugia in the Middle Ages, when the Baglioni and their rivals fought in the great square of the Cathedral; but it was not at all like Penn's City of Peace, which he had founded as an asylum of the oppressed, where no sword was to be drawn, and no man persecuted for his creed." Ibid., 353.

75. *Life*: a literary and humorous magazine, not the picture magazine of the mid-twentieth century.

"The neglect of history," she wrote more than sixty years ago, "practised by educators who would escape its authority, stands responsible for much mental confusion." "I used to think that ignorance of history meant only a lack of cultivation and a loss of pleasure. Now I am sure that such ignorance impairs our judgment by impairing our understanding, by depriving us of standards, or the power to contrast, and the right to estimate."[76] "In the remote years of my childhood," she wrote, "the current events, that most interesting and valuable form of tuition which, nevertheless, is unintelligible without some knowledge of the past, was left out of our limited curriculum. We seldom read the newspapers (which I remember as of an appalling dullness), and we knew little of what was happening in our day. But we did study history, and we knew something of what had happened in other days than ours; we knew and deeply cared."[77]

History is the best fare for one's imagination; it also provides for a thoughtful conservatism whose absence, especially in America, she regretted.[78] "Political conservatism may be a lost cause in modern democracy; but temperamental conservatism dates from the birth of man's reasoning powers, and will survive the clamour and chaos of revolutions."[79] For "innovations to which we are not committed are illuminating things."[80] "The reformer whose heart is in the right place, but whose head is elsewhere, represents a waste of force. . . ."[81] "It is well that the past yields some solace to the temperamental conservative, for the present is his only on terms he cannot easily fulfill. His reasonable doubts and his unreasonable prejudices block the path of

76. *Points of Friction*, 7, 10. "We can know nothing of any nation unless we know its history."

77. "It was not possible for a child who had lived in spirit with Saint Geneviève to be indifferent to the siege of Paris in 1870. It is not possible for a child who has lived in spirit with Jeanne d'Arc to be indifferent to the destruction of Rheims Cathedral in 1914," *Points of Friction*, 25–26.

78. ". . . even a conservative American, if such anomaly exists . . ." *In the Dozy Hours*, 101.

79. *Points of Friction*, 102.

80. Ibid., 99.

81. *Counter-Currents*, 32. "A moderate knowledge of history—which, though discouraging, is also enlightening—might prove serviceable to all the enthusiasts who are engaged in making over the world. Many of them (in this country, at least) talk and write as if nothing in particular had happened between the Deluge and the Civil War." Ibid., 21.

contentment. He is powerless to believe a thing because it is an eminently desirable thing to believe. He is powerless to deny the existence of facts he does not like. He is powerless to credit new systems
with finality. The sanguine assurance that men and nations can be
legislated into goodness, that pressure from without is equivalent to
a moral change within, needs a strong backing of inexperience. 'The
will,' says Francis Thompson, 'is the lynch-pin of the faculties.' We
stand or fall by its strength or its infirmity."[82]

> To cheat ourselves intellectually that we may save ourselves spiri-
> tually is unworthy of the creature that man is meant to be.
> And to what end! Things are as they are, and no amount of
> self-deception makes them otherwise. The friend who is incapa-
> ble of depression depresses us as surely as the friend who is inca-
> pable of boredom bores us. Somewhere in our hearts is a strong,
> though dimly understood, desire to face realities, and to measure
> consequences, to have done with the fatigue of pretending. it is
> not optimism to enjoy the view when one is treed by a bull; it is
> philosophy. The optimist would say that being treed was a valu-
> able experience. The disciple of gladness would say that it was
> a pleasurable sensation. The Christian Scientist would say there
> was no bull, though remaining—if he were wise—on the treetop.
> The philosopher would make the best of a bad job, and seek what
> compensation he could find. He is of a class apart.[83]

"Human experience," she wrote during the First World War, "is
very, very old. It is our sure monitor, our safest guide. To ignore it
crudely is the error of those ardent but uninstructed missionaries
who have lightly undertaken the re-building of the social world."[84]
She belonged to the rare company of realistic idealists, whose
knowledge of history and whose self-knowledge go hand in hand—
which provided her with the necessary balance in perceiving, and
describing, people and places and scenes to which she would be otherwise sentimentally inclined. "Touraine," she once wrote, "is full

---

82. *Points of Friction*, 97–98.
83. Ibid., 122–23.
84. *Counter-Currents*, 137. "Great events, however lamentable, must be looked at greatly."
Ibid., 105.

of beauty, and steeped to the lips in historic crimes."[85] This kind of demanding realism was part of her religion: "It was Cardinal Newman who first entered a protest against 'minced' saints, against the pious and popular custom of chopping up human records into lessons for the devout. He took exception to the hagiological license which assigns lofty motives to trivial actions."[86]

She was a *moraliste,* not a Puritan. She believed in the virtues of cultivating human self-discipline; but also in the virtue of cultivating human pleasure. In 1890 she wrote: "Why should the word 'pleasure,' when used in connection with literature, send a cold chill down our strenuous nineteenth century spines? It is a good and charming word, caressing in sound and softly exhilarating in sense."[87] Also: "Joy is a delightful, flashing little word, as brief as is the emotion it conveys."[88] And about an emotion: ". . . when a happy moment, complete and rounded as a pearl, falls into the tossing ocean of life, it is never wholly lost."[89] Her taste for pleasure was as fine as it was strong. In her essay on Horace, she wrote, about his retreat in the country, that it was "what was then called the simple life; but, as compared with the crude and elemental thing which goes by that name in this our land today, it is recognizable as the austere luxury of a very cultivated poet."[90] She generally despised preaching, especially Puritan preaching. "'Christ died for a select company that was known to Him, by name, from eternity,' wrote the Reverend Samuel Willard, pastor of the South Church, Boston, and author of that famous theological folio, *A Compleat Body of Divinity.* 'The bulk of mankind is reserved for burning,' said Jonathan Edwards genially; and his Northampton congregation took his word for it. That these gentlemen knew not more about Hell and its inmates than did Dante is a circumstance which does not seem to have occurred to anyone. A preacher has some advantage over a poet."[91] And here is a prize:

---

85. *Americans and Others,* 142.
86. Ibid., 72.
87. *Points of View,* 139.
88. *Points of Friction,* 109.
89. *Points of View,* 147.
90. *Eight Decades,* 60.
91. Ibid., 75.

Agnes Edwards, in an engaging little volume on Cape Cod, quotes a clause from the will of John Bacon of Barnstable, who bequeathed to his wife for her lifetime the "use and improvement" of a slave-woman, Dinah. "If, at the death of my wife, Dinah be still living, I desire my executors to sell her, and to use and improve the money for which she is sold in the purchase of Bibles, and distribute them equally among my said wife's and my grandchildren."

There are fashions in goodness and badness as in all things else; but the selling of worn-out women for Bibles goes a step beyond Mrs. Stowe's most vivid imaginings.[92]

She did not like Mrs. Stowe.[93] She cared little for Bostonians,

92. Ibid., 86–87. About the "painful and precocious" diary of "young Nathaniel Mather, who happily died before reaching manhood, but not before he had scaled the heights of self-esteem, and sounded the depths of despair. When a boy, a real human boy, laments and bewails in his journal that he whittled a stick upon the Sabbath Day, 'and, for fear of being seen, did it behind the door, a great reproach of God, and a specimen of that atheism I brought into the world with me'—we recognize the fearful possibilities of untempered sanctimony." Agnes Repplier, *Varia* (Boston, 1897), 36.

93. From "Books That Have Hindered Me": "The last work to injure me seriously as a girl, and to root up the good seed sown in long years of righteous education, was *Uncle Tom's Cabin*, which I read from cover to cover with the innocent credulity of youth; and, when I had finished, the awful conviction forced itself upon me that the Thirteenth Amendment was a ghastly error, and that the war had been fought in vain. Slavery, which had seemed to me before undeviatingly wicked, now shone in a new and alluring light. All things must be judged by their results: and if the result of slavery was to produce a race so infinitely superior to common humanity; if it bred strong, capable, self-restraining men like George, beautiful, courageous, tender-hearted women like Eliza, visions of innocent loveliness like Emmeline, marvels of acute intelligence like Cassy, children of surpassing precocity and charm like little Harry, mothers and wives of patient, simple goodness like Aunt Chloe, and, finally, models of all known chivalry and virtue like Uncle Tom himself—then slavery was the most ennobling institution in the world, and we had committed a grievous crime in degrading a whole heroic race to our narrower, viler level. It was but too apparent, even to my immature mind, that the negroes whom I knew, or knew about, were very little better than white people; that they shared in all the manifold failings of humanity, and were not marked by any higher intelligence than their Caucasian neighbors. Even in the matters of physical beauty and mechanical ingenuity there had been plainly some degeneracy, some falling off from the high standard of old slavery days. Reluctantly I concluded that what had seemed so right had all been wrong indeed, and that the only people who stood preeminent for virtue, intellect, and nobility had been destroyed by our rash act, had sunk under the enervating influence of freedom to a range of lower feeling, to baser aspirations and content. It was the greatest shock of all, and the last." *Points of View*, 75–76.

including Emerson:[94] "Unlike Emerson, we are glad to be amused, only the task of amusing us grows harder day by day."[95] Her "amusing" was a rapier word with double edges: "It is amusing to hear Bishop Copleston, writing for that young and vivacious generation who knew not the seriousness of life, remind them pointedly that 'the task of pleasing is at all times easier than that of instructing.' It is delightful to think that there ever was a period when people preferred to be pleased rather than instructed."[96]

"Any book which serves to lower the sum of human gaiety is a moral delinquent" (proof that she could be flippant when she wanted to be).[97] She could be as impatient with the cant of the modern critic as with that of the ancient Puritan preacher:

> It is the most significant token of our ever-increasing "sense of moral responsibility in literature" that we should be always trying to graft our own conscientious purposes upon those authors who, happily for themselves, lived and died before virtue, colliding desperately with cakes and ale, had imposed such depressing obligations.
>
> "*Don Quixote*," says Mr. Shorthouse with unctuous gravity, "will come in time to be recognized as one of the saddest books ever written"; and if the critics keep on expounding it much longer, I truly fear it will.[98]

She herself counted the "obnoxious word 'ethics' six times repeated in the opening paragraph of one review, and have felt too deeply disheartened by such an outset to penetrate any further."[99] Her strong heart as well as her appetite found the vague and bland

---

94. About John Fiske, the greatly respected Boston historian: "He cannot for a moment forget how much better he knows; and instead of an indulgent smile at the delightful follies of our ancestors, we detect here and there through his very valuable pages something unpleasantly like a sneer." *Books and Men*, 58–59. "Longfellow wrote a 'Drinking Song' to water which achieved humour without aspiring to it, and Dr. Holmes wrote a teetotaler's adaptation of a drinking song, which aspired to humour without achieving it." *Points of Friction*, 206.
95. Agnes Repplier, *Books and Men* (Boston, 1890), 119.
96. *Points of View*, 105.
97. Witmer, 257.
98. *Points of View*, 3.
99. Ibid., 118–19.

white sauce of ethical culture repellent. "There is," she wrote, "nothing new about the Seven Deadly Sins. They are as old as humanity. There is nothing mysterious about them. They are easier to understand than the Cardinal Virtues."[100]

She had a compound attitude toward Quakers. She had a genuine feeling for their humaneness. Unlike most people—unlike, alas, many Philadelphians—she much preferred the melancholy Penn over the ambitious Franklin.[101] She had a good deal of respect for "that old-time Quakerism, gentle, silent, tenacious, inflexible, which is now little more than a tradition in the land, yet which has left its impress forever upon the city it founded and sustained."[102] Yet the unimaginative tightness of the Quaker mind grated on her nerves. She admired Elizabeth Drinker for her singularly detailed and disciplined diary of Philadelphia during the Revolution; but she was exasperated with her self-imposed limitations, with that whalebone corseting of a soul. "The most striking characteristic of our Quaker diarist is precisely this clear, cold, unbiased judgment, this sanity of a well-ordered mind. What she lacks, what the journal lacks from beginning to end, is some touch of human and ill-repressed emotion, some word of pleasant folly, some weakness left undisguised and unrepented. The attitude maintained throughout is too judicial, the repose of heart and soul too absolute to be endearing. . . ."[103] Because Agnes Repplier could not stomach Puritans, she stood for tolerance; because she was not a Quaker, tolerance could also leave her cold. "The languid indifference . . . which we dignify by the name of tolerance, has curtailed our interest in life."[104] (She would have agreed with her contemporary compatriot and potential confrère, the Philadelphia literary gentleman Logan

---

100. *Counter-Currents*, 136.
101. She instinctively understood the connection between the utilitarianism of a Franklin and the sentimentalism of the Brownings, a century later. She cited "the robust statement of Benjamin Franklin: 'I approved, for my part, the amusing one's self now and then with poetry, so far as to improve one's language, but no farther.' What a delicious picture is presented to our fancy of a nineteenth-century Franklin amusing himself and improving his language by an occasional study of 'Sordello.'" *Eight Decades*, 127.
102. *Compromises*, 128.
103. Ibid., 151.
104. *Eight Decades*, 81.

Pearsall Smith, who fled to England from the bosom of Quaker-dom: "Only among people who think no evil can Evil monstrously flourish.") "There are always men and women," she wrote, "who prefer the triumph of evil, which is a thing they can forget, to pro-longed resistance, which shatters their nerves. But the desire to escape an obligation, while very human, is not generally thought to be humanity's noblest lesson."[105] She was not an abstract moralist; she had, as we have seen, a stern sense of duty. She was impatient with stupidity—and impatience has not been a Quaker or Phila-delphia habit. "Sonorous phrases like 'reconstruction of the world's psychology,' and 'creation of a new world atmosphere,' are mental sedatives, drug words, calculated to put to sleep any uneasy appre-hensions. They may mean anything, and they do mean nothing, so that it is safe to go on repeating them."[106] "The combination of a sad heart and a gay temper, which is the most charming and the most lovable thing the world has got to show"; this was emphatically not a Quaker combination.[107]

Her mind, in many ways, represented the best of combinations: she was a realistic idealist and a tough-minded romantic. I wrote before that she *chose* to regard her childhood as not particularly unhappy: a choice which was conscious, not a subconscious one, for which all Freudian terms such as "sublimation" or "repression" would be woe-fully insufficient. She, who had no children, thought and knew a good deal about the trials and tribulations of childhood, and she wrote some of her finest essays about children's minds. She detested people who wrote books such as the one "with the somewhat ominous title *Children's Rights.*"[108] She understood, because she loved, the imagina-tion of children (". . . no child can successfully 'make believe,' when he is encumbered on every side by mechanical toys so odiously complete that they leave nothing for the imagination to supply").[109]

---

105. *Points of Friction*, 6.

106. Ibid., 75–76.

107. Ibid., 115.

108. *In the Dozy Hours*, 50.

109. Ibid., 53–54. Reminiscing about her convent days: "The very bareness of our sur-roundings, the absence of all appliances for play, flung us back unreservedly upon the illimitable resources of invention." Agnes Repplier, *In Our Convent Days* (Boston and New York, 1905), 148.

Because she was not a sentimentalist, she understood how very complex the minds of children (not at all little adults, as Americans are wont to believe, and to treat them) are:

> The merriment of children, of little girls especially, is often unreal and affected. They will toss their heads and stimulate one another to peals of laughter which are a pure make-believe. When they are really absorbed in their play, and astir with delicious excitation, they do not laugh; they give vent to piercing shrieks which sound as if they were being cut in little pieces. These shrieks are the spontaneous expressions of delight; but their sense of absurdity, which implies a sense of humor, is hard to capture before it has become tainted with pretense.[110]

A passage worth an entire library confected by child psychologists.

It was a kind of participant knowledge: neither objective, nor subjective, but personal. So was her understanding of the psychology of nations. "National traits," she wrote, "are, as a matter of fact, as enduring as the mountaintops. They survive all change of policies, all shifting of boundary lines, all expansion and contraction of dominion."[111] She understood how the struggles of nations are more important and decisive matters than are the struggles of classes; that the sympathies and the antipathies which the images of certain nations inspire are deep-seated and weighty matters, more profound than the superficial and current categories of "international relations." She understood that Anglophilia and Francophilia and Germanophilia were not merely the results of ethnic or ancestral memories; that they were more than political preferences. They were cultural preferences, representing certain inclinations of spirit and mind. On the highest level of her own cultural preferences Agnes Repplier aspired to those peaks of sensitivity which were unique for that Anglo-French civilization that, around 1900, may have marked the pinnacle of the Bourgeois Age.

The *entente cordiale* between these two great Western European nations existed in her mind decades before their alliance became a

---

110. Agnes Repplier, *Under Dispute* (Boston and New York, 1923), 303–304.
111. *Eight Decades*, 253.

reality on the battlefield, and well before it had become a reality in the form of a treaty. This was no coincidence. She, who was not particularly interested in politics, sensed that Germany represented a danger, not only to the British and the French, but to the kind of civilization she cherished. This is why her impatient and, on occasion, insistent, admonitory writings during the First World War should not be considered as if they were odd political excursions during her literary career, which is what some of her critics took them to be. She was convinced that a victory of Germany over France and Britain would be a disaster to the entirety of Western civilization, and she was bitterly impatient with the majority of her countrymen who were unwilling to face this condition, comforting themselves instead with pious sentiments.

How she loved England! "I, without one drop of English, Scotch, Welsh, or Irish blood in my veins, have come into the matchless inheritance of the English tongue and of English letters, which have made the happiness of my life."[112] She had no sympathy with the frequently narrow Anglophobia of Irish Catholics in the United States;[113] she had even less sympathy with the kind of redskin American nationalism which, wishing to fill the Indian land, preferred to turn its broad back on the English heritage. But she met with the same cold and shrouded obstacles with which so many lovers of England had had their chilly encounters: the English were diffident, with gray ice over their faces.[114] She wrote a beautiful essay about

---

112. From her address to the English-Speaking Union (Witmer, 116). When she first set foot in England: "After French, Dutch, German, Flemish, to say nothing of American, the mother tongue was made doubly blessed by being so sweetly spoken. . . . The charming intonations of the English fill me with wonder and regret. Why can't I speak in that way?" Stokes, 100. Later she would qualify her unconditional admiration for English speech, and for certain English characteristics. Throughout her life, however, she determined to spell certain words in the English way: "fervour," "harbour," "humour," etc. (She must have had a recurrence of trouble with proofreaders.)

113. She preferred the English to the Irish people, as she preferred the King James Bible to the Douay. Around 1600 the English tongue "had reached its first splendour, with the tenderness, vigor, and warmth of a language fresh from the mint. If all other English were to be blotted out from the world, the King James Bible would preserve intact its beauty and its power." Witmer, 148. (What would she say today?)

114. She had a fine correspondence with Andrew Lang, the eccentric critic and essayist, whose letters to her were full of unexpected small delights. When she finally met Lang

the relationship of England and America, "The Estranging Sea." She, who understood the English so well, felt their unwillingness to respond, to the marrow of her bones. It was an unrequited love.

She was sixty years old when, in 1915, she asked her friend Dr. White to take her to France to serve in the American Ambulance Hospital.[115] (He, wisely enough, refused.) She hated the sanctimonious William Jennings Bryan ("a past master of infelicitous argument, and very ugly to boot"). She did not like Germans, and she would have agreed with the wag who said that Wagner's music was better than it sounds; she did not like their heaviness;[116] she did not like Schopenhauer, "the great apostle of pessimism" who made "so much headway in reducing sadness to a science." She could be critical of the faults of the French, and especially of their talent for egocentricity: "When Voltaire sneered at the *Inferno,* and thought

---

in London she found him "sulky, and irresistibly charming; tall, lean, grey and very handsome." Stokes, 119. He was lean and gray indeed. On one occasion he asked Agnes Repplier to pay for their tea. At the end of her visit he bade her goodbye and never wrote to her again.

115. In 1914 she composed a pamphlet, together with J. William White, entitled: "Germany and Democracy, the Real Issue, the Views of Two Average Americans, a reply to Doctor Dernburg." (Dr. Dernburg had presented the case for Germany in the *Saturday Evening Post*.) The pamphlet was subsequently republished in England, France, and Holland. "In good truth," she wrote, "all German apologists, writing to enlist the sympathy of Americans, should be made to understand the value of an understatement. If they would claim a little less, we could believe a great deal more. . . ." Stokes, 175.

116. As early as 1902 she wrote: "There is a power of universal mastery about the traveling Teuton which affronts our feebler souls. We cannot cope with him; we stand defeated at every turn by his restless determination to secure the best. The windows of the railway carriages, the little sunny tables in the hotel dining-rooms, the back seats—commanding the view—of the Swiss funiculaires; all these strong positions he occupies at once with the strategical genius of a great military nation. No weak concern for other people's comfort mars the simple straightforwardness of his plans, nor interferes with their prompt and masterly execution. Amid the confusion and misery of French and Italian railway stations, he plays a conqueror's part, commanding the services of the porters, and marching off triumphantly with his innumerable pieces of hand luggage, while his fellow tourists clamour helplessly for aid. 'The Germans are a rude, unmannered race, but active and expert where their personal advantages are concerned,' wrote the observant Froissart many years ago. He could say neither more nor less were he traveling over the Continent to day." *Compromises*, 187–88.

But, then, she also wrote: "'Potter hates Potter, and Poet hates Poet,'—so runs the wisdom of the ancients—but tourist hates tourist with a cordial Christian animosity that casts all Pagan prejudices in the shade." Ibid., 185.

Hamlet the work of a drunken savage, he at least made a bid for the approbation of his countrymen, who, as Schlegel wittily observes, were in the habit of speaking as though Louis XIV had put an end to cannibalism in Europe."[117] Her initial sympathies were monarchical and aristocratic and romantic: when she first visited Paris she kissed the tattered cassock of Archbishop Darboy (murdered during the Commune in 1871) "when no one was looking. Republican France held no place in her heart."[118] She changed her mind about this; she rallied to the cause of the French Republic before, during, and after the First World War.[119]

During the war she would write scathingly about suffragettes and pacifists.[120] "The Honourable Bertrand Russell," she wrote, "whose annoyance at England's going to war deepened into resentment at her winning it (a consummation which, to speak the truth, he did his best to avert). . . ."[121] She read in the newspapers about a high-flown American project: a "World Conference for Promoting Concord between All Divisions of Mankind," "a title," she added, "that leaves nothing, save grammar, to be desired."[122] After the war she went to a Philadelphia dinner party with her friends the Pennells. Joseph Pennell was unkempt and boisterous, wishing to shake the Philadelphia bourgeois.[123] "Mark my words!" he roared across

---

117. *Books and Men*, 189.

118. Witmer, 92.

119. Her then young admirer, Constance O'Hara, told about a Monsignor Kieran who "preached a fine sermon . . . rich with classical allusions and splendid imagery that got off the subject only once or twice when he thundered at the French for their anti-clericalism. He always got that in—despite Agnes Repplier, the bluestocking, looking at him coldly from her pew, and thinking no doubt scornful thoughts about Irish Catholics." Constance O'Hara, *Heaven Was Not Enough* (Philadelphia, 1955), 41–42.

120. "When the news of the Belgian campaign sickened the heart of humanity, more than one voice was raised to say that England had, by her treatment of militant suffragists (a treatment so feeble, so wavering, so irascible, and so soft-hearted that it would not have crushed a rebellious snail), forfeited her right to protest against the dishonouring of Belgian women." *Points of Friction*, 141–48. "The only agreeable thing to be recorded in connection with Europe's sudden and disastrous war is the fact that people stopped talking about women, and began to talk about men." *Cross-Currents*, 98.

121. *Points of Friction*, 143.

122. *Cross-Currents*, 71.

123. Husband of Agnes Repplier's childhood friend Elizabeth Robins, a painter, engraver, and etcher of considerable talent: a large and saturnine man, wishing to combine

the table. You'll all live to see the day when the German Army and the British Army march arm in arm down Chestnut Street!"

> An impressive silence followed this astounding declaration. Then, leaning forward ever so slightly in her place, Agnes Repplier spoke up in a voice that was deadly calm. "Oh, dear Mr. Pennell," she said slowly and distinctly, "do have them come down Pine Street. Nothing ever happens on Pine Street."[124]

She believed in the uniqueness of Western civilization. She was neither an American isolationist nor a Pan-Americanist: "friendship and alliance with those European states whose aspirations and ideals respond to our own aspirations and ideals, are as consistent with Americanism as are friendship and alliance with the states of South America, which we are now engaged in loving. It is not from Bolivia, or Chile, or Venezuela, or the Argentine that we have drawn our best traditions, our law, language, literature, and art."[125] "You cannot make the word 'freedom' sound in untutored ears as it sounds in the ears of men who have counted the cost by which it has been preserved through the centuries."[126] She was the finest of Americans. Her mind was cosmopolitan in its scope, she was a devoted Anglophile and Francophile; yet she had nothing in common with her contemporary American exiles, whether of the rarefied or of the merely spoiled kind. She knew more about France and the French than a whole slew of American expatriates; yet she would not have retired to a salon-equipped château even if she had all the money in the world. She was more like Willa Cather than she was like Edith Wharton, even as she was unlike any of her contemporaries. She saw in the United States the potentiality for what was best in the world: not the last best hope of mankind, not the seat of world government, but something somberer and greater: the representative and the repository of the heritage of Western civilization.

Therefore, with all the refined qualities of her mind, she detested and feared American vulgarity less than she detested and feared

---

throughout his life the attributes of artist and aristocrat, with indifferent success.

124. Stokes, 188.
125. *Cross-Currents*, 291–92.
126. *Points of Friction*, 24–25.

American sentimentalism (she would have agreed with Wilde, who said that sentimentality was the Bank Holiday of cynicism), beneath the superficialities of which she would instantly detect the deeper element of a corruption of purpose:

> We are rising dizzily and fearlessly on the crest of a great wave of sentiment. When the wave breaks, we may find ourselves submerged, and in danger of drowning; but for the present we are full of hope and high resolve. Forty years ago we stood in shallow water, and mocked at the mid-Victorian sentiment, then ebbing slowly with the tide. We have nothing now in common with that fine, thin, tenacious conception of life and its responsibilities. . . . A vague humanity is our theme. . . .[127]

So she wrote in 1915. "Americans returning from war-stricken Europe in the autumn of 1914 spoke unctuously of their country as 'God's own land,' by which they meant a land where their luggage was unmolested."[128] She, who habitually kept her ironic talent in restraint, let out the reins when it came to evidence of American self-satisfaction. An American critic, a Mr. Haweis, "guided by that dangerous instinct which drives us to unwarranted comparisons,"

> does not hesitate to link the fame of Knickerbocker's *New York* with the fame of *Gulliver's Travels,* greatly to the disadvantage of the latter. "Irving," he gravely declares, "has all the satire of Swift, without his sour coarseness." It would be as reasonable to say, "Apollinaris has all the vivacity of brandy, without its corrosive insalubrity."[129]

"That failure in good sense which comes from too warm a self-satisfaction" raised her ire even at the age of eighty-one, when she recalled the national temper around 1900:

> Those were good days in which to live. Our skirmish with Spain was over, and we talked about it and wrote about it in terms that would have befitted Marathon. Mr. Hennessy is as enthusiastic

---

127. *Cross-Currents*, 1.
128. Ibid., 67.
129. *In the Dozy Hours*, 105. Apollinaris: a mineral water.

about our "histing the flag over the Ph'lippeens" as if he had not just found out that they were islands, and not, as he had previously supposed, canned goods. A sense of well-being permeates Mr. Dooley's pages. The White House cat is named "Gold Bonds"; mortgages spell security; the price of whisky, "fifteen cents a slug," remains immovable in days of peace and war; the "almighty dollar" has the superb impregnability that once attached itself to Roman citizenship; and devout men breathe a prayer that Providence may remain under the protection of the American flag.[130]

She read a letter from Walter Hines Page, printed after the First World War: "In all the humanities, we are a thousand years ahead of any people here.... God has as yet made nothing or nobody equal to the American people; and I don't think He ever will or can." "Which is a trifle fettering to omnipotence," she would add.[131]

She was over seventy when she wrote that "like the little girl who was so good that she knew how good she was, we are too well-informed not to be aware of our preeminence in this field." In the spring of 1925 the American Ambassador to the Court of St. James's delivered himself of a speech before the Pilgrims' Dinner in London. "In it he defined with great precision the attitude of the United States toward her former allies. His remarks, as reported, read like a sermon preached in a reformatory."[132] Her fine indignation carried over into the twenties, and beyond. Her preferences became slightly more conservative;[133] she was concerned with the ultimate effects

---

130. Agnes Repplier, *In Pursuit of Laughter* (Boston, 1936), 180. Twenty years earlier she wrote: "When Mr. Carnegie thanked God (through the medium of the newspapers) that he lived in a brotherhood of nations—'forty-eight nations in one Union,'—he forgot that these forty-eight nations, or at least thirty-eight of them, were not always a brotherhood.

Nor was the family tie preserved by moral suasion. What we of the North did was to beat our brothers over the head until they consented to be brotherly. And some three hundred thousand of them died of grievous wounds and fevers rather than love us as they should." *Cross-Currents*, 65–66.

131. Agnes Repplier, *To Think of TEA!* (Boston, 1932), 79.

132. *Eight Decades*, 240.

133. In 1919 she wrote: "If the principles of conservatism are based on firm supports, on a recognition of values, a sense of measure and proportion, a due regard for order—its prejudices are indefensible. The wise conservative does not attempt to defend them; he only clings to them more lovingly under attack. He recognizes triumphant science in

of admitting an unlimited number and variety of immigrants to the United States, and wrote sharply about this. Yet she kept her irascibility at the American trait of self-congratulation burning with a glow. "It is a bearable misfortune to be called un-American, because the phrase still waits analysis," she wrote in 1924.[134] In 1927 she spoke about "Success and Ideals." "Every message, every address, every editorial, every sermon had faithfully echoed this chant of triumph over the unparalleled prosperity of 1926 and the magnificent prospects of 1927. We are the super-state and we have been assiduously taught that, to be good and happy and prosperous, is to fulfill the designs of a singularly partial Providence."[135] "It is not efficiency but a well-balanced emotional life which creates an enjoyable world." And the American "lacked the moral and intellectual humility, which would bring him an understanding of tragedies in which he has no share and supremacies in which he sees no significance."[136] Here is Agnes Repplier, the so-called conservative period piece, writing in the twenties. Walter Lippmann and the American liberal and intellectual consensus would agree to all the above. She would, however, lash out at silliness from every quarter, no matter how intellectually fashionable or timely. In 1931, the *New Republic* "says that the United States is a belligerent country. Assuredly not! Bullying, perhaps, but not belligerent."[137] One source of her best qualities was her instant contempt for any kind of intellectual opportunism. "The man who never tells an unpalatable truth 'at the wrong time' (the right time has yet to be discovered) is the man whose success in life is fairly well assured,"[138] Agnes Repplier wrote in 1924 a sentence that alone is worth the contents of an, as

---

the telephone and the talking machine, and his wish to escape these benefactions is but a humble confession of unworthiness. He would be glad if scientists, hitherto occupied with preserving and disseminating sound, would turn their attention to suppressing it, would collect noise as an ashman collects rubbish, and dump it in some only place, thus preserving the sanity of the world." *Points of Friction*, 100.

134. *Under Dispute*, 75.
135. Witmer, 159.
136. Ibid., 157, 158.
137. Agnes Repplier, *Times and Tendencies* (Boston and New York, 1931), 35.
138. *Under Dispute*, 83. She admired this quality in others, watching them with a gimlet eye. "Mr Philip Guedalla, whose charm as a historian lies in his happy detachment—for the time—from the prejudices of his day . . ." *Times and Tendencies*, 39.

yet unwritten, volume on the vice of the twentieth century, which is intellectual opportunism.

"Stupidity," she wrote wisely, "is not the prerogative of any one class or creed."[139] She knew that most stupidity is not the result of neuro-cerebral incompetence but that it is self-induced and willful.[140] "What the world asks now are state reforms and social reforms—in other words, the reformation of our neighbors. What the Gospel asks, and has always asked, is the reformation of ourselves—a harassing and importunate demand."[141] Democracy "is not the final word of progress. . . . Democracy is rational but not luminous."[142]

She preferred Theodore Roosevelt to Wilson:

> Nothing is easier than to make the world safe for democracy. Democracy is playing her own hand in the game. She has every intention and every opportunity to make the world safe for herself. But democracy may be divorced from freedom, and freedom is the breath of man's nostrils, the strength of his sinews, the sanction of his soul. It is as painful to be tyrannized over by a proletariat as by a tsar or by a corporation, and it is in a measure more disconcerting, because of the greater incohesion of the process. It is as revolting to be robbed by a reformer as by a trust.[143]

She loved her country, and knew all its faults: "a mad welter of lawlessness, idleness, and greed; and, on the other hand, official

---

139. *Points of Friction*, 72.

140. 1931: "A young Englishman, teaching in an American school, said that what struck him most sharply about American boys was their docility. He did not mean by this their readiness to do what they were told, but their readiness to think as they were told, in other words, to permit him to do their thinking for them." *Times and Tendencies*, 305–306.

141. *Points of Friction*, 78–79.

142. "I do strive to think well of my fellow man, but no amount of striving can give me confidence in the wisdom of a Congressional vote." Witmer, 160.

143. *Points of Friction*, 74–75. Thirty years earlier she wrote: "It is an interesting circumstance in the lives of those persons who are called either heretics or reformers, according to the mental attitudes or antecedent prejudices of their critics, that they always begin by hinting their views with equal modesty and moderation. It is only when rubbed sore by friction, when hard driven and half spent, that they venture into the open, and define their positions before the world in all their bald malignity." *Points of View*, 136. In 1892: ". . . the sanguine socialist of to-day, who dreams of preparing for all of us a lifetime of unbroken ennui." *Essays in Idleness*, 167.

extravagance, administrative weakness . . . and shameless profiteer-
ing. Our equilibrium is lost, and with it our sense of proportion. We
are Lilliput and Brobdingnag jumbled together, which is worse than
anything Gulliver ever encountered."[144] Certain American assertions drove her to despair. "Mr. Rockefeller is responsible for the
suggestion that Saint Paul, were he living today, would be a captain
of industry. Here again a denial is as valueless as an assertion."[145] Yet
she saw, and wished to encourage with every nerve of her being, the
finer potentialities of the American mind:

> When we leave the open field of exaggeration, that broad area
> which is our chosen territory, and seek for subtler qualities in
> American humour, we find here and there a witticism which,
> while admittedly our own, has in it an Old-World quality. The
> epigrammatic remark of a Boston woman that men get and for-
> get, and women give and forgive, shows the fine, sharp finish of
> Sydney Smith or Sheridan. A Philadelphia woman's conversation,
> that she knew there could be no marriages in Heaven, because—
> "Well, women were there no doubt in plenty, and some men; but
> not a man whom any woman would have,"—is strikingly French.
> The word of a New York broker, when Mr. Roosevelt sailed for
> Africa, "Wall Street expects every lion to do its duty!" equals in
> brevity and malice the keen-edged satire of Italy.[146]

And of American speech:

> If some Americans can speak superlatively well, why cannot
> more Americans speak pleasingly? Nature is not altogether to
> blame for our deficiencies. The fault is at least partly our own.
> The good American voice is very good indeed. Subtle and sweet
> inheritances linger in its shaded vowels. Propriety and a sense of
> distinction control its cadences. It has more animation than the

---

144. *Points of Friction*, 106.
145. Ibid., 241.
146. *Americans and Others*, 47–48. Her appreciation for American humor was not
restricted to such odd samples of esprit from the upper classes: "the indolent and luminous genius of Mr. Dooley has widened our mental horizon. Mr. Dooley is a philosopher,
but his is the philosophy of the looker-in, of that genuine unconcern which finds Saint
George and the dragon to be both a trifle ridiculous." Ibid., 49–50.

English voice, and a richer emotional range. The American is less embarrassed by his emotions than is the Englishman; and when he feels strongly the truth, or the shame, or the sorrow his words convey, his voice grows vibrant and appealing. He senses his mastery over a diction, "nobly robust and tenderly vulnerable." The former and finished utterances of an older civilization entrance his attentive ear.[147]

She would not care for that quintessentially modern American-intellectual type, the social scientist;[148] but she would care even less for the unctuous foreigner who bilks and misleads Americans by offering credit to their worst intellectual vices:

> That astute Oriental, Sir Rabindranath Tagore, manifested a wisdom beyond all praise, in his recognition of American audiences. As the hour for his departure drew nigh, he was asked to write, and did write, a "Parting Wish for the Women of America," giving graceful expressions to the sentiments he knew he was expected to feel. The skill with which he modified and popularized an alien point of view revealed the seasoned lecturer. He told his readers that "God has sent woman to love the world," and to build up a "spiritual civilization." He condoled with them because they were "passing through great sufferings in this callous age." His heart bled for them, seeing that their hearts "are broken every day, and victims are snatched from their arms, to be thrown under the car of material progress." The Occidental sentiment which regards man as simply an offspring, and a fatherless offspring at that (no woman, says Olive Schreiner, could look upon a battle-field without thinking, "So many mothers' sons!") came as naturally to Sir Rabindranath as if he had been to the manner born. He was content to see the passion and pain, the sorrow and heroism of men, as reflections mirrored in woman's

---

147. *Times and Tendencies,* 225.

148. In a letter to Harrison Morris, 1912: "You know everything and everybody. Please tell me what is the American Social Science Association, of which I have been asked to become a member. It has dues and gives medals. Shall I accept?" She adds a postscript: "I see by looking again at the card, the name of the thing is the National Institute of Social Sciences. What are social sciences?"

soul. The ingenious gentlemen who dramatize Biblical narratives for the American stage, and who are hampered at every step by the obtrusive masculinity of the East, might find a sympathetic supporter in this accomplished and accommodating Hindu.[149]

Miss Repplier was a solitary person. She would have agreed with the French maxim *"On trouve rarement le bonheur en soi, jamais ailleurs"*—one finds happiness rarely in oneself, never elsewhere—but her *bonheur* was seldom, if ever, separable from the conscious activity of her mind. Her adult work was all of a piece. Her adult life was all of a piece. Only they existed on different planes. People who did not know Agnes Repplier may have thought (indeed, they often did) that she was an eccentric dowager, an aristocrat of sorts, all dove-gray silk, instructing the world, keeping her impatience and brilliance, like a pair of greyhounds, on display and on the leash. Agnes Repplier was a *grande dame* of letters all right, but her character was not that of an aristocrat; she was a bourgeoise, which did not bother her much.[150]

She had, as I wrote before, few pretensions. Or, to be exact, she had a hundred strong convictions for each of her pretensions—an attractive ratio.

She was not happy, because her life was not easy. She had little money.[151] She earned almost all her income by writing—writing erudite essays, and hardly ever compromising her high standards—a truly extraordinary achievement. Around the age of thirty-two, as we have seen, she reached a high plateau, and from there on, her essays flowed from her pen during those solitary mornings and she had no trouble publishing anything. Her main outlet was the *Atlantic,* but for more than twenty-five years she also wrote for *Life,* the *Yale Review, Century Magazine, Forum, Harper's,* and so on. The recognition of her work brought her other benefits. She could travel

---

149. *Points of Friction,* 160–61.
150. She did not, like Edith Sitwell, wear eccentric and Gothic costumes; she had, however, a predilection for Turkish rings.
151. "Real biting poverty, which withers lesser evils with its deadly breath . . ." *Essays in Idleness,* 144. Fortunately enough, this was not her experience. Her mother left a small inheritance. As early as the year 1887 she earned by her writings more than $1,000, a small but respectable sum for a writer in those days.

to Europe. She first crossed the Atlantic in 1890 with her sister on the steamer *Normania*. During the next ten years she was able to visit Europe three more times, for ever longer periods, as the chaperone of two accommodating young girls, the Boone sisters from Eden Hall (who were the wards of Cardinal Gibbons of Baltimore). Between the thirty-sixth and seventy-fifth years of her life she visited Europe half a dozen times, usually in the company of friends, the last time as a member of the official American delegation to the Ibero-American World Exhibition in Seville in 1929, a trip which she enjoyed at least as much as (perhaps even more than) her first, and of which she wrote a short and witty account. Knowledgeable, expectant, perceptive, thoroughly aware of her surroundings and of the people, yet always ready for new impressions and experiences, she was an excellent traveler,[152] and an excellent companion, so far as we can tell. She crisscrossed the United States on innumerable occasions, mostly on lecturing engagements. Her public life corresponded to the age of the public lecture, a peculiarly American form of instructional entertainment. She did not like to lecture; she was far less confident at the lectern than at her desk; but lecturing produced an income that she could not afford to relinquish.[153] After most of these trips she returned to Philadelphia bone-tired. Her finances required that she accept lecturing invitations even after she had reached seventy.

She was not a domestic woman. She was thoroughly urban, fond of good food and wines, smoking innumerable cigarettes (and, on occasion, small black cigars). She did not know how to cook. Her domestic life was not comfortable. After ten years of successful writing, she, her sister, and her brother were able to move from West

---

152. She wrote in the rubric of her passport: "Face, broad; Complexion, sallow; Mouth, too large." Stokes, 122. She was unduly conscious of what she considered the inadequacies of her looks. Her mouth was beautifully shaped.

153. About her trials on the lecturing circuit she wrote to Mrs. Schuyler Warren (see below) in April 1914: "Boston is even more mad about prostitutes than Philadelphia and New York. She talks about little else, tells blood-curdling stories, which bear every evidence of ripe invention, and the Dedham Club at which I lectured had actually had a real live 'white slave' (at least she claimed to be one, but she may have been only bragging) to address them last month. Now how can a respectable old lady like myself compete with such an attraction! . . ." Ibid., 172.

Philadelphia to downtown Philadelphia, renting apartments succes-
sively on Spruce, Chestnut, and Pine Streets.[154] In 1921 they moved
to 920 Clinton Street, the house which eventually became her trade-
mark; one of those old Philadelphia streets with red brick houses
of good proportions and solidity.[155] For the first time in her life she
found a house that suited her character, her image, her personality.
Yet the perfection of the milieu was external rather than internal.
The interior was dusky, Victorian, not particularly distinguished,
full of old bibelots.[156] Her surroundings stood still even when her
mind did not.

She would receive single visitors in Clinton Street from time
to time; she would never entertain there. (Later she would invite
friends for lunch at the Acorn Club.)[157] Yet her friends meant the
world to her—literally, not merely figuratively speaking. She relished the friendship and the intellectual companionship of men.
She was thoroughly at home with them; they, in turn, relished the
masculine strength and directness of her mind. She was not a professional intellectual; she belonged to that select minority of strong
minds who disdain being considered "intellectual," as if mental
refinement were some kind of skill. Yet she came into her own at a
time when there was a perceptible tendency among men and women
who were attracted to the intellectual life to seek some comfort

154. At that time she lived but a few houses away from Boies Penrose, with whom she
had very little in common. On Chestnut Street (2035) she lived but a few doors from the
house (2005) where she had lived as a child.

155. In 1931 a college girl asked for an interview with "Miss Repplier of Clinton Street."

   "Our glance wanders momentarily through the lace-curtained windows. Again there
is that feeling of time gone backward. A black carriage, proud with metal trappings, is
passing. A coachman, resplendent in white cord breeches, black coat and cockaded top
hat. A fine sleek horse stepping daintily—Clinton Street, perhaps the only thoroughfare in Philadelphia where a horse and carriage is not an anachronism, but a commonplace." J. O'K. in the *Grackle*, the literary magazine of Chestnut Hill College, fall 1931.
The writer probably did not know that Agnes Repplier, who disliked automobiles, was
one of the very last Philadelphians to hire a horse-drawn carriage from a livery stable, as
late as the early 1930s.

156. In 1893 she had written: "It is a painful thing, at best, to live up to one's bricabrac
if one has any; but to live up to the bricabrac of many lands and of many centuries is a
strain which no wise man would dream of inflicting upon his constitution." *In the Dozy
Hours*, 113.

157. I like the Acorn Club," she said on one occasion. "They never do anything."

and warmth in each other's company in what was otherwise a very indifferent world. During winter evenings in the late eighties and nineties Agnes Repplier was part of a small Philadelphia circle of such people, of whose limitations she was amiably, rather than condescendingly, aware.[158] Around 1890 she met four patrician gentlemen, each of whom had a great influence in her life. Harrison Morris, later editor of *Lippincott's Magazine*, became her lifelong friend and literary adviser; Horace Howard Furness, the Shakespeare scholar, cherished her friendship and treated her as an ornament at the gatherings in his suburban house "Lindenshade."[159] S. Weir Mitchell, the talented patrician physician and writer, received her at his more formal entertainments with a kind of avuncular deference; J. William White actually became her occasional collaborator. Like Mitchell, White was part of the Philadelphia medical tradition, at the peak of its reputation around the turn of the century. He was an attractive man and an excellent surgeon. He probably saved her life. He diagnosed cancer in her left breast. He removed it in a masterly operation.[160] She was then forty-three years of age. They were close friends for the next two decades, very close during the First World War. Both were thoroughly convinced Francophiles and Anglophiles. They collaborated on political pamphlets. White went off to France in 1915.[161] He died in Philadelphia a year later. Agnes Repplier wrote his short memorial biography.

Her friendships with women were long-lasting and profound. Elizabeth Robins was her oldest friend, from their convent days. She was a complicated woman, consumed by social ambition, a Quakeress with aristocratic aspirations, tending to subordinate her undoubted intelligence to certain pretensions. After she married

---

158. There was a Browning Society: "We encouraged each other in mediocrity." Yet this society "endeavoured to keep letters alive, which was certainly a noble enterprise, even if in Philadelphia it was much like keeping a selection of corpses moving about." Stokes, 101. She was a founding member of the Contemporary Club in 1886.

159. His "astoundingly prudish wife" was not an asset during their gatherings. Agnes Repplier to A. Edward Newton, May 10, 1930 (ALS in Princeton University Library).

160. To cover the upper portion of a thin scar Agnes Repplier wore a black, sometimes velvet choker for the rest of her life. It became her very well.

161. That year she dined with White and Theodore Roosevelt. "Heavenly! There were seven men. I was the only woman." Witmer, 111.

Pennell, Elizabeth and Agnes drifted a little apart. The former may have resented the fact that the girl who once was Minnie now outshone her in the literary world. Agnes Irwin, who, as we have seen, thought it best to disembarrass herself of little Agnes in her school, recognized her talents nevertheless at an early age; her solid support and affection for the young girl blossomed into the best kind of friendship, with reciprocal affection resting on the solid foundation of mutual respect and esteem. "Miss Agnes" Irwin died suddenly in 1914; her school remains her monument even now; another monument is the fine short biography that Agnes Repplier wrote after her death. Cornelia Frothingham was a New England woman, an in-law of the Brinley family in Philadelphia; in spite of her sometimes tiresome insistence on civic virtues and self-improvement, this neurotic woman[162] and Agnes Repplier became close friends, traveling often to Europe, Nova Scotia, and Maine together. Mrs. Schuyler Warren was the mistress of a sort of literary salon in New York circa 1905; well-read, exceptionally handsome, and rich. Agnes Repplier took great pleasure in her company. Two close Philadelphia friends were Caroline Sinkler and Cecilia Beaux, the painter. During the last quarter of her life Miss Repplier often appeared in public together with Miss Frances Wister, a formidable Philadelphia patroness of the arts; their friendship was extraordinary perhaps only because of Miss Wister's enthusiasm for music, to which Miss Repplier was, perhaps by nature, indifferent.[163]

There were people who believed that this bluestocking, this lifelong spinster, had, like her contemporary Willa Cather, a secret longing for people of her own sex. I do not believe this to be true. The evidence of a handful of letters to her friends, perhaps especially to Mrs. Warren and to Miss Frothingham, is insufficient, save for those who are hopelessly inclined to the attribution of sexual

---

162. "Cornelia Frothingham was ill for ten weeks with a nervous collapse, all the more serious because it had no cause." Agnes Repplier to Mrs. Wilson Farrand, Easter Monday 1913 (ALS in Princeton University Library).

163. If Miss Repplier could be deaf to the unwitting language of music, Miss Wister could on occasion be deaf to the unwitting humor of words. She gave a sherry party in honor of Marcel Tabuteau, the famous oboist of the Philadelphia Orchestra. She proposed a toast: "For years," she said, "he delighted me every Friday afternoon with his little instrument."

motives to every expression of human sentiment.[164] The contrary evidences are more impressive. We have seen how thoroughly she enjoyed masculine company and its attentions. Her occasional references about sexual attraction in her writings are sane and healthy compounds of the commonsensical and the Gallic. They are devoid of sentimentality; with a touch of the *femme moyenne sensuelle* they are much closer to Jane Austen than to the Brontës, and much closer to Colette than to George Sand. When President Eliot of Harvard pronounced Becky Sharp a despicable creature, she corrected him impatiently:[165] to the contrary, she said, the heroine of *Vanity Fair* had many admirable qualities. In some of her writing, passages exist that suggest her healthy sensuality, or at least her natural appetite for it. She wrote of a pampered cat, who grew so tired of his dull orderly life that "he ran away with a vagabond acquaintance for one long delicious day of liberty, at the close of which, jaded, spent, starved, and broken, he crept meekly back to bondage and his evening cutlet."[166] At the same time she had a very clear understanding of the virtues of restraint—especially in art:

> In French fiction, as Mr. Lang points out, "love comes after marriage punctually enough, but it is always love for another." The inevitableness of the issue startles and dismays an English reader, accustomed to yawn gently over the innocent prenuptial dallyings of Saxon man and maid. The French storywriter cannot and does not ignore his social code which urbanely limits courtship. When he describes a girl's dawning sentiment, he does so often with exquisite grace and delicacy; but he reserves his portrayal of the master passion until maturity gives it strength, and circumstances render it unlawful. His conception of his art imposes no scruple which can impede analysis. If an English novelist ven-

---

164. One of the few examples: when visiting Clarens, Switzerland, with Cornelia Frothingham, she wrote (in 1902): "We want to live here together." Stokes, 146.

165. Her friend Agnes Irwin on Eliot of Harvard: "Wherever he is, he lowers the temperature."

166. Agnes Repplier, *The Fireside Sphinx* (Boston, 1901), 301. About the Westminster cats in London: their bad behavior "has given rise to the pleasant legend of a country house whither these rakish animals retire for nights of gay festivity, and whence they return in the early morning, jaded, repentant, and forlorn." *Essays in Idleness*, 23.

tures to treat of illicit love, the impression he gives is of a blind, almost mechanical force, operating against rather than in unison with natural laws; those normal but most repellent aspects of the case which the Frenchman ignores or rejects. His theory of civilization is built up largely—and wisely—on suppression.[167]

She regretted that she never married; and she learned not to make an issue of it.[168] She was a spinster, and she learned not to mind it. She was appalled at the crudity with which American humorists treated spinsters, and wrote a sensible little essay about spinsterhood. "It is not an easy thing to be happy. It takes all the brains, all the soul, and all the goodness we possess. We may fail of our happiness, strive we ever so bravely; but we are less likely to fail if we measure with judgment our chances and our capabilities. To glorify spinsterhood is as ridiculous as to decry it. Intelligent women marry or remain single, because in married or in single life they see their way more clearly to content. They do not, in either case, quarrel with fate which has modelled them for, and fitted them into, one groove rather than another; but follow, consciously or unconsciously, the noble maxim of Marcus Aurelius: 'Love that only which the gods send thee, and which is spun with the thread of thy destiny.'"[169] She admired that stoic Roman ruler. Horace, she wrote on another occasion, was like Marcus Aurelius, "able to be alone; but he was far too wise to make of himself that lopsided thing called a recluse."[170] So was she.

She was impatient with the self-conscious respect and the superficial sentimentalism with which American men treated their women. There were many things wrong with ancient Rome, but "she was far from being a matriarchy like the United States. She was not a nation of husbands, but a nation of men."[171] "The superlative complacency of American women is due largely to the oratorical adulation of American men—an adulation that has no more sub-

---

167. *Compromises*, 51.
168. Her friends "gave her so much, [but] they were not able to give her what she craved most. Once she said with strong feeling. 'I never have been first with anyone.'" Witmer, 107.
169. *Compromises*, 184.
170. *Eight Decades*, 59.
171. Ibid., 54.

stance than has the foam on beer."[172] She was an intelligent feminist, who took a long-range view of things. "Since Adam delved and Eve span, life for all of us has been full of labour; but as the sons of Adam no longer exclusively delve, so the daughters of Eve no longer exclusively spin. In fact, delving and spinning, though admirable occupations, do not represent the sum total of earthly needs. There are so many, many other useful things to do, and women's eager finger-tips burn to essay them all."[173] "Perhaps the time may even come when women, mixing freely in political life, will abandon that injured and aggressive air which distinguishes the present advocate of female suffrage," she wrote in 1894.[174] The Michigan magistrate who in 1918 "gave orders that a stalwart male angel presiding over the gateway of a cemetery should be recast in feminine mould may have been an erring theologian and doubtful art-critic; but that he was a stout-hearted American no one can deny."[175]

She knew the follies of the exclusively male, as well as the exclusively female, viewpoint. "'Never,' said Edmond de Goncourt, 'has a virgin, young or old, produced a work of art.' One makes allowance for the Latin point of view. And it is possible that M. de Goncourt never read *Emma.*"[176] But "the pitfall of the feminist is the belief that the interests of men and women can ever be severed; that what brings sufferings to the one can leave the other unscathed."[177] "In Mr. St. John Ervine's depressing little drama, *Mixed Marriage,*

---

172. *Points of Friction*, 192.
173. *Varia*, 28.
174. *In the Dozy Hours*, 72.
175. *Points of Friction*, 167. "*Qui veut faire l'ange fait la bête,*' said Pascal; and the Michigan angel is a danger signal. . . . No sane woman believes that women, as a body, will vote more honestly than men; but no sane man believes that they will vote less honestly. They are neither 'the gateway to hell,' as Tertullian pointed out, nor the builders of Sir Rabindranath Tagore's 'spiritual civilization.' They are neither the repositories of wisdom, nor the final word of folly." Ibid., 201–02. "'God help women when they have only their rights!' exclaimed a brilliant American lawyer; but it is in the 'only' that all savour lies. Rights and privileges are incompatible. Emancipation implies the sacrifice of immunity, the acceptance of obligation. It heralds the reign of sober and disillusioning experience. Women, as M. Faguet reminds us, are only the equals of men; a truth which was simply phrased in the old Cornish adage, 'Lads are as good as wenches when they are washed.'" Ibid., 202–203.
176. *Points of Friction*, 82.
177. *Cross-Currents*, 123.

which the Dublin actors played in New York some years ago, an old woman, presumed to be witty and wise, said to her son's betrothed: 'Sure, I believe the Lord made Eve when he saw Adam could not take care of himself'; and the remark reflected painfully upon the absence of that humorous sense which we used to think was the birthright of Irishmen. The too obvious retort, which nobody uttered, but which must have occurred to everybody's mind, was that if Eve had been designed as a caretaker, she had made a shining failure of her job."[178] "The too obvious retort" of a fine conversationalist. "Whenever Adam's remarks expand too obviously into a sermon, Eve, in the most discreet and wife-like manner, steps softly away, and refreshes herself with slumber. Indeed, when we come to think of it, conversation between these two must have been difficult at times, because they had nobody to talk about."[179] She had a finely tuned appetite for malicious humor in conversation, including the eternal topic of how and why certain people are attracted to each other, in which she, rightly, saw the essence of sex. She did not take Freud seriously, which was a good thing. In her essay on "Three Famous Old Maids," the Misses Austen, Edgeworth, and Mitford, she described their "serene, cheerful, and successful lives . . . all rounded and completed without that element we are taught to believe is the mainspring and prime motor of existence."[180]

Her fierce independence of mind,[181] as we have seen, rested on the understanding that freedom is not merely the absence of restraints but that, to the contrary, it springs from the restraints one imposes on oneself. Her independence was sustained, rather than compromised, by her religion. She was a Roman Catholic with a very independent mind, a rarity in her country in her times, but no less a Catholic for that. Weaker or more self-indulgent women than Agnes Repplier could find it comforting to turn against the memories of

---

178. *Points of Friction*, 183.
179. *Essays in Idleness*, 164.
180. Witmer, 90.
181. She found independence attractive in every sense. It attracted her to cats, about which she wrote (too often for my taste: at least three essays, and an entire book): she liked the dormant savage energy beneath their lazy composture, and their total absence of docile loyalties.

an unhappy childhood that culminated in cold convent days and expulsion, to explain to themselves and to the world that they could sustain no inner nourishment from those rigid pieties whose hypocritical and superstitious nature they claimed to know only too well. At the same time, the majority of Catholics during Agnes Repplier's life, "when respectability stalked unchecked," chose not to think much, if at all, about the deep differences between what they believed and what they professed to believe. Some of the middle-class Catholics in Philadelphia did not like her, and pronounced some of her writings scandalous. She, on her part, disliked many of the German and Irish Catholics, a petulant kind of dislike that flared especially high during the First World War. The vulgarized Americanisms of some of the clergy haunted her throughout her entire life.[182] Yet even during her lifetime the Church was a house of many mansions. Not all American Catholics were parochial.[183] Cardinal Gibbons, many of the bishops, the heads and the nun-teachers of the small Catholic academies and colleges welcomed her with eagerness and affection. Catholic universities awarded their highest honors to her. The Catholic community of Philadelphia, indeed of the United States—it was more of a community then than it is now—eventually took pride in the achievement of this solitary woman, who was, after all, one of their own. She patronized and befriended the handsome and civilized priest Henry Drumgoole, choosing him for her escort to many a gathering. The Monsignori Drumgoole,[184] Sigourney Fay, Edward

---

182. In 1931: "Linguistic idiosyncrasies are social idiosyncrasies. I thought of this when I heard an American prelate, a man of learning and piety, allude in a sermon 'to the most important and influential of the saints and martyrs.' It sounded aggressively modern. 'Powerful' is a word well fitted to the Church Triumphant. . . . But 'important' has a bustling accent, and an 'influential' martyr suggests a heavenly banking-house." *Times and Tendencies*, 222–23.

183. "The one Catholic who made me feel better about the situation was Miss Agnes Repplier. She was Philadelphia—and it was her co-religionists who rejected this witty and wonderful woman, not the inner circle where she was a fêted and sought-after personage. When I was a child she had an apartment with her brother Louis and her sister Mary at Twenty-first and Pine Streets. She was a slight woman with keen grey eyes behind noseglasses that gave her a Pecksniffian expression and she had then a nervous jerk to her head." O'Hara, 110

184. In 1919 Archbishop Dougherty removed Msgr. Drumgoole from St. Charles Seminary to the rectorate of a workingman's parish, St. Gregory's. "The good and devout

Hawks were priests after her heart (the last two converts from Anglicanism), representing a higher and more elegant and broad-minded Catholicism that was definitely not isolationist; a minority among the clergy, they supported the British and French cause during the entire First World War.

The character of Agnes Repplier was compendious enough to encompass a taste for the baroque as well as for the classical, even though she had a profound distaste for easy enthusiasms. Her philosophy of life was reflected in "The Chill of Enthusiasm," one of her favorite essays. "If we had no spiritual asbestos to protect our souls, we should be consumed to no purpose by every wanton flame," she wrote.

> If our sincere and restful indifference to things which concern us not were shaken by every blast, we should have no available force for things which concern us deeply. If eloquence did not sometimes make us yawn, we should be besotted by oratory. And if we did not approach new acquaintances, new authors, and new points of view with life-saving reluctance, we should never feel that vital regard which, being strong enough to break down our barriers, is strong enough to hold us for life.[185]

Yet, with all her self-restraint, reserve, and irony, she was not a rationalist. "If knowledge alone could save us from sin, the salvation of the world would be easy work."[186] She had a respect for emotions,

---

people, most of whom worked on the Pennsylvania Railroad, were astounded at their new Rector, and soon indignant. Archbishop Dougherty had exposed a congregation of hard working people to one of the most brilliant men in the Church. They yearned for the comfortable mugginess of the religion they knew, and Monsignor Drumgoole, with his assistant Father Edward Hawks, the converted Anglican, made it a dazzling, golden thing. It was perhaps as well the Monsignor Sigourney Fay, another converted Anglican, died the year before Monsignor Drumgoole became Rector of St. Gregory's, for Father Fay was something of an aesthete, a lover of epigrams, and, devoted to Monsignor Drumgoole, would often have been in residence at St. Gregory's. The puritanical Archbishop would have something to think about, since Monsignor Fay, a close friend of Cardinal Gibbons, was not sparing with the perfume he used. He achieved a brief fame as Father Darcy in Scott Fitzgerald's *This Side of Paradise*, the novel that heralded the arrival of the twenties." Ibid., 132.

185. *Eight Decades*, 265.
186. *Cross-Currents*, 145.

and the New Englanders' dichotomy of Reason vs. Emotion made no sense to her.[187] Her understanding of life—and not only of letters—was spacious enough for her to comprehend the reasons of the heart.

Like Dr. Johnson's, her life was in many ways a triumph of character. Her accomplishment may be summed up in one short sentence: She was the Jane Austen of the essay. That she is not so recognized is a great—and one hopes, temporary—loss. Her essays are always lucid, often profound, and worth rereading. Few of them show the marks of her age. In spite of her quickly faded reputation, there is little of her writing that is a period piece.

We must, however, recognize the essence of a certain kind of truth within that epithet, even though we must qualify it. From her first essay, published in the *Atlantic* in 1886, to the last, published there fifty-four years later (in 1940), there is hardly any difference in the style or in the quality of her writing. Agnes Repplier did not grow. She reached a high and exceptional level of expression when she, against extraordinary odds, first earned her national reputation. She kept up this high level, with few exceptions, until the end of her industrious life. To sustain this was achievement enough; and there may have been an internal relationship between the scope of her art and that of her life. She took pleasure in her own writings (during the last years of her life she would, on occasion, request that her nurse read some of them to her aloud, only to ask that the volume be quickly put back on the shelves when the bell rang, announcing a visitor), but she never let herself be carried away by a wave of unwonted self-confidence; she never overestimated her talents.[188] She did not try her hand at a novel, or a play, or even at a compendious work of literary criticism. The small essay remained her genre; she was satisfied with it, just as her social ambitions never

---

187. ". . . our great-grandfathers, who were assuredly not a tender-hearted race . . . cried right heartily over poems, and novels, and pictures, and plays, and scenery, and everything, in short, that their great-grandsons would not now consider as worthy of emotion." *Books and Men*, 113.

188. She said often that she did not expect most of her writings to survive. On October 18, 1930, she wrote to A. Edward Newton about her *Essays in Miniature*: ". . . a horrid little book" (ALS in Princeton University Library).

bloomed beyond the particular comforts she found in the often dull but always cozy quietude and familiarity of Philadelphia. "My niche may be small, but I made it myself," she would say. Much of the wit and the wisdom in her essays was not grasped even by her closest friends. She knew this. Yet she did not long for wider intellectual or literary companionship. She was content with the genuineness of the affection from her friends whose intellectual sensitivities may have been wanting, here and there, but whose personal sensitivities were not. In this respect—and in this respect only—she was like Edith Wharton, who once said about the society of Old New York that it was a bottle now empty but at the bottom of which there still remained a fine kind of lees, an essence of rarefied and unspoken sentiments.

There is another, related, element to consider. Her first books of essays were composed and published when she had passed the age of thirty. From her solitary reading she brought forth an immense accumulation of intellectual capital, upon which, assisted by her prodigious memory, she could draw for the next fifty years, replenishing it with ease. This capital was large enough not to be exhausted. Thus she was unaffected by the disease that affects American native talent: the brilliant early accomplishment unequaled in later years, never again blossoming in maturity. It was not her genius which was precocious; it was her maturity. Perhaps it was because of this precocious maturity—a rare accomplishment, to the point of being an oxymoron—that she remained unaffected by senility even in her eighties.

Because of this maturity she knew the limitations of public recognition. In this Philadelphia was, as usual, wanting—or, rather, slow.[189] (After she made her reputation in Boston, through the *Atlantic,* a certain lady in Philadelphia would occasionally ask her friends whether they knew a "Miss A. Riplear.") Unlike many other Philadelphia artists, she took this without much agitation. There is a passage in her fine little history of Philadelphia which applies very well to herself. "Philadelphia, like Marjorie Fleming's stoical turkey,

---

189. The first Philadelphia Award, carrying $10,000, established by Edward W. Bok, was accorded to Cornelius McGillicuddy (Connie Mack), the manager of the Philadelphia Athletics baseball team.

is 'more than usual calm,' when her sons and daughters win distinction in any field. She takes the matter quietly, as she takes most other matters, preserving with ease her mental balance, and listening unmoved to the plaudits of the outside world. This attitude is not wholly wise nor commendable, inasmuch as cities, like men, are often received at their own valuation, and some degree of self-assertion converts many a wavering mind. If the mistaking of geese for swans produces sad confusion, and a lamentable lack of perspective, the mistaking of swans for geese may also be a dangerous error. The birds languish, or fly away to keener air, and something which cannot be replaced is lost. Yet anything is better than having two standards of merit, one for use at home and one for use abroad; *and the sharp discipline of quiet neglect is healthier for a worker than that loud local praise which wakes no echo from the wider world.*"[190] The italics are mine.

Gradually, slowly, the neglect disappeared. After 1900 she was well recognized, well respected, on occasion celebrated.[191] She often said that she enjoyed her years between forty and sixty the most. But after the First World War, which, as we saw, was a searing experience for her mind, she complained more and more often of being tired, especially from her lecturing.[192] Yet her writing remained lively and sharp.[193] She found a certain satisfaction in her Clinton Street house. In her seventy-fifth year she embarked on her official trip to Spain, where she outwalked and outtalked many of the younger members of the American delegation. She was seventy-seven when she saw the Gershwin musical *Of Thee I Sing,* which she enjoyed thoroughly; she was pleased with the fact that her compatriots delighted in see-

---

190. *Philadelphia: The Place and the People*, 390–91,

191. She was vexed by the public celebrity of a distant cousin, who had become a society reporter on the *Evening Ledger*: "Agnes Repplier Junior, who often dispensed with the youthful appendage, was a comely, amiable young woman, not particularly intelligent, and as it turned out, not averse to reaping a little advantage from the hazards of mistaken identity." Witmer, 123. Her marriage eliminated this vexation.

192. Between 1912 and 1916 she lost many of her closest friends: Furness, Mitchell, the Irwin sisters, and Dr. White.

193. *Under Dispute* (Boston, 1924) and *Times and Tendencies* contain some of her best writing, to wit, "The Unconscious Humour of the Movies" in the latter.

ing "the inglorious nature of their absurdities."[194] As she gave up lecturing, she depended only on her writing. It was then, in the last decade of her writing career, that she turned out a number of books in which we can detect, here and there, a certain decline of verve. Between the seventy-fourth and seventy-seventh years of her life she wrote three biographies, as well as a book on cats and a book on tea.[195] They were followed by a book on laughter, which she wrote and had published after her eightieth birthday. The motto under the title read: *"Un gros rire vaut mieux qu'une petite larme."* A big laugh is worth more than a small tear. This is not the motto of a Genteel Lady of Letters.

In Pursuit of Laughter showed some of the marks of tiredness. Miss Repplier was becoming a bit predictable, and on occasion even repetitious. If *In Pursuit of Laughter* was not a potboiler, well, it was a *pot-au-feu*: a *pot-au-feu* put together by someone thoroughly at home with Gallic and American cooking, with the inherent qualities of all kinds of condiments and meat. "Our passionate loyalty to our humourists, our tolerance of the 'comic' in newspapers and cinemas," she wrote of her fellow Americans, "proves our need of laughter; but we are not gay. The appalling grin with which men and women are photographed for the press is as remote from gaiety as from reason."[196]

On her eightieth birthday the Cosmopolitan Club, of which in 1886 she had been a founding member, gave her a dinner (she was, in reality, eighty-two). The book collector A. Edward Newton was the toastmaster; there were many speeches in her honor. That year (1937) Houghton Mifflin published her own selection of her best essays, entitled *Eight Decades*. We encountered it before; there she did a sleight-of-hand about her age. *Eight Decades* begins with a forty-page autobiography. It is sprightly and colorful, amusing and witty, spangled with small particles of glitter that would be characteristic of the ornament of a woman half her years. Yet it tells very little about herself and her life. She was profoundly aware of the

---

194. *In Pursuit of Laughter*, 191.
195. *Père Marquette* (Garden City, NY, 1929), *Mère Marie of the Ursulines* (Garden City, NY, 1931), *Junípero Serra* (1933).
196. *In Pursuit of Laughter*, 221.

limitations of autobiographies, and she would not abandon the kind of rectitudinous reticence that accompanied her through her life.[197] During the following year she was found to be suffering from acute anemia. She also feared that her memory was fading, which worried her far more than anemia. She now retired to her bed. For the first time in her life she would not go to Mass on Sunday. "No, I won't. God is a good deal more understanding than relatives." "I am light-headed and heavy-footed." "All my time is now wasted. It has no meaning. Work is over."[198] This was an exaggeration. Her last essay, on the Housmans, was published in the *Atlantic* in January 1940. That year she was complimented and charmed by a young Philadel-phia scholar, George Stokes, who had begun writing a biographical study of her. She received him in Clinton Street, sometimes staying in bed, puffing on innumerable cigarettes. The scene should remind us for the last time: she, the contemporary of literary women such as Mrs. Humphrey Ward and Julia Ward Howe, had nothing in com-mon with them; she had many things in common with her younger contemporary Colette.

She lived to see her beloved France conquered and humiliated anew by a Germany much more brutal than that of the Kaiser or the heavy-footed tourists; she lived to see England alone against the wall, in its finest hour. But the fires of her anger now had died down; the awful scenes and issues of the Second World War flowed on the surface of her mind. Like the aged Hilaire Belloc, the erstwhile fiery Francophile and Germanophobe, everything she had proclaimed

---

197. "The Happiness of Writing an Autobiography": ". . . even the titles of certain auto-biographical works are saturated with self-appreciation. We can see the august simper with which a great lady in the days of Charles the Second headed her manuscript: 'A True Relation of the Birth, Breeding and Life of Margaret Cavendish, Duchess of Newcastle. Written by Herself.' Mr. Theodore Dreiser's *A Book about Myself* sounds like nothing but a loud human purr. The intimate wording of *Margot Asquith, an Autobiography* gives the key to all the cheerful confidences that follow. Never before or since has any book been so much relished by its author. She makes no foolish pretence of concealing the pleasure that it gives her; but passes on with radiant satisfaction from episode to episode, extract-ing from each in turn its full and flattering significance. The volumes are as devoid of revelations as of reticence. If at times they resemble the dance of the seven veils, the reader is invariably reassured when the last veil has been whisked aside, and he sees there is nothing behind it." *Under Dispute*, 90–91.
198. Witmer, 164.

about the danger of the Western nations from Germany came true; but she could no longer rouse herself to an indignant passion comparable to hers during the First World War. Unlike Belloc, she was not senile. She was eighty-eight years old when a bequest brought her an increase in comfort. She moved to an apartment in Overbrook. Meals, including breakfast, were brought to her. She had fallen in her bedroom and moved very little. Yet her mind was amazingly sharp. Reporters from the Philadelphia newspapers came to interview her on her birthdays; she waved them away with a kind of petulant charm. She had the pleasure of the company of her intellectual niece; and she lived to see the publication of a biographical study of her by Professor Stokes. She lived to be ninety-five. "Her face was a picture of distinguished intellect, reticence, sensitiveness, and tolerance, yet she never seemed old. She did not regret or complain, for a lifetime of stoicism was not easily discarded. She still possessed ardor and contemplation, and when death came to her, he came softly, imperceptibly, hardly distinguishable from his half-brother, sleep."[199]

"She was the Jane Austen of the essay. That she is not so recognized is a great—and, one hopes, temporary—loss." This I wrote now about thirty years ago, in my chapter about Agnes Repplier, in my book *Philadelphia 1900-1950: Patricians and Philistines*, the chapter which now serves for the introduction of the present volume. But the loss prevails. There has not been a revival of interest in Agnes Repplier. That is why I am grateful to ISI Books to entrust me with this, necessarily selective, collection of her essays.

Re-reading essay after essay, book after book by her for the purpose of this volume, I think that I can surmise the main reasons for this neglect. One simple explanation: in 1981, when my book was published, there were still some Philadelphians who remembered her name, and even a few who had read her writings.[200] Not now.

---

199. Ibid., 170.

200. I cannot resist the temptation to recount here an episode (on which I have been dining out ever since). Philadelphia, as Agnes herself often said, is not and has not been

But I think there is another, deeper reason. The fundament of her essays is, of course, her independence of mind. But, both beyond and beneath her—probably inimitable—style is the substantial matter of her illustrations of her arguments from the treasure-trove of her astonishing knowledge of English and French and American literature and history, her quoting and citing (and how effortlessly!) writers whom she knew so very well, but her later potential readers not at all.

In sum, not only the quality but the quantity of her knowledge was, and remains, stunning.

This condition may impress modern readers of Agnes Repplier as quite old-fashioned. But allow me to state that "old-fashioned" means something different from "antiquated". There is nothing antiquated in Agnes's style, which is direct, telling, and vigorous. It will strike a civilized reader with fresh gusts of air, and one gust of spirit after another. So she wrote most of her essays, some of them more than one hundred years ago. It is remarkable how little her writing style changed through more than eighty years. She had a superb ear (and memory) for poetry; but she never wrote poems. She wrote at least four good biographies, history here and there, but mostly essays. It was not easy for me to select some of them for this present book, where I have been governed by the need to select some of them because of their topics even more than because of the excellence of their style.

I re-read about thirty of her volumes (I found, suddenly and happily, that at least one dozen of them are in my possession, some of them with her own signature on their title pages). I even found a small gem of a pamphlet, printed privately, reproducing Thackeray's own drawings made when he had visited a friend in Philadelphia, *A Book of Drawings by William Makepeace Thackeray. A series of metamorphoses made in Philadelphia, 1853, for the children of William B. Reed, 1925. With a note by Agnes Repplier.* At the end of yet another excellent short essay she wrote: "For to Thackeray, humour was a

a very bookish city. In 1981, after the then customary presentation of my Philadelphia book at an author's reception at the Union League, a Philadelphia gentleman came up to me at the bar of a downtown restaurant: "I hear you wrote a wonderful book" he said, "I'm going to borrow it."

moral emancipation, and cynicism a delicate adjustment of reflection to experience . . . He loved great cities, and complex civilizations, and crowded canvases, and the supreme irony of truth. This knowledge lent wisdom to his pen and gaiety to his pencil. We learn and we laugh, and what better things are there in the world for us to do?" Eighty-four years later: surely better than watch and grin.

Philadelphia: A Short History

1

Introduction to *Philadelphia**

O ut of the mists that mercifully conceal those early school days which, being forgotten, are unduly praised, comes the spectre of a little American history with green sides and a red back, an odious little history, arranged in questions and answers like a catechism, and wholly destitute of anything that could arouse childish interest or quicken childish enthusiasm. One page and one only lingers in my memory, as a return for the many gloomy hours wasted in the companionship of this book,—a page containing a print of West's picture, of the "Great Treaty" at Shackamaxon.

Our grandfathers loved this picture, and implicitly believed all the details of the incident it portrays. We have outgrown our grandfathers' narrow artistic standards, and their broad historic credulity; and the agreeable consciousness of such double progress enriches our self-esteem. Yet it is a pleasant scene that West painted in those easy, ignorant days, when impressionism had still to be invented, and people had not begun to make a fetich of truth. The "Treaty Elm" spreading its mighty branches, as proud and as honored as England's "Royal Oak." William Penn, years older than his age, dressed as he never did dress in early manhood, benignantly blessing everybody. Venerable Friends, in the loosest and longest of coats, holding a parchment deed of mighty bulk, the document

* From *Philadelphia: The Place and the People,* 1898.

which has been lost for more than two hundred years. Boxes and bales of goods scattered on the sward. Indian braves solemnly inspecting their contents. Indian squaws and pappooses grouped picturesquely in the foreground. The whole composition suggesting an entertainment midway between a church fair and an afternoon tea, placid, decorous, satisfactory, and sincere.

This was the peaceful fashion in which the little Quaker colony took her infant steps, this was the atmosphere which nurtured her tender youth. And now, after two centuries have rolled slowly by, something of the same spirit lingers in the quiet city which preserves the decorum of those early years, which does not jostle her sister cities in the race of life, nor shout loud cries of triumph in their ears, nor flaunt magnificent streamers in the breeze to bid the world take note of each pace she advances.

Every community, like every man, carries to old age the traditions of its childhood, the inheritance derived from those who bade it live. And Philadelphia, though she has suffered sorely from rude and alien hands, still bears in her tranquil streets the impress of the Founder's touch. Simplicity, dignity, reserve, characterize her now as in Colonial days. She remembers those days with silent self-respect, placing a high value upon names which then were honored, and are honored still. The pride of the past mingles and is one with the pride of the present. The stainless record borne by her citizens a hundred and fifty years ago flowers anew in the stainless record their great-great-grandsons bear today; and the city cherishes in her cold heart the long annals of the centuries, softening the austerity of her presence for these favored inheritors of her best traditions. She is not eager for the unknown; she is not keen after excitement; she is not enamored of noise. Her least noticeable characteristic is enthusiasm. Her mental balance cannot lightly be disturbed. *Surtout pas trop de zêle,* she says with Talleyrand; and the slow, sure process by which her persuasions harden into convictions does not leave her, like a derelict, at the mercy of wind and wave. She spares herself the arduous labor of forming new opinions every morning, by recollecting and cherishing her opinions of yesterday. It is a habit which promotes solidity of thought.

To those who by right of heritage call themselves her sons, and even to such step-children as are, by nature or grace, attuned to the chill tranquility of their foster mother, Philadelphia has a subtle charm that endures to the end of life. In the restful atmosphere of her sincere indifference, men and women gain clearness of perspective, and the saving grace of modesty. Few pedestals are erected for their accommodation. They walk the level ground, and, in the healthy absence of local standards, have no alternative save to accept the broad disheartening standards of the world. Philadelphians are every whit as mediocre as their neighbors, but they seldom encourage each other in mediocrity by giving it a more agreeable name. Something of the old Quaker directness, something of the old Quaker candor,—a robust candor not easily subdued,—still lingers in the city founded by the "white truth-teller," whose word was not as the words of other men,—spoken to conceal his thoughts, and the secret purpose of his soul.

Deep is the debt of gratitude which the City of Peace owes to the many hands that have labored for two hundred years in her behalf; but deepest of all is her debt to Penn who knew her little but who loved her well, whom she thrust aside from her councils, and forgot in his hour of need, but whose influence lingers today in that atmosphere of serenity which is the finest characteristic of Philadelphia. More impetuous towns speed like meteors on their paths, dazzling the western world by their velocity, and dazzled themselves by their own glitter and glory; but the Quaker City sees them rush by without envy, without ambition, without distaste, without emotions of any kind. She knows, and she has known for many years, what is best for her; and if this best be ever out of reach, it is not by mere swiftness of step that she can hope to overtake it. She is content to grow slowly if she can grow symmetrically, and if grace and strength keep pace with her increasing bulk. She is content to face the future if she can hold closely to the past, recalling its lessons, valuing its traditions, respecting its memory, and loving in her cold, steadfast fashion the living links which connect her with her honorable history, with her part in the great story of the nation.

2

How the Quaker City Spent Its Money*

For nearly a century the history of Philadelphia is a placid record of unbroken good fortune. The tireless wrangling of two great conflicting interests injured the province very little, and gave her that most precious boon,—a standing quarrel which could be taken up by the combatants whenever they had leisure to engage in it. Had the Assembly and the Proprietary party worked together in accord, the colonists would have suffered grievously from the benumbing of those angry passions which childhood is bidden to restrain, but which make life a thing of abounding interest to healthily contentious men. The Indian wars, though they cost Pennsylvania both troops and money, left the city undevastated by the horrors which dyed deep with blood the annals of less fortunate communities. The stubborn and conservative Quakers guarded their town—Penn's precious legacy—with a wise watchfulness, and she waxed fairer and stronger every year. Her prosperity was not, indeed, a matter of sudden acquisition, like the affluence of New Zealand, where, Mr. Froude assures us, the laborers eat hothouse grapes. It was built up on solid foundations of industry and thrift, having Franklin's maxims for its weekday sermons, and Franklin's shining example to illustrate the text. The man who amassed his fortune penny by penny, and retired from business at the early age of forty-two, with

* From *Philadelphia: The Place and the People*, 1898.

a modest income of three thousand dollars, taught his neighbors a triple lesson of assiduity, economy, and moderation. It is only to be regretted that the edifying spectacle of colonial honor and enterprise should be marred by the dark shadow of privateering. In the Spanish war, and in King George's war, the virtuous Quaker City sent forth these armed marauders to snatch what prey they could; and that she was proud of their success, and pointed them out with elation to strangers visiting her busy docks, proves the exactness of Sydney Smith's cynical observation anent the stanch moral support to be derived from the most dubious of theories.

The increasing wealth of the province manifested itself in farmhouses so strongly and admirably built that time leaves no impression on their massive walls; in countryseats more spacious and beautiful than could be found in any other State save Virginia; in the fast-growing luxury of town life; and in a sane philanthropy, devoid of whims and sentiment. The charity of the Quakers has always extended to the bodies as well as to the souls of men. In 1713, when the city was still in its infancy, they built "for the habitation and succor of the poor and unfortunate," the pretty rural cottages long known as the Quaker almshouses. Each cottage had its patch of ground, where the aged inmates—unashamed by the stigma of pauperism—cultivated bright flowers and healing herbs. It was a peaceful haven, affording, not only shelter, but, as an old historian earnestly assures us, "opportunities for study and meditation." We smile when we read the words, but we sigh, too, recalling the bleak desolation, the abiding horror of a modern almshouse, and comparing it with the decent privacy of the happier poor nearly two hundred years ago, when the wisdom of our forefathers drew a deep line of distinction between the old and helpless, "the afflicted of God," and the sturdy beggar or shameless wench, for whom was made sharper and sterner provision. It is to the Quaker almshouse.

Home of the homeless,
Then in the suburbs it stood, in the midst of meadows and woodlands,

that tradition points as the final meeting place of Gabriel and Evangeline; and antiquarians who disprove the story with aggressive and importunate details might find a better use for their time and knowledge. In the graveyard of old St. Joseph's—hidden away in Willing's Alley from the wrath of hostile creeds—the lovers slept side by side; and the clamor of a great city echoed but faintly through the narrow, walled-in strip of consecrated ground, where, after so many years of sorrowful wandering, their faithful hearts found rest.

What the college was to the Episcopal and Proprietary party in Philadelphia, the Pennsylvania Hospital was to the Quakers,—a party stronghold, as well as a cherished and admirably administered institution. On its ancient corner-stone was cut deep this cheerful and devout inscription:—

In the year of Christ MDCCLV,
George the second happily reigning,
(For he sought the happiness of his people)
Philadelphia flourishing,
(For its inhabitants were public-spirited)
    This Building
By the bounty of the government,
And of many private persons,
    Was piously founded
For the relief of the sick and the miserable.
May the God of Mercies bless the undertaking.

Of the public spirit here gratefully commemorated, the erection of this hospital gives abiding proof. When, in 1750, Dr. Thomas Bond and a few charitable citizens realized the necessity of providing shelter for "sick and distempered strangers," their appeal for funds met with an immediate response. The Assembly voted at different times five thousand pounds to help them with the work. All classes endeavored honestly to assist. A special subscription was asked from "rich widows and other single women," and they answered nobly by raising a fund sufficient for the purchase of drugs. Although most of the money came from the Quakers, who kept the hospital always under their control, yet other churches contributed with amazing generosity. The pious freelance, Whitefield, collected, after an ardent and persuasive sermon, one hundred and seventy pounds. England, ever liberal to colonial charities, lent such material aid that the directors found their burden almost easy to bear. An Act of Parliament gave to the hospital all the unclaimed funds remaining in the hands of the trustees of the Pennsylvania Land Company in London, and this extraordinary windfall amounted to thirteen thousand pounds. The Proprietors, Thomas and Richard Penn, gave a portion of the land on which the building was erected, and an annuity of forty pounds a year. Finally, Dr. John Fothergill of London sent a beautifully articulated human skeleton, and so admirable a collection of anatomical models and drawings that the thrifty Friends refused to exhibit them gratuitously to the public. They were placed in a room apart, and Dr. Shippen explained them learnedly every other Saturday afternoon to such seekers after knowledge as were willing to pay a dollar for its acquisition.

It does not surprise us to find the name of Benjamin Franklin on the first board of managers. In point of fact, a Philadelphia board of managers which did not include Franklin would have been as great an anomaly as a Roman or a Florentine church without a trace of Michelangelo. It was Franklin who drew up the very sensible rules for the direction of the hospital, Franklin who was elected president of the board in 1756, and Franklin who characteristically proposed the distribution of tin boxes, lettered in gold, "Charity for the Hospital," and destined to receive the chance donations of benevolent friends and visitors. A penny given was a penny made, and the yearly reports of the institution show how much of its income was derived from the small contributions of well-wishers whose narrow means forbade a larger dole. Gifts of various kinds were proffered by prominent citizens; among them a second skeleton (skeletons were rare enough to be held in high esteem) which, being presented by Miss Deborah Morris, after the death of her brother, Dr. Benjamin Morris, was, we are assured, "gratefully received, and honorably deposited in the apothecary's shop."

The site on which the hospital was erected—not without long

contention, for the Proprietors had wished to donate a less available piece of ground—was admirably chosen, and the building itself, like all other important buildings of the time, is a model of dig-nified simplicity, finely proportioned, and free from meretricious decoration. It is well for us who live in an age of over-ornamentation that we can rest our weary eyes upon the graceful severity of colo-nial architecture where nothing needless can be found. The ample lawn was shaded by two rows of beautiful trees planted by Hugh Roberts, one of the first managers, in 1756, and among them grew and flourished a scion of the famous Treaty Elm, pleasantly refuting the slanderous tongues which mocked that historic monument, that mute witness of a nation's peace.

The prosperity of the hospital was unbroken, its efficiency unim-paired, until the dark days which followed the Revolution, when the terrible depreciation of the currency, the chaotic confusion of the public service, and the determination of the legislature to tax charitable institutions, crippled and well-nigh ruined it. Resolute labor and resolute resistance on the part of the managers averted the impending shipwreck, but years dragged by before the old sphere of quiet usefulness was even partially regained. It is pleasant to record that at this juncture the First Troop of Philadelphia City Cavalry gave to the Pennsylvania Hospital the entire sum received by it for services during the Revolutionary war; and the maternity ward for poor married women was built and endowed with this money. A very different, but equally welcome donation was the picture of "Christ Healing the Sick," which Benjamin West generously presented to the institution in 1817, and which awakened such enthusiasm in the hearts of our uncritical grandfathers that the adroit managers of the hospital—mindful still of Dr. Franklin's maxims—placed it on exhibition, and realized nearly twenty thousand dollars from the eager crowds who thronged to see it. The big canvas is a replica of the painting originally intended by West for Philadelphia; but which, when it was seen in London, excited, we are told, "such a glow of admiration that nobles and commons, rich and poor, united in the determination to retain it in the country." Verily, an artist so blessed by the patronage, so burdened by the praises of his own generation, might well afford indifference to the acrimonious verdicts of posterity.

It was not in philanthropy alone, in the building of almshouses, libraries and hospitals, that the rich colonists of the Quaker City found a use for their ample incomes. They spent their money, after a reasonable fashion, upon creature comforts, and in moderate display. Within their red brick houses, "stately and three stories high, in the mode of London," writes Gabriel Thomas as early as 1696, reigned security and modest affluence. Balconies and sundials lent to these demure homes an occasional air of gayety and picturesqueness. "Everything necessary for the Support of Life throughout the whole Year," might be found in the far-famed Philadelphia markets; and, if we may trust the evidence of colonial letters and diaries, more ingenuous and less jubilant as a rule than colonial chroniclers, our forefathers heartily enjoyed the good things which Providence had kindly placed at their disposal. In the published journal of Jacob Hiltzheimer, who lived to see the Revolution, and was apparently but little interested in that great crisis, we find such scandalous entries as this: "Feb. 14th, 1766. At noon went to William Jones's, to drink punch; met several of my friends, and got decently drunk. The groom could not be accused of the same fault." Whether this means that the groom drank not at all, or that his libations went beyond the limits of decency, does not very clearly appear; but noon seems an early hour to settle down seriously to punch, even on Saint Valentine's day. On other occasions we read that Mr. Hiltzheimer went with his two sons and Daniel Wister to Joseph Galloway's place, "to eat turtle,"—a more innocent indulgence; that on the tenth of May he saw a "ten-pound race between Joseph Hogg's and John Buckingham's horses"; and that—being well disposed to divers sorts of entertainment—he found equal pleasure in bull-baiting, and in witnessing the performance of *Romeo and Juliet*, at the Old Southwark Theatre. An opportunity for special festivity was the King's birthday, June 4th, when he dined on the green banks of the Schuylkill, in company with three hundred and eighty loyal citizens, all in most jovial humor. Any number of healths were drunk at this gay repast, "among them Dr. Franklin's, which gave great satisfaction to everybody." A long boat was then dragged to the water's edge and launched, while the firing of "many great guns" announced King George's birthday to the town.

No one was better disposed towards a moderate conviviality than Franklin himself, for all his maxims and apothegms. In that old house on High Street where he lived and died, where, in the garden, he flew his immortal kite, and where he attached his own lightning rod to his own wall, thereby greatly entertaining his curious neighbors, there reigned always hospitality and good cheer. True, he sent his sister Jane a spinning wheel instead of the coveted tea table, desiring her to be a "notable housewife." True, he recommended the *Whole Duty of Man*, and the *Young Lady's Library*, as proper reading for his daughter Sally, in place of the novels for which her spirit yearned. But, nevertheless, there remains now in the possession of the Pennsylvania Historical Society that delightful punch keg which could be rolled so easily from guest to guest, and which carried the generous liquor circling around Franklin's board. A curious little keg this, pretty, portly, and altogether unlike other punch bowls left us from colonial days. And what of that often quoted letter written by Franklin in England to his wife, and promising her, not spinning wheels and decorous dull books, but the foreign crockery dear to the hearts of all colonial dames. Yet not every spouse would have felt pleased by this dubious compliment from an absent husband.

"I also forgot to mention among the china a large fine jug for beer, to stand in the cooler. I fell in love with it at first sight; for I thought it looked like a fat jolly dame, clean and tidy, with a neat blue and white calico gown on, good-natured and lovely, and put me in mind of—somebody."

Praise is not always charming. Had Mrs. Franklin loved poetry as well as she loved her husband, which happily does not seem to have been the case, she would have felt more pain than pleasure at hearing her merits extolled by him in such halting verses as these:—

Not a word of her face, of her shape, or her air,
Or of flames, or of darts, you shall hear;

I beauty admire, but virtue I prize,
That fades not in seventy year.

In peace and good order my household she guides,
Right careful to save what I gain;
Yet cheerfully spends, and smiles on the friends
I've the pleasure to entertain.

Well, the lines show at least that Franklin did like to entertain his friends, and that it gladdened him to see his wife lay aside her customary frugality on those blithesome occasions, when the punch keg went rolling round. Mrs. Franklin—being but a woman, albeit a great man's helpmate—found perchance a keener joy in furnishing her house than in feeding her husband's guests. There is a delightful blending of conscious thrift and timorous extravagance in the account she writes him of her modestly garnished chambers.

> The chairs downstairs are plain horsehair, and look as well as Paduasoy, and are admired by all. In the little south room is a carpet I bought cheap for its goodness, and nearly new. In the parlor is a Scotch carpet which has much fault found with it. In the north room, where we sit, we have a small Scotch carpet, the small bookcase, brother John's picture, and one of the King and Queen. In the room for our friends we have the Earl of Bute hung up, and a glass.

The simplicity of the philosopher's surroundings contrasted sharply with the beauty and elegance of more pretentious dwellings; with Edward Shippen's house, for example, which is described by a contemporary chronicler as a veritable palace of delights, girt by an ample park, "and having a very famous and pleasant summer house erected in the middle of his garden, abounding with tulips, pinks, carnations, roses, and lilies, not to mention those that grew wild in the fields; and also a fine lawn upon which reposed his herd of tranquil deer."

A herd of deer reposing on South Second Street seems as strange an anomaly as the concealed staircase, the "priest's escape," in

James Logan's countryseat, "Stenton." Who in that dignified and law-abiding household could ever have needed to escape, save from importunate visitors, or from the friendly Indians who came again and again to Logan, as to their truest ally, seeking counsel and aid in their difficulties. It was not unusual for several hundred Indians to stay a week encamped in the Stenton woods, and treated always with the greatest kindness and hospitality by the master of the house, whose public duties left him scant leisure for rest. Small wonder that Cannassetego, chief of the Onondagas, bewailed the approaching end of their most trusted friend, and touchingly entreated the Council that when Logan's soul went to God, another might be chosen in his place, "of the same prudence and ability in counseling, and of the same tender disposition and affection for the Indians."

The beauty of Stenton lay in its broad lands, its superb avenue of hemlocks, which tradition pleasantly but mendaciously asserted to have been planted by William Penn, its lofty wainscoted rooms, its generous fireplaces, ornamented with blue and white tiles, its graceful staircase,—that test of colonial architecture,—its air of dignified and scholarly repose. Here, in the well-lit library, were ranged those noble old books which subsequently became the city's legacy; and looking at them with love and pride, their owner felt a not unreasonable regret that no one in the future was likely to cherish them as he did. "I have four children now with me," he writes to Thomas Story in 1734, "who I think take more after their mother than me, which I am sure thou wilt not dislike in them; yet if they had more of a mixture, it might be of some use to bring them through the world; and it sometimes gives me an anxious thought that my considerable collections of Greek and Roman authors, with others in various languages, will not find an heir in my family to use them as I have done, but after my decease may be sold or squandered away."

If ghosts can reasonably rejoice as well as groan and rattle chains, then must the spirit of James Logan, scholar and statesman, have exulted over the patient toil of his grandson's wife, heir of his name though not of his blood, as she faithfully and intelligently sorted, copied and annotated the important letters stored in the Stenton library, and wrought from them a lasting record of his life and work.

The "Penn and Logan Papers," with their wealth of historic and colonial interest, might never have seen the light, had not Deborah Logan worked year after year with unwearied and unrewarded fidelity in those too scant hours of leisure which the mistress of a large and busy household could dare to call her own.

We think of Quakers now as clad perpetually in sober drab, with close bonnets or broad-brimmed hats; but for many years after the founding of Philadelphia they wore no exclusive costumes, contenting themselves with avoiding in a general way the allurements of fashion and finery. Hence the stern warnings, the sharp reproofs directed from time to time against those daughters of Eve who yearned after fancy fig leaves, who let their hair stray wantonly over their brows, or sought to widen their modest petticoats with the seductive crinoline. As Thomas Chalkley vigorously but vainly remarked, "If Almighty God should make a woman in the same Shape her hoop makes her, Everybody would say truly it was monstrous; so according to this real truth they make themselves Monsters by art."

Nor were the female Friends averse to glowing colors, remembering perhaps Penn's sky-blue sash which gave them warrant for their weakness. Their silk aprons rivaled the rainbow, and not infrequently their gowns were of red or green, instead of that dove-like hue which Whittier loved and praised. Sir Godfrey Kneller's portrait of Sarah, elder daughter of James Logan of Stenton, and wife of Isaac Norris of Fairhill, shows us a stately young woman dressed in deep blue, and with the air of an English court beauty rather than a colonial Quaker matron. Thomas Lloyd's daughter, Mary, who married Isaac Norris the elder, is also painted in a blue gown relieved with crimson; and her granddaughter, Mary Dickinson, appears all in red, that deep seducing red which the Paris artists of today love better than any other shade. These women, despite their partiality for vivid tints, were strict Quakers, but Quakers upon whom the rigid rules of an exclusive costume had yet to be imposed. Perhaps Mrs. Dickinson was one of the last to rejoice in the glory of color, for we find *her* daughter, Maria Logan, painted in the orthodox dress of the Friends, and presenting a curious contrast to her resplendent kinsfolk. There is ample evidence to show that the scarlet cloaks so popular in provincial England (who does not remember poor ill-fated Sylvia's?) found their way over the ocean, and created much disturbance among the sober-minded and austere. That one of these gay garments, "almost new, with a double cape," was stolen from Franklin's house in 1750, proves that the philosopher did not seek to restrain the natural longing of wife and daughter for the shining, booths of Vanity Fair.

Gayer and gayer grew the Quaker City that had been so demure in childhood. Coaches emblazoned with heraldic devices rolled through the ill-paved streets. In the bitter cold of winter days the frozen Delaware was covered with merry throngs; and there is a pleasant flavor of colonial simplicity in the interesting information, wafted along a century and more, that the best skaters of their day were General Cadwalader and Massey the biscuit maker. In the bitter cold of winter nights, wax candles shone softly down on Philadelphia's sons and daughters, as they met for the famous Dancing Assemblies that date from 1749, and lend an air of prim worldliness to the uneventful annals of the town. Dancing seems never to have been regarded with the same stern disapprobation that made the theater a forbidden joy. Whitefield, indeed, who was impartially opposed to cakes and ale in any shape, waged an earnest crusade against this, as against all other diversions, and set himself the serious task of remodeling the nature of youth. But before he came to make a dull world duller, the colonists who were not Quakers had smiled indulgently upon such harmless mirth; and the Quakers, though not dancing themselves, had been serenely content that others should. Mr. Richard Castelman, writing in 1710, records with a grateful heart the kindness and courtesy of "the facetious Mr. Staples, the dancing master, who was the first stranger of Philadelphia that did me the honor of a visit. To his merry company I owe the passing of many a sad hour, that might have hung heavy upon the hands of a man deprived of friends and fortune in an alien land."

Thirty years later, we find several dancing masters prepared to teach "fashionable English and French dances, after the newest and politest manner practiced in London, Dublin, and Paris"; and, with the perfection of such accomplishments, there came naturally in time subscription balls, in which the graces thus acquired, could be properly shown to the world. These balls, if they somewhat scandalized the elect, were favored with the approbation and patronage of the Episcopal clergy, who were well disposed towards any form of entertainment which the Quakers rejected, and of which the Presbyterians disapproved. The Assemblies were not scenes of wild dissipation, nor was there any excessive extravagance to provoke the direful eloquence of the pulpit. They began at precisely six o'clock in the evening, and by midnight the dancers were all wending their ways homeward. The old subscription ticket cost forty shillings; and for this moderate outlay a gentleman could take the lady of his choice to sixteen or eighteen entertainments, the dances being given every Thursday night in the winter and early spring. The supper was of the very lightest order, consisting, it was said, "chiefly of something to drink"; a not inadequate description of a repast where five gallons of rum and two hundred limes were consumed in punch, and nine shillings' worth of "milk bisket" represented the solid food,—a half-pennyworth of bread to this intolerable deal of sack. Card tables were prepared for the amusement of those who did not dance, and who appear to have been less patient then than now, and less disposed to play a purely passive part.

The invitations were often printed on the undecorated backs of common playing cards, blank cards of any kind being exceedingly scarce, and spades and hearts being only too abundant in an age which had not yet learned to repudiate gambling as a sadly unprofitable vice. No wife nor daughter of mechanic or tradesman was suffered to enter the Assemblies which were rigidly aristocratic, and no flippant coquetry was permitted to interfere with the decorous order of procedure. The ladies who arrived earliest had places duly assigned them in the first set, and those who followed were distributed throughout other sets, either at the discretion of the directors, or according to the numbers they drew,—a melancholy arrangement, fraught, like the modern dinner, with many painful possibilities. It was Miss Polly Riché who in 1782 first revolted against this stringent rule, and insisted on standing up in any set she fancied, thus precipitating a quarrel between the gentlemen who supported her recusancy and the managers of the Assembly. But what other conduct could have been expected in 1782? Cornwallis had surrendered; the war of the Revolution was practically at an end; independence had been won, and Philadelphia was slowly struggling to emerge from chaos into a new law and order. An evil time this for conservatives, as Miss Polly Riché doubtless understood; so she struck her little blow for liberty, and struck it not in vain. The exaltation of freedom manifested itself on all sides in a general disposition to obey nobody, and the hour was ripe for revolt.

3

Lords of Misrule*

A city which has been for nine months in the hands of a foreign enemy is always a pitiable sight. Armies are demoralizing
things, and it is only after they have taken their departure that the
full extent of the mischief they have wrought becomes apparent to
every eye. Sober thrift and quiet rectitude have well-nigh vanished.
The industrious artisan has become a midnight brawler; the once
decent young housewife walks the streets, an outcast, with her bas-
tard baby in her arms. Restlessness and discontent are in the very
air, and the old, dull, decorous life has become distasteful, alike to
men and women. Poor Philadelphia, bruised, and sore, and shaken,
needed a firm and kindly rule to bring her back to health; but having suffered sadly from her foes, she found herself, on the return of
friends, to be in a far worse case than ever. It is true there were not
wanting men who, like Morris, and Wilson, and Dr. Rush, strove
hard to stem the tide of violence, and to save their city from an ignoble reign of terror, which had not even the saving grace of mistaken
enthusiasm. But loud-voiced demagogues held the public ear; and
the mob, so long repressed by the presence of an unsympathetic sol-
diery, was once more happy and alert. There was a fierce demand for
vengeance upon Tories, and the selection of a few victims to appease

---

* From *Philadelphia: The Place and the People*, 1898.

the people became a matter of immediate necessity. The men picked out for this purpose were well chosen, being too poor and humble to have troublesome friends, yet not so absolutely insignificant as to make their execution a matter of no moment to anybody. They were both Quakers, a happy stroke of diplomacy, and both were charged with the same offence. Carlisle, a carpenter, had kept one of the city gates during the English occupancy; and Roberts, a miller, though no such important post was ever assigned him, had enlisted under General Howe's command, and would have been wiser had he departed with the rest of the troops.

These two carefully selected malefactors were tried in the criminal court for high treason, and condemned to death. The jury that brought in the verdict of guilty recommended them to mercy, and petitions for their pardon were signed by many hundreds of citizens, including prominent Whigs. But the mob, like the Minotaur, demanded its dole, and on the fourth of November, Elizabeth Drinker writes sadly in her diary:—

> They have actually put to death, hanged on the commons, John Roberts and Abraham Carlisle, this morning. An awful day it has been.

General Arnold was placed by Washington in command of Philadelphia, and at once began that life of costly and formal elegance which gave universal dissatisfaction, and to supply the money for which he plunged deeper and deeper into speculations. It is not always an easy matter to content civilians, who have ever been wont to complain loudly of the wantonness of soldiers; and we find the irascible Christopher Marshall inveighing with much bitterness against the officers of Washington's staff: "Careless of us, but carefully consulting where they shall go to spend the winter in jollity, gaming, and carousing;" a reproach to which the wind-swept hills of Valley Forge could have made answer true. Arnold's unpopularity, however, was a serious matter. In social life he had many friends, and his marriage with Miss Margaret Shippen allied him closely to the most prominent families in Philadelphia; but the people in general—not the rabble, but the respectable portion of the community—were deeply angered by his pride, and regarded his suddenly acquired wealth with equal envy and mistrust. Joseph Reed, the president of the Executive Council and the acknowledged leader of the Constitutionalists, was his avowed enemy; and the quarrels between these two opposing powers relieved Philadelphia of any oppressive dulness during the autumn and early winter of 1779. Reed accused Arnold of gross venality; Arnold accused Reed of inciting riots, and laid upon his shoulders—unjustly—the blame for the shameful inertness which permitted a mob of only two hundred men to destroy what property it pleased on the fourth of October, and to shoot Captain Campbell at the window of his own house.

In truth, it was a time of reckless agitation, and the spirit of revolt against all authority, public or private, was rapidly undermining common safety and domestic restraint. Elizabeth Drinker writes on one page of her journal: "Our great men, or the men in power, are quarrelling very much among themselves;" and on the next, with a ludicrous appreciation of her own personal discomfort in this fine, strange atmosphere of freedom: "Our new maid had a visitor all day, and has invited her to lodge with her, without asking leave. Times are much changed, and maids have become mistresses."

We hear a great deal during the next few years, both in letters and journals, about the vexatious behavior of servants. Marshall grows eloquent on the subject, and confesses that his wife has been made ill more than once by sheer anxiety for a little lass who has been bound to them, and who persists, notwithstanding many exhortations and corrections, in staying out all night. The streets of Philadelphia, once so quiet and secure, were no longer safe for any woman after the twilight hour. The country roads, once peaceful as those of Arcady, were now infested by prowling soldiers, deserters, and highwaymen. The history of the Doans, five robber brothers, "strong, handsome, generous, and humane,"—if we may trust contemporary records,—affords a pleasing illustration of the time. These famous and very popular outlaws were Tory sympathizers who, in the beginning of the war, hoped to preserve a strict neutrality; but who found themselves soon objects of suspicion and attack. They were heavily fined for non-attendance on militia duty, their stock was sold, their farm was confiscated. They then resolved to follow the memorable examples of Dick Turpin and Claude Duval, and, taking the road, became a terror to the whole countryside. Like their models, they were capriciously generous, giving freely to the poor what they stole from the rich; and the small farmers of the neighborhood, whose political principles were of the vaguest order, had no fault to find with men who never took so much as a turnip from their fields, and who often assisted them in the profitable but perilous business of supplying food to the hungry English soldiers. Women, with their customary disregard for dull integrity, looked upon the five brothers as heroes of romance; and children, listening eagerly to tales of their intrepid exploits, resolved to be highwaymen themselves as soon as ever they were grown. "The Doans," we are told, "delighted to injure public property, but did no harm to the weak, the poor, or the peaceful."

Even public property, however, deserves some sort of protection, and even the rich weary in time of being despoiled. When the depredations of these spirited outlaws became too heavy for endurance, a strong body of militia was sent to assist the sheriff in tracking them down. They were hunted day and night, were finally brought to bay, and made a most desperate resistance. Two were shot dead by the soldiers, one escaped, and two were brought prisoners to Philadelphia, and hanged without delay. In the city they excited profound sympathy. "Many temperate people," says their historian, "expressed great commiseration for them"; and the memory of their courage and their kindness surviving the memory of their misdeeds, they grew in time to be considered as upholders of a lost cause, rather than criminals brought to justice, and expiating their offences against society upon the gallows tree.

None of this sentimental regard was evinced for another class of lawbreakers, whose transgressions were of the mildest order, and who sinned against the community, only that they might obey the troublesome dictates of their consciences. The Quakers could not and would not serve in the militia. Strict members of the Society held it unlawful to offer an armed resistance to any authority, however tyrannous and oppressive. This subjected them to heavy fines, which, unhappily, they thought it, not only inconvenient, but wrong, to pay. Certain taxes levied for military purposes were also regarded by them as iniquitous, and they opposed to all such measures their old weapon of passive, impregnable obstinacy. In colonial days, wise men like Benjamin Franklin had known how to circumvent these ill-timed scruples; and the Quakers had not always been averse to the diplomacy which wrested from them measures they could not openly concede, and saved them from a dangerous rupture with conflicting powers. But the men now holding authority were in no humor for dallying with the disaffected, or making allowances for perverse conscientiousness. The Friends, moreover, were exceedingly unpopular with the mob, which was sure to applaud any severe measures passed against them. Already many prominent members of the Society had suffered banishment and confiscation. Those who remained were liable at any time to have their houses searched for English goods, or their furniture dragged away to be sold for an unpaid fine. The entries in Elizabeth Drinker's diary show her to have lost in this manner so many of her household chattels, that the reader wonders she had pot or pan, chair or table, left in her pillaged home. There is something irresistibly pathetic in the sight of any woman despoiled of those belongings to which she clings with an affection man seldom understands; and our sympathy for this Quaker housewife is all the keener because she utters no word of complaint, but states as briefly as possible, and without comment, the losses she suffers day by day.

On the fourteenth of June, 1779, she writes: "George Pickering came this afternoon for the non-association fine, which came to thirteen pounds, which is thirteen shillings, as the money now is exchanged twenty to one. He took a looking glass worth between forty and fifty shillings, six new-fashioned pewter plates, and a three-quart pewter basin; little or nothing the worse for the wear."

Again, in the early autumn, she makes a similar entry: "This morning, in meeting time, (myself at home) Jacob Franks and a son of Cling, the vendue master, came to seize for the Continental tax. They took from us one walnut dining table, one mahogany tea table, six handsome walnut chairs with open backs, crow feet, a shell on the back and on each knee,"—how lovingly minute this description!—"a mahogany-framed sconce looking glass, and two large pewter dishes. They carried them off in a cart from the door to Cling's."

Poor mistress of an empty house who watched her well-kept chairs dragged off in this ignominious way to public execution, and whose grief at losing them was heightened by the knowledge that the miserable sums for which they were to be sold bore no proportion to their value! There is real bitterness—though still no open outcry—in the brief note of May 1, 1780: "Jeremiah Baker took a mahogany folding card table from us this morning, for a Northern Liberty tax amounting to about eighteen shillings. The table was worth between three and four pounds."

How very much easier and more agreeable to have paid the eighteen shillings, we cannot help thinking; but there is no tyrant so oppressive as an inexorable conscience, and it is plain that this alternative never even presented itself to the minds of the unfortunate Quakers, despoiled by the strong hand of the law.

All this time, the depreciation of the currency, the scarcity of provisions, the alarmingly high prices demanded for the bare necessities of life, and the growing unwillingness of merchants to sell at any price, were fast bringing Philadelphia to a condition of absolute distress. The angry Constitutionalists clung to the notion that the remedy for these evils lay in stringent legislation, and they resolved to bully the state back into its old prosperity. It was not possible, indeed, for the Committee of Inspection to make butter, sorely though the butter was needed; but it *was* possible to pass a law, forbidding any man to pay more than fifteen shillings a pound for it. Neither could the members of the Committee grow wheat, though the poor cried out for bread; but they could devise another law, forbidding farmers and traders to sell their grain privately, or to ask its full value in the open markets. Nothing is easier than this kind of legislation, and nothing more purely inefficacious.—"There shall be in England seven half-penny loaves sold for a penny; the three-hooped pot shall have ten hoops; and I will make it felony to drink small beer." Rather than part with goods at a loss, the merchants closed their shops, the importers concealed their stores, the farmers brought no more provisions for the hungry townsfolk to eat.

Congress, meanwhile, was helping liberally to lead the country to financial dishonor and ruin by repeated issues of worthless paper,—five millions one month, ten millions another, twenty millions the next, until the currency became so absolutely valueless as to pass into a familiar proverb,—"not worth a Continental." By the close of the war, four hundred dollars of American money would not bring four English shillings; but as early as 1780, a man might come perilously nigh starvation while his pockets were lined with notes. "I have more money than ever I had, but I am poorer than ever I was," complained a writer in Dunlap's *Packet;* and his state was the state of all. An apprentice lad named Leyham, having served two months in the militia, received two hundred dollars for his pay. He bought a pair of shoes for one hundred dollars, invested another hundred in a sleigh ride, and went empty handed home. A Philadelphia barber of a humorous turn of mind papered the walls of his shop with the depreciated currency, to the huge delight of his customers. At the sale of Cornelius Land's household effects, a frying pan brought one hundred and twenty-five dollars; a wood saw, one hundred and eighty-five dollars; three steel forks, one hundred and twelve dollars, and an old clock, eleven hundred dollars. Silk sold in the Philadelphia shops at one hundred dollars a yard, tea at sixty dollars a pound. A bill of Colonel Allen's has come down to us from this happy period, and illustrates the formidable cost of articles which could never have been considered luxuries.

1 Pair Boots	$600.00
6 3/4 yds. Calico, at 885 per Yard	$752.00
6 yds. Chintz, at $150 do.	$900.00
4 1/2 yds. Moreen, at $100 do.	$450.00
4 Handkerchiefs, at $100 each	$400.00
8 yds. Quality Binding, at $4 per Yard	$32.00
1 Skein Silk	$10.00
	$3,144.00

Jan. 5th, 1781.

Quite a little fortune for such a modest account. How many thousands of dollars must a woman have crowded into her purse, when she went forth to do a morning's shopping!

It seems incredible that men could be found willing to play their parts in this financial farce, and to thrust the dismal diversion upon others. But in the spring of 1781 a new issue of paper currency was ordered, and, at the same time, stringent laws were passed to compel the people to receive it. Any one who expressed a preference for real money, when this make-believe money was offered to him, should be taught by heavy fines the wickedness of such unpatriotic discrimination. A small minority of Anti-Constitutionalists, led by Robert Morris and Thomas Mifflin, did, indeed, oppose the measure with all their strength; and, knowing too well such opposition was in vain, Morris prepared and offered to the Assembly a protest, in which he expressed in no unfaltering terms the contempt of a sane and honorable man for such wanton destruction of the public credit. The time was soon to come when the finances of the country were to be in his capable hands; but, even in the present chaotic confusion, he labored hard to bring about some semblance of law and order. The Bank of Pennsylvania, which was founded solely in the interest of Washington's army, was due largely to his ability and munificence. Without its help, the ragged and hungry troops must have either disbanded or starved in their quarters. The Bank of North America, chartered by Congress as well as by the Assembly, was organized upon his plans, and controlled by his policy. In the days of our deepest humiliation it restored credit, quickened commerce, supplied some measure of integrity, and saved us from financial ruin. Its history, however, belongs to a later period, when foreign foes had yielded their place to domestic enemies, less easily reckoned with, and far less easily subdued.

In January, 1779, Congress celebrated with a great civic banquet the long desired and long delayed alliance with France. It had been no easy task for Franklin to cement this alliance, and to make of sentimental friendship a firm national bond. The French, indeed, had received him with effusive delight. He was the idol of the hour. His house at Passy was the resort of statesmen, scientists, and scholars. If he appeared in the streets, the mob shouted itself hoarse in his honor; when he went to court, fair ladies dropped wreaths upon his head, which must have been inexpressibly embarrassing. Wits praised his conversation, dandies, his dress, and poets dedicated to him verses that were fully as bad as his own. His benignant features were painted over and over again, and his portraits set in lockets, rings, and snuff-boxes. Learned academicians shed tears of joy on seeing him embraced by Voltaire. The enthusiasm he aroused extended itself to the country he represented; and the cause of the colonists was pronounced to be the cause of justice, liberty, and humanity. Yet none the less, France hesitated long ere she sent her aid to these admirable patriots, the success of whose arms seemed then more than doubtful; and French capitalists prudently declined to lend a single franc to men whose courage and principles they ardently admired, but whose financiering was open to objections. From the universal admiration for all things pertaining to America, the American currency was most unkindly omitted.

It cannot be denied that the allurements of a brilliant society, and the still more congenial companionship of learned men, beguiled Franklin into an occasional neglect of his mission. He wrote some excellent pamphlets which few people read, and which convinced nobody; and he assured his friends at home that nothing but their own success would persuade France to become their ally. This was true. Burgoyne's surrender at Saratoga did more service than a year's hard talking. For the first time, French strategists thought it worth while to lend aid to the colonies, in the hope of injuring Great Britain. The treaty which recognized the independence of the United States was signed February sixth, 1778; the following month, Franklin was formally received at court as an American commissioner; and, on the thirteenth of April, D'Estaing sailed with his fleet from Toulon.

The arrival in France of that clear-headed man of affairs, John Adams, brought order out of chaos, and gave a less sentimental basis to the friendship between the two nations. Franklin was appointed our minister; and, while Adams toiled like a clerk in the commissioner's office, the philosopher played chess with Mme. Brillon, or wrote his famous "Bagatelles" for the amusement of that vivacious slattern, Mme. Helvetius. He was now over seventy, and had merited a few years of trifling by a lifetime of arduous and useful labor. Leisure he enjoyed, as well as the lively and affectionate society of women. The enthusiasm manifested by France for himself, and for his work, awakened in his heart corresponding sentiments of cordiality; and he had no fault to find with this Arcadian and misrepresented nation, save that it took too much snuff, and wore too much powder on its hair,—offences so venial they could hardly have merited a revolution for their nemesis. At times, amid the pleasures and honors of his official life, he sighed for his old home, and begged to be recalled; but his popularity was so great, and his name carried with it such weight and influence in diplomatic circles, that it was not deemed expedient to permit his return until 1785, when Thomas Jefferson was sent to fill his place.

The alliance with France infused fresh hope and courage into the hearts of the despondent Americans. On the twenty-fifth of August, 1780, the Chevalier de Luzerne gave a grand entertainment to the members of Congress and other prominent citizens, in honor of the French king's birthday. Our enthusiasm for our allies was mounting fast to fever heat, and, indeed, the country sorely needed any emotion which could enliven or sustain it. Confidence was lost. Our troops, ill fed, ill clad, unpaid, were sullen and mutinous, held in their ranks with difficulty, notwithstanding the brutal punishments inflicted on deserters, and accustomed to revenge their own hardships upon the farmers and country people whom they plundered without mercy. The feeble resources of the revenue had been taxed to the utmost. Political leaders, impotent for good, were quarrelling fiercely among themselves, and Philadelphia was the chosen arena for their disgraceful strife. "It is obvious," wrote Reed to Washington, "that the bulk of the people are weary of the war"; and Washington sadly confessed in return that never before had he seen the discontent so general and so alarming. The French officers were angry and aghast at the forlorn condition of our affairs, which seemed hopeless to men who could not understand what splendors of endurance and action still lay behind that "slough of Despond." "Send us ships, troops, and money," wrote Rochambean to Vergennes; "but do not depend upon these people, nor upon their means."

When the skies were darkest, and brave hearts were heaviest, came the news of Arnold's proposed treachery, casting a taint of dishonor upon the whole country, and adding a burden of bitter humiliation to the accumulated disasters of the war. The plot, indeed, was discovered, West Point was saved, and André died a shameful death on the bleak hillside of Tappan.

> He was not slain with the sword,
> Knight's axe, or the knightly spear;

and the tragic sharpness of his fate has made imperishable the name of the blithe young soldier whose race was so swiftly run. He is truly the world's conqueror whose name the world holds dear. Not years of honorable work, well done and amply rewarded, win this capricious and undying regard; but rather the sudden snatching away of life full to the brim of gladness, and gay courage, and the promise of noble things. André's remains were carried over the sea in 1821, and interred in the south aisle of Westminster Abbey, where sleep the best and bravest of England's soldier sons. The inscription on his monument states simply that he was beloved by his fellow officers, and that he died for his country and his king.

In Philadelphia, where Arnold was so well known, and where the proudest and happiest period of his life had been passed, the news of his treason awakened a fierce but easily allayed excitement. His estate was immediately confiscated, and everything that belonged to him was publicly sold. His wife entreated permission to remain under her father, Mr. Edward Shippen's, protection; but this grace was denied her, and she received orders from the Executive Council to leave Pennsylvania within two weeks. She joined her husband in New York, and subsequently went with him to London, where Sir Banastre Tarleton was wont to declare her the handsomest woman in Great Britain. The Philadelphia mob solaced itself by hanging Arnold in effigy, and expended much wit in devising a figure with two faces, which held a mask in its hand, and represented the traitor. This puppet was dragged in a cart through the streets, accompanied by a picturesque and, it was hoped, accurate facsimile of the devil, and preceded by a band of music making all the noise it could. The populace was so well amused by the procession, and by the hanging and burning of the effigy, that it neglected its usual pastimes. No Tories were stoned, no doors nor windows broken, no property of any kind destroyed, though many citizens, as guiltless as the puppet, passed anxious hours before the peaceful rising of the sun.

In September, 1781, the French troops under Count Rochambeau passed through Philadelphia on their way south, where the repeated successes of the American arms had given a new aspect to the war, and filled despondent hearts with hope. The splendid appearance of these foreign allies, their martial bearing, their debonair gayety and good humor won universal admiration. The regiment De Soissonnais especially, in its picturesque uniform with rose-colored facings and white and rose-colored plumes, lent a most welcome air of brightness and wellbeing to our forlorn, threadbare army, which had never been fine, and which was now pathetically shabby. The Frenchmen were reviewed by Chief Justice McKean, who wore on this occasion a brave suit of black velvet which must have cost at least five thousand dollars of Continental currency. General Washington, Count Rochambeau, and M. de Luzerne were present; and the universal satisfaction was vastly increased when it was made known that four hundred thousand crowns had come over from France, and that there was once more a prospect of our own troops wearing—not rose-colored plumes, but sound shoes and decent breeches. So great was the public joy over this brighter outlook, that the mob in buoyant mood surrounded the residence of M. de Luzerne, and kept him awake all night by shouting lustily for King Louis XVI.

Before the allied armies left for the south, news of a still more important character was brought to cheer them on their way. The French fleet under the command of Count de Grasse had crossed the seas in safety, and lay awaiting further orders in the Chesapeake. It was this fleet which, closing in on the Virginia coast, cut off from the English army all chance of escape by water, and compelled Lord Cornwallis to surrender to General Washington at Yorktown, October 19, 1781. On the twenty-third of October, two hours before sunrise, the word was carried by an express rider into sleepy Philadelphia; and a German watchman, who was the first to hear the news, proceeded tranquilly on his rounds, announcing at intervals to such as lay awake to listen: "Past three o'clock, and Lord Cornwallis is taken."

4

The Promise of the Bell*

Christmas in Philadelphia

When from the wooden steeple of the Philadelphia State House (the nation's birthplace, and the most sacred spot on American soil) the Liberty Bell rang out its message of freedom "throughout the land," it did more than proclaim the Declaration of Independence, and it did more than summon the colonists to defend that independence with their lives. It promised them in a beautiful and borrowed phrase the reward of their valor. It affirmed their inalienable right to "life, liberty, and the pursuit of happiness"; thus linking with bare existence two things which give it worth, thus striving to ennoble and embellish the length of years which lie between man's cradle and his grave.

Never was a phrase more profoundly English or more profoundly Greek in its rational conception of values. It means a vast deal more than the privilege of casting a ballot, which privilege has been always praised and glorified beyond its deserts. "The liberty to discover and pursue a natural happiness," says Santayana, "the liberty to grow wise, and live in friendship with the gods and with one another, was the liberty vindicated by the martyrdom of Thermopylæ, and by the victory of Salamis." It is also the liberty which England has always prized and cherished, and which has promoted

---

* From *The Promise of the Bell: Christmas in Philadelphia*, 1924.

the thoroughly English qualities of "solidity and sense, independence of judgment, and idiosyncrasy of temperament." To the colonists it opened a fair vista, a widening of their somewhat restricted
horizon, a very definite and shining goal, well worth their resolute
endeavor.

When on the 23rd of October, 1781, three hours before sunrise,
a watchman called through the quiet streets of Philadelphia, "Past
three o'clock, and Lord Cornwallis is taken," the city awoke to a
refreshing sense of safety and exhilaration. The war was not over;
but victory was assured, and, with it, life and liberty. There remained
the pursuit of happiness, and it was undertaken in good faith, and
without undue delay. A sober and sedate community, kept in order
by Quaker dominance, Philadelphians had always shown a singular
capacity for enjoying themselves when they had the chance. They
had danced twelve hours at the Mischianza,—a notable achievement. They had promoted horse racing, condoned bull baiting, and
had been "decently drunk" from time to time at punch parties on
the river. Now, deeming pleasure to be one approach to happiness,
they opened the old Southwark theater, which had led a life of sore
vicissitudes, rechristened it cautiously the Academy of Polite Science, and gave a performance of Beaumarchais's *Eugénie*, in honor
of Washington, who graced the occasion with his presence. He was
escorted to his box by attendants bearing wax candles in silver
candlesticks, a deferential courtesy which made him distinctly and
desirably visible to the audience in the dimly lit theater.

Nothing in the way of entertainment came amiss to people
whose hearts were at ease, and who were unspoiled by wealth or
poverty. They went to Washington's rigidly formal receptions. They
danced as gaily, if not as long, at the Assembly balls, and at the less
august tradesmen's balls, as they had danced at the Mischianza and
at the Fête du Dauphin. They dined well with such hosts as Robert Morris and William Bingham. They opened hospitable doors to
strangers, who sometimes thought them dull; "the men grave, the
women serious," wrote Brissot de Warville in 1788. They feasted on
Christmas Day, and they built bonfires on the Fourth of July. They
rode to hounds. They began the long career of parades and proces-

sions which have always been dear to the city's heart, and which the famous New Year Mummers have by now carried to the wonder point of gaiety, brilliancy, and burlesque.

Eating and drinking were the fundamentals of enjoyment in the Quaker town, as they have been in all cities and in all ages of the world. But it was eating and drinking relished "as the sane and exhilarating basis of everything else"; and its most precious asset was companionship. When the Chevalier de Luzerne drank twelve cups of tea during the course of a winter afternoon call upon Mrs. Robert Morris, it was not because he doted on the beverage. No Frenchman has ever shared Dr. Johnson's passion for tea. It was for love of the warm brightly lit rooms (warm rooms were no everyday indulgence in the era of open fires and Franklin stoves), and for love of his agreeable hostess, and of the animated and purposeful conversation. When John Adams "drank Madeira at a great rate" at the house of Chief Justice Chew, "and found no inconvenience in it," it was not because he was a tippler; but because the generous wine quieted his anxious thoughts, and stimulated him to match mind with mind in the sympathetic society of his friends.

Indeed, the drinking of Madeira was in the nature of a ceremonial rite. Even in the days of Penn no serious business was enacted, no compact sealed, no social gathering complete without this glass of wine. It signified good-fellowship and goodwill; and when Penn returned to England for the last time, he left his little store of wine in the cellar of the Letitia House "for the use and entertainment of strangers," which was a gracious thing to do.

According to Dr. Weir Mitchell, Philadelphia was famous for its Madeira, which, being a temperamental wine, throve best in that serene atmosphere, and in the careful hands of Philadelphians. It was kept by preference in demijohns, and lived in moderate darkness under the roof, where it "accumulated virtues like a hermit." For seventy years—the allotted years of man—it could be trusted to acquire merit. After that period, it began—like man—to deteriorate. When its owner was compelled by circumstance to house it in the cellar, it was suffered to rest and revive for a day or two in a warm room on its way to the dining table; and the bottles were carried with infinite tenderness lest the wine be bruised in the transit. A crust of bread was placed by every glass to "clean the palate" before drinking. Elizabeth Robins Pennell tells us that, in her grandfather's old-fashioned household, Madeira was the wine of ceremony, dedicated to the rites of hospitality, sacred to the stranger, to whom it was offered like the bread and salt of the Arab, and with whom it established (if the stranger knew anything about wine) a bond of sympathy and understanding.

When in the winter of 1799 the directors of the Mutual or "Green Tree" Assurance Company were holding their annual dinner, word was brought them of Washington's death. They charged their glasses, rose to their feet, and gravely drank to his memory. In the century and a quarter which have intervened since then, the rite has been yearly repeated. Even today, though the toast may no longer be drunk, the diners rise, the words are spoken, and the dead leader is honored by the living.

How cordial, how dignified, how intelligent was this hospitality practiced by men who were pursuing happiness along tranquil and rational lines! How immaculately free from the grossness of Georgian drunkenness, and from the grossness of Victorian gluttony! It is true that boned turkey and terrapin were making their way to tables where wild ducks and venison had always been plentiful, and where dairy products, made perfect by practice, were admittedly the finest in the land. But it was companionship and conversation, "the liberty to grow wise and live in friendship with one another," which citizens prized, and which strangers recognized and remembered. Philadelphia, said the poet Moore, was the only American city in which he felt tempted to linger. It was the silver talk, alternating with golden silence, which made the nights speed by when friend met friend, and the wreckage of years was forgotten.

> And the men that were boys when I was a boy
> Shall sit and drink with me.

The Wistar parties were born naturally into a world where social intercourse was pleasant and esteemed. First a few friends dropped casually in upon Dr. Caspar Wistar, and sat by his fire on winter nights. Then he asked a few more. By 1811 the custom was an established one, and every Saturday night Dr. Wistar entertained his guests, among them any foreigners of distinction who chanced to be visiting Philadelphia. His house at Fourth and Prune Streets was spacious; the supper he provided was simple and sufficient. In 1818 he died, and his friends wisely resolved to perpetuate his name by perpetuating his hospitality. A hundred years is a respectable age for any social observance to reach in the United States; but Philadelphians reckon such things by centuries. Their tenacity in clinging to old customs, and maintaining them unchanged, is a valiant and poignant protest against the ills done to their town by modernity.

For more than any other American city, Philadelphia has suffered the loss of her comeliness, a comeliness that was very dear to those who first heard the promise of the Bell. "After our cares for the necessities of life are over," said the wise Franklin, "we shall come to think of its embellishments." In the pursuit of a rational happiness, Philadelphians devoted time, thought, and money to the embellishment of their daily lives. They had an unerring taste in architecture and decoration. Their portraits were painted by good artists, Peale and Stuart and Sully. Trim gardens lent brilliancy of color to their handsome, sober homes. They made of "Faire Mount" hill a thing of beauty, a little spot of classic grace and charm, which artists loved, and politicians ruthlessly destroyed—perhaps because it was the only thing in the nature of an eminence to break the level surface on which Penn laid out his checkerboard town.

To the casual visitor of today, Philadelphia seems an ugly and shabby city, set in the fields of Paradise. Surroundings of exceptional loveliness have lured the town dweller from his narrow streets, from soot and grime and perpetual racket, to pursue happiness in the clean and composed life of the country. And as more and more citizens seek every year this method of escape, the abandoned city grows more and more downcast and forlorn. It is to be forever regretted that its oldest streets, lined with houses of unsurpassable dignity, should have degenerated into filthy slums, where an alien population violates every tradition of reticence and propriety. Christ Church, Gloria Dei, and Saint Peter's still stand inviolate, keeping their dirty neighbors at arm's length with green churchyards and cherished slips of lawn. Indeed, churchyards, which were once in disfavor, have come to be highly commended. They interpose their undesecrated neatness between many an ancient place of worship and its elbowing associates.

To the visitor who is not casual, to a few careful observers like Mrs. Pennell and Christopher Morley, and to those Philadelphians who love her pavements better than turf, and her brick walls better than trees, Penn's city has a charm which enterprise and immigrant are equally powerless to destroy. It is a beauty faded with years, and dimmed by neglect, and it lies hidden away in quiet nooks and corners; but none the less is it apparent to the eye of the artist and the antiquarian. The Bell, the joyous, old Liberty Bell; is, indeed, housed with appropriate splendor. It has been carried over the country in a series of triumphant processions, and many thousands of Americans have greeted it with reverence. But the deepening fissure in its side now calls imperatively for rest; and Independence Hall—a remarkably agreeable example of colonial architecture—is the Mecca of patriotic pilgrims. All the year round they come to look upon the room where the Declaration of Independence was signed, and upon the Bell which rang its message to the land.

Today that message rings the knell of the past, and the deathless promise of the future:

Tho' much is taken, much abides.

Life, though it is beset by greater perils; liberty, though it is restricted by an excess of legislation; and the pursuit of happiness, though it is turned into new, and possibly nobler, channels. The old society "in which men looked up without envy or malice, and even found life richer from the thought that there were degrees of excellency and honor," has been replaced by a society in which perpetual change has bred dissatisfaction and insecurity. But more clearly than before the note of a real democracy, of a sense of comradeship, of a natural, cheerful, irresponsible interest in one another, has been struck in what was once the City of Brotherly Love. It gives to Christmas something which earlier Christmases never knew; a coming together of people whose lives are, by force of circumstance, apart, a closing in of circles which are commonly and necessarily remote.

For a week before the feast, the great pioneer department store of America sets aside a half hour in the morning and a half hour at dusk for community singing of Christmas hymns and carols. The rush of business is suspended, the giant organ peals forth the familiar strains, and men, women, and children, crowded into every inch of available space, sing with all their might, "God Rest Ye Merry, Gentlemen," "Come, All Ye Faithful," and "While Shepherds Watch'd Their Flocks by Night." Nobody claims the sounds they make are beautiful; but nobody denies they are inspiriting.

> If unmelodious was the song,
> It was a hearty note, and strong.

People who surge around counters to do their Christmas shopping are indifferent, not to say inimical, to one another; but people who stand shoulder to shoulder singing the same words are impelled by the force of crowd psychology to good feeling and mutual understanding.

Charity is an old, old virtue, and Christmas has always been its sacred season; but it is not charity which now makes the householder put Christmas candles in his windows, to give the passerby a sense of recognition and intimacy. It is not charity which rears the great municipal Christmas tree for all the town to see, or provides the great municipal concert on Christmas Eve for all the town to hear—and join in if it pleases. It is not charity which lights the "Community Christmas Trees" on country roads, and leaves them shining softly in the darkness as a reminder of goodwill. It is not charity which sends little groups of men and women, accompanied by a sober deaconess to sing carols in the few quiet streets which Philadelphia has preserved unspoiled. These singers ask for no recompense. They are forging a link in the bond of healthy human emotions. They are adding their share to the little intimacies of the world.

"Life, liberty, and the pursuit of happiness." "Inalienable rights" the Signers termed them, which yet have never been without assailants. What strange vicissitudes the Bell has witnessed, and what strange meanings have been read into its message! But its promise still holds good. If we never grow wise as the Greeks grew wise, if we never lay hold of the "natural happiness" which is the birthright of Englishmen, we may yet surpass Greece and England in the grace of friendship. It will be something different from friendship with our friends; it will be friendship with our neighbors. It will be—I hope—disunited from duty, and composed of simple, durable materials,—tolerance, good-nature, and a sweet reasonableness of approach. It will read a generous meaning into qualities which are common to all of us, displeasing to most of us, and intelligible only to the wide-eyed few who interpret the heart of humanity.

Americans & Politics

5

The Chill of Enthusiasm[*]

Surtout, pas de zèle.—Talleyrand

There is no aloofness so forlorn as our aloofness from an uncontagious enthusiasm, and there is no hostility so sharp as that aroused by a fervor which fails of response. Charles Lamb's "D—n him at a hazard," was the expression of a natural and reasonable frame of mind with which we are all familiar, and which, though admittedly unlovely, is in the nature of a safeguard. If we had no spiritual asbestos to protect our souls, we should be consumed to no purpose by every wanton flame. If our sincere and restful indifference to things which concern us not were shaken by every blast, we should have no available force for things which concern us deeply. If eloquence did not sometimes make us yawn, we should be besotted by oratory. And if we did not approach new acquaintances, new authors, and new points of view with life-saving reluctance, we should never feel that vital regard which, being strong enough to break down our barriers, is strong enough to hold us for life.

The worth of admiration is, after all, in proportion to the value of the thing admired,—a circumstance overlooked by the people who talk much pleasant nonsense about sympathy, and the courage of our emotions, and the open and generous mind. We know

---

[*] From *Americans and Others*, 1912.

how Mr. Arnold felt when an American lady wrote to him, in praise of American authors, and said that it rejoiced her heart to think of such excellence as being "common and abundant." Mr. Arnold, who considered that excellence of any kind was very uncommon and beyond measure rare, expressed his views on this occasion with more fervor and publicity than the circumstances demanded; but his words are as balm to the irritation which some of us suffer and conceal when drained of our reluctant applause.

It is perhaps because women have been trained to a receptive attitude of mind, because for centuries they have been valued for their sympathy and appreciation rather than for their judgment, that they are so perilously prone to enthusiasm. It has come to all of us of late to hear much feminine eloquence, and to marvel at the nimbleness of woman's wit, at the speed with which she thinks, and the facility with which she expresses her thoughts. A woman who, until five years ago, never addressed a larger audience than that afforded by a reading club or a dinner party, will now thrust and parry on a platform, wholly unembarrassed by timidity or by ignorance. Sentiment and satire are hers to command; and while neither is convincing, both are tremendously effective with people already convinced, with the partisans who throng unwearyingly to hear the voicing of their own opinions. The ease with which such a speaker brings forward the great central fact of the universe, maternity, as an argument for or against the casting of a ballot (it works just as well either way); the glow with which she associates Jeanne d'Arc with federated clubs and social service; and the gay defiance she hurls at customs and prejudices so profoundly obsolete that the lantern of Diogenes could not find them lurking in a village street,—these things may chill the unemotional listener into apathy, but they never fail to awaken the sensibilities of an audience. The simple process, so highly commended by debaters, of ignoring all that cannot be denied, makes demonstration easy. "A crowd," said Mr. Ruskin, "thinks by infection." To be immune from infection is to stand outside the sacred circle of enthusiasts.

Yet if the experience of mankind teaches anything, it is that vital convictions are not at the mercy of eloquence. The "oratory of conviction," to borrow a phrase of Mr. Bagehot's, is so rare as to be hardly worth taking into account. Fox used to say that if a speech read well, it was "a damned bad speech," which is the final word of cynicism, spoken by one who knew. It was the saving sense of England, that solid, prosaic, dependable common sense, the bulwark of every great nation, which, after Sheridan's famous speech, demanding the impeachment of Warren Hastings, made the House adjourn "to collect its reason,"—obviously because its reason had been lost. Sir William Dolden, who moved the adjournment, frankly confessed that it was impossible to give a "determinate opinion" while under the spell of oratory. So the lawmakers, who had been fired to white heat, retired to cool down again; and when Sheridan—always as deep in difficulties as Micawber—was offered a thousand pounds for the manuscript of the speech, he remembered Fox's verdict, and refused to risk his unballasted eloquence in print.

Enthusiasm is praised because it implies an unselfish concern for something outside our personal interest and advancement. It is reverenced because the great and wise amendments, which from time to time straighten the roads we walk, may always be traced back to somebody's zeal for reform. It is rich in prophetic attributes, banking largely on the unknown, and making up in nobility of design what it lacks in excellence of attainment. Like simplicity, and candor, and other much-commended qualities, enthusiasm is charming until we meet it face to face, and cannot escape from its charm. It is then that we begin to understand the attitude of Goethe, and Talleyrand, and Pitt, and Sir Robert Peel, who saved themselves from being consumed by resolutely refusing to ignite. "It is folly," observed Goethe, "to expect that other men will consent to believe as we do"; and, having reconciled himself to this elemental obstinacy of the human heart, it no longer troubled him that those whom he felt to be wrong should refuse to acknowledge their errors.

There are men and women—not many—who have the happy art of making their most fervent convictions endurable. Their hobbies do not spread desolation over the social world, their prejudices do not insult our intelligence. They may be so "abreast with the times" that we cannot keep track of them, or they may be basking serenely in some Early Victorian close. They may believe buoyantly in the Baconian cipher, or in thought transference, or in the serious purposes of Mr. George Bernard Shaw, or in anything else which invites credulity. They may even express their views, and still be loved and cherished by their friends.

How illuminating is the contrast which Hazlitt unconsciously draws between the enthusiasms of Lamb which everybody was able to bear, and the enthusiasms of Coleridge which nobody was able to bear. Lamb would parade his admiration for some favorite author, Donne, for example, whom the rest of the company probably abhorred. He would select the most crabbed passages to quote and defend; he would stammer out his piquant and masterful half sentences, his scalding jests, his controvertible assertions; he would skillfully hint at the defects which no one else was permitted to see; and if he made no converts (wanting none), he woke no weary wrath. But we all have a sneaking sympathy for Holcroft, who, when Coleridge was expatiating rapturously and oppressively upon the glories of German transcendental philosophy, and upon his own supreme command of the field, cried out suddenly and with exceeding bitterness: "Mr. Coleridge, you are the most eloquent man I ever met, and the most unbearable in your eloquence."

I am not without a lurking suspicion that George Borrow must have been at times unbearable in his eloquence. "We cannot refuse to meet a man on the ground that he is an enthusiast," observes Mr. George Street, obviously lamenting this circumstance; "but we should at least like to make sure that his enthusiasms are under control." Borrow's enthusiasms were never under control. He stood ready at a moment's notice to prove the superiority of the Welsh bards over the paltry poets of England, or to relate the marvelous Welsh prophecies, so vague as to be always safe. He was capable of inflicting Armenian verbs upon Isopel Berners when they sat at night over their gipsy kettle in the dingle (let us hope she fell asleep as sweetly as does Milton's Eve when Adam grows too garrulous); and he met the complaints of a poor farmer on the hardness of the times with jubilant praises of evangelicalism. "Better pay three pounds an acre, and live on crusts and water in the present enlightened days," he told the disheartened husbandman, "than pay two shillings an acre, and sit down to beef and ale three times a day in the old superstitious ages." This is *not* the oratory of conviction. There are unreasoning prejudices in favor of one's own stomach which eloquence cannot gainsay. "I defy the utmost power of language to disgust me wi' a gude denner," observes the Ettrick Shepherd; thus putting on record the attitude of the bucolic mind, impassive, immutable, since earth's first harvests were gleaned.

The artificial emotions which expand under provocation, and collapse when the provocation is withdrawn, must be held responsible for much mental confusion. Election oratory is an old and cherished institution. It is designed to make candidates show their paces, and to give innocent amusement to the crowd. Properly reinforced by brass bands and bunting, graced by some sufficiently august presence, and enlivened by plenty of cheering and hat flourishing, it presents a strong appeal. A political party is, moreover, a solid and self-sustaining affair. All sound and alliterative generalities about virile and vigorous manhood, honest and honorable labor, great and glorious causes, are understood, in this country at least, to refer to the virile and vigorous manhood of Republicans or Democrats, as the case may be; and to uphold the honest and honorable, great and glorious Republican or Democratic principles, upon which, it is also understood, depends the welfare of the nation.

Yet even this sense of security cannot always save us from the chill of collapsed enthusiasm. I was once at a great mass meeting, held in the interests of municipal reform, and at which the principal speaker was a candidate for office. He was delayed for a full hour after the meeting had been opened, and this hour was filled with good platform oratory. Speechmaker after speechmaker, all adept in their art, laid bare before our eyes the evils which consumed us, and called upon us passionately to support the candidate who would lift us from our shame. The fervor of the house rose higher and higher. Martial music stirred our blood, and made us feel that reform and patriotism were one. The atmosphere grew tense with expectancy, when suddenly there came a great shout, and the sound of cheering from the crowd in the streets, the crowd which could not force its way into the huge and closely packed opera house. Now there are few things more profoundly affecting than cheers heard from a distance, or muffled by intervening walls. They have a fine dramatic quality, unknown to the cheers which rend the air about us. When the chairman of the meeting announced that the candidate was outside the doors, speaking to the mob, the excitement reached fever heat. When some one cried, "He is here!" and the orchestra struck the first bars of "Hail Columbia," we rose to our feet, waving multitudinous flags, and shouting out the rapture of our hearts.

And then,—and then there stepped upon the stage a plain, tired, bewildered man, betraying nervous exhaustion in every line. He spoke, and his voice was not the assured voice of a leader. His words were not the happy words which instantly command attention. It was evident to the discerning eye that he had been driven for days, perhaps for weeks, beyond his strength and endurance; that he had resorted to stimulants to help him in this emergency, and that they had failed; that he was striving with feeble desperation to do the impossible which was expected of him. I wondered even then if a few common words of explanation, a few sober words of promise, would not have satisfied the crowd, already sated with eloquence. I wondered if the unfortunate man could feel the chill settling down upon the house as he spoke his random and undignified sentences, whether he could see the first stragglers slipping down the aisles. What did his decent record, his honest purpose, avail him in an hour like this? He tried to lash himself to vigor, but it was spurring a broken-winded horse. The stragglers increased into a flying squadron, the house was emptying fast, when the chairman in sheer desperation made a sign to the leader of the orchestra, who waved his baton, and "The Star Spangled Banner" drowned the candidate's last words, and brought what was left of the audience to its feet. I turned to a friend beside me, the wife of a local politician who had been the most fiery speaker of the evening. "Will it make any difference?" I asked, and she answered disconsolately; "The city is lost, but we may save the state."

Then we went out into the quiet streets, and I bethought me of Voltaire's driving in a blue coach powdered with gilt stars to see the first production of *Irène*, and of his leaving the theatre to find that enthusiasts had cut the traces of his horses, so that the shouting mob might drag him home in triumph. But the mob, having done its shouting, melted away after the irresponsible fashion of mobs, leaving the blue coach stranded in front of the Tuileries, with Voltaire shivering inside of it, until the horses could be brought back, the traces patched up, and the driver recalled to his duty.

That "popular enthusiasm is but a fire of straw" has been amply demonstrated by all who have tried to keep it going. It can be lighted to some purpose, as when money is extracted from the enthusiasts before they have had time to cool; but even this process—so skillfully conducted by the initiated—seems unworthy of great and noble charities, or of great and noble causes. It is true also that the agitator—no matter what he may be agitating—is always sure of his market; a circumstance which made that most conservative of chancellors, Lord Eldon, swear with bitter oaths that, if he were to begin life over again, he would begin it as an agitator. Tom Moore tells a pleasant story (one of the many pleasant stories embalmed in his vast sarcophagus of a diary) about a street orator whom he heard address a crowd in Dublin. The man's eloquence was so stirring that Moore was ravished by it, and he expressed to Sheil his admiration for the speaker. "Ah," said Sheil carelessly, "that was a brewer's patriot. Most of the great brewers have in their employ a regular patriot who goes about among the publicans, talking violent politics, which helps to sell the beer."

Honest enthusiasm, we are often told, is the power which moves the world. Therefore it is perhaps that honest enthusiasts seem to think that if they stopped pushing, the world would stop moving,—as though it were a new world which didn't know its way. This belief inclines them to intolerance. The more keen they are, the more contemptuous they become. What Wordsworth admirably called "the self-applauding sincerity of a heated mind" leaves them no loophole for doubt, and no understanding of the doubter. In their volcanic progress they bowl over the non-partisan—a man and a brother—with splendid unconcern. He, poor soul, stunned but not convinced, clings desperately to some pettifogging convictions which he calls truth, and refuses a clearer vision. His habit of remembering what he believed yesterday clogs his mind, and makes it hard for him to believe something entirely new today. Much has been said about the inconvenience of keeping opinions, but much might be said about the serenity of the process. Old opinions are like old friends,—we cease to question their worth because, after years of intimacy and the loss of some valuable illusions, we have grown to place our slow reliance on them. We know at least where we stand, and whither we are tending, and we refuse to bustle feverishly about the circumference of life, because, as Amiel warns us, we cannot reach its core.

6

Americanism*

Whenever we stand in need of intricate knowledge, balanced judgment, or delicate analysis, it is our comfortable habit to question our neighbors. They may be no wiser and no better informed than we are; but a collective opinion has its value, or at least its satisfying qualities. For one thing, there is so much of it. For another, it seldom lacks variety. Two years ago the *American Journal of Sociology* asked two hundred and fifty "representative" men and women "upon what ideals, policies, programs, or specific purposes should Americans place most stress in the immediate future," and published the answers that were returned in a Symposium entitled, "What is Americanism?" The candid reader, following this symposium, received much counsel, but little enlightenment. There were some good practical suggestions; but nowhere any cohesion, nowhere any sense of solidarity, nowhere any concern for national honor or authority.

It was perhaps to be expected that Mr. Burghardt Du Bois's conception of true Americanism would be the abolishment of the color line, and that Mr. Eugene Debs would see salvation in the sweeping away of "privately owned industries, and production for individual profit." These answers might have been foreseen when the questions

---

* From *Counter-Currents*, 1916.

were asked. But it was disconcerting to find that all, or almost all, of the "representative" citizens represented one line of civic policy, or civic reform, and refused to look beyond it. The prohibitionist discerned Americanism in prohibition, the equal suffragist in votes for women, the biologist in applied science, the physician in the extirpation of microbes, the philanthropist in playgrounds, the sociologist in eugenism and old-age pensions, and the manufacturer in the revision of taxes. It was refreshing when an author unexpectedly demanded the extinction of inherited capital. Authorship seldom concerns itself with anything so inconceivably remote.

The quality of miscellaneousness is least serviceable when we leave the world of affairs, and seek admission into the world of ideals. There must be an interpretation of Americanism which will express for all of us a patriotism at once practical and emotional, an understanding of our place in the world, and of the work we are best fitted to do in it, a sentiment which we can hold—as we hold nothing else—in common, and which will be forever remote from personal solicitude and resentment. Those of us whose memories stretch back over half a century recall too plainly a certain uneasiness which for years pervaded American politics and American letters, which made us unduly apprehensive, and, as a consequence, unduly sensitive and arrogant. It found expression in Mr. William Cullen Bryant's well-known poem, "America," made familiar to my generation by school readers and manuals of elocution, and impressed by frequent recitations upon our memories.

> O mother of a mighty race,
> Yet lovely in thy youthful grace!
> The elder dames, thy haughty peers,
> Admire and hate thy blooming years;
>   With words of shame
> And taunts of scorn they join thy name.

There are eight verses, and four of them repeat Mr. Bryant's conviction that the nations of Europe united in envying and insulting us. To be hated because we were young, and strong, and good, and beautiful, seemed, to my childish heart, a noble fate; and when a closer acquaintance with history dispelled this pleasant illusion, I parted from it with regret. France was our ally in the Revolutionary War. Russia was friendly in the Civil War. England was friendly in the Spanish War. If the repudiation of state debts left a bad taste in the mouths of foreign investors, they might be pardoned for making a wry face. Most of them were subsequently paid; but the phrase "American revoke" dates from the period of suspense. By the time we celebrated our hundredth birthday with a world's fair, we were on very easy terms with our neighbors. Far from taunting us with shameful words, our "haughty peers" showed on this memorable occasion unanimous good temper and good will; and *Punch*'s congratulatory verses were among the most pleasant birthday letters we received.

The expansion of national life, fed by the great emotions of the Civil War, and revealed to the world by the Centennial Exhibition, found expression in education, art, and letters. Then it was that Americanism took a new and disconcerting turn. Pleased with our progress, stunned by finding that we had poets, and painters, and novelists, and magazines, and a history, all of our own, we began to say, and say very loudly, that we had no need of the poets, and painters, and novelists, and magazines, and histories of other lands. Our attitude was not unlike that of George Borrow, who, annoyed by the potency of Italian art, adjured Englishmen to stay at home and contemplate the greatness of England. England, he said, had pictures of her own. She had her own "minstrel strain." She had all her sons could ask for. "England against the world."

In the same exclusive spirit, American school boards proposed that American schoolchildren should begin the study of history with the colonization of America, ignoring the trivial episodes which preceded this great event. Patriotic protectionists heaped duties on foreign art, and bade us buy American pictures. Enthusiastic editors confided to us that "the world has never known such storehouses of well-selected mental food as are furnished by our American magazines." Complacent critics rejoiced that American poets did not sing like Tennyson, "nor like Keats, nor Shelley, nor Wordsworth"; but that, as became a new race of men, they "reverberated a synthesis of all the poetic minds of the century." Finally, American novelists assured us that in their hands the art of fiction had grown so fine and rare that we could no longer stand the "mannerisms" of Dickens, or the "confidential attitude" of Thackeray. We had scaled the empyrean heights.

There is a brief paragraph in Mr. Thayer's *Life and Letters of John Hay*, which vividly recalls this peculiar phase of Americanism. Mr. Hay writes to Mr. Howells in 1882: "The worst thing in our time about American taste is the way it treats James. I believe he would not be read in America at all if it were not for his European vogue. If he lived in Cambridge, he could write what he likes; but because he finds London more agreeable, he is the prey of all the patriotisms. Of all vices, I hold patriotism the worst, when it meddles with matters of taste."

So far had American patriotism encroached upon matters of taste, that by 1892 there was a critical embargo placed upon foreign literature. "Every nation," we were told, "ought to supply its own second-rate books,"—like domestic sheeting and ginghams. An acquaintance with English authors was held to be a misdemeanor. Why quote Mr. Matthew Arnold, when you might quote Mr. Lowell? Why write about Becky Sharp, when you might write about Hester Prynne? Why laugh over Dickens, when you might laugh over Mark Twain? Why eat artichokes, when you might eat corn? American schoolboys, we were told, must be guarded from the feudalism of Scott. American speech must be guarded from the "insularities" of England's English. "That failure in good sense which comes from too warm a self-satisfaction" (Mr. Arnold does sometimes say a thing very well) robbed us for years of mental poise, of adjusted standards, of an unencumbered outlook upon life.

It is strange to glance back upon a day when we had so little to trouble us that we could vex our souls over feudalism and fiction; when—in the absence of serious problems—we could raise pronunciation or spelling into a national issue. Americanism has done with trivialities, patriotism with matters of taste. Love for one's country is not a shallow sentiment, based upon self-esteem. It is a profound and primitive passion. It may lie dormant in our souls when all goes well. It may be thwarted and frustrated by the exigencies of party government. It may be dissevered from pride or pleasure. But it is part of ourselves, wholly beyond analysis, fed upon hope and fear, joy and sorrow, glory and shame. If, after the fashion of the world, we drowsed in our day of security, we have been rudely and permanently awakened. The shadow of mighty events has fallen across our path. We have witnessed a great national crime. We have beheld the utmost heights of heroism. And when we asked of what concern to us were this crime and this heroism, the answer came unexpectedly, and with blinding force. The sea was strewn with our dead, our honor was undermined by conspiracies, our factories were fired, our cargoes dynamited. We were a neutral nation at peace with the world. The attack made upon our industries and upon our good name was secret, malignant, and pitiless. It was organized warfare, without the courage and candor of war.

The unavowed enemy who strikes in the dark is hard to reach, but he is outside the pale of charity. There was something in the cold fury of Mr. Wilson's words, when, in his message to Congress, he denounced the traitors "who have poured the poison of disloyalty into the very arteries of our national life," which turned that unexpansive state paper into a human document, and drove it straight to the human hearts of an injured and insulted people. Under the menace of disloyalty, Americanism has taken new form and substance; and our just resentment, like the potter's wheel, has molded this force into lines of strength and resistance. We have seen all we want to see of "frightfulness" in Europe, all we want to see of injustice, supported by violence. We are not prepared to welcome any scheme of terrorization in the interests of a foreign power, or any interference of a foreign power with our legitimate fields of industry. Such schemes and such interference constitute an inconceivable affront to the nation. Their stern and open disavowal is the shibboleth by which our elections may be purged of treachery, and our well-being confided to good citizenship.

Of all the countries in the world, we and we only have any need to create artificially the patriotism which is the birthright of other nations. Into the hearts of six millions of foreign-born men—less than half of them naturalized—we must infuse that quality of devotion which will make them place the good of the state above their personal good, and the safety of the state above their personal safety. It is like pumping oxygen into six million pairs of lungs for which the common air is not sufficiently stimulating. We must also keep a watchful eye upon these men's wives,—when they are so blessed,—and concentrate our supreme energy on uncounted millions of children, whose first step toward patriotism is the acquirement of a common tongue.

We are trying fitfully, but in good faith, to work this civic miracle. Americanization Day is but one expression of the nation-wide endeavor. When Cleveland invited all her citizens who had been naturalized within a twelvemonth to assemble and receive a public welcome, to sit on a platform and be made much of, to listen to national songs and patriotic speeches, and to take home, every man, a flag and a seal of the city, she set a good example which will be widely followed. The celebrations at Riverside, California, and New York City's Pageant of the Nations had in view the same admirable end. Sentiment is not a substitute for duty and discipline; but it has its uses and its field of efficacy. Such ceremonies perseveringly repeated for twenty years might work a change in the immigrant population of today, were we secure from the fresh millions which threaten us tomorrow. That the Fourth of July should be often selected for these rites is perhaps inevitable; it is a time when patriotism assumes a vivid and popular aspect; but Heaven forbid that we should rechristen Independence Day, Americanization Day! However ready we may be to welcome our new citizens, however confident we may be of their value to the Republic, we are not yet prepared to give them the place of honor hitherto held by the signers of the Declaration of Independence. The name which perpetuates the memory of that deed is a sacred name, and should be preserved no less sacredly than the national life which was then committed to our keeping.

It is no insult to the immigrant to say that he constitutes one of the perils of Americanism. How can it be otherwise? Assume that he is a law-abiding citizen, that he knows nothing of the conspiracies which have imperiled our safety, that he does not propose to use his vote in the interests of a foreign power, and that the field of hyphenated politics has no existence for him. For all these boons we are sufficiently grateful. But how far does he understand the responsibilities he assumes with the franchise, how far does he realize that he has become part of the machinery of the state, and how far can we depend upon him in our hour of need? He knows, or at least he has been told, that he may not return home to fight for his own country, if he seeks American citizenship. He must resist a natural and a noble impulse as the price of his coveted "papers." But will there spring in his heart a noble, though not very natural, impulse to fight for us if we call our sons to arms? Can we hope that his native intelligence, unshackled by any working knowledge of our language, will grasp our national policy and our national obligations; and that—free from conscription—he will voluntarily risk his life in behalf of a government for which he has no inheritance of fidelity?

We have opened our doors to unrestricted immigration, partly because capitalists want plenty of cheap labor, which is not a good reason; and partly because the immigrants want to come, which is not a sufficient reason. They also—despite the heart-rending conditions depicted by Miss Frances Kellor—want to stay. Those who return to the higher standards of Europe do not materially affect the situation. They stay, and either surmount their difficulties, or, succumbing to them, fill our asylums, hospitals, and almshouses. For many years, foreign economists must have looked with relief at the countless thousands of derelicts who were supported by the United States instead of by their own governments. But even the satisfaction we have thus afforded does not wholly justify our course. Is it worth our while to fill the air with clamor over eugenics and birth control, to build barriers around a marriage license, and to dramatize impassioned pleas for sterility, when the birthrate of the Republic is nobody's concern? If the survival of the fittest means as much to the commonwealth as to the family, why should we fiddle over pathology while the nation burns?

Miss Keller is not the only kind-hearted American who holds her countrymen to blame for the deficiencies of the immigrant. Her point of view is a common one, and has some foundation in fact. She censures us even for his dirt, though if she had ever listened to the vitriolic comments of the police, she might revise her judgment on that score. "Can't you *do* anything?" I once asked a disconsolate guardian of the peace, who stood on a fine hot day contemplating the forth-flung garbage of the Israelite. To which he made answer: "Did ye iver thry to clane out a sthable wid a toothpick?" And as this had not been one of my life's endeavors, I offered no further comment. But Miss Kellor touches a vital truth when she says that Americans will never weld a mass of heterogeneous humanity into a nation, until they are able to say what they want that nation to be, and until they are prepared to follow a policy intelligently outlined. In other words, Americanism is not a medley of individual theories, partial philanthropies, and fluid sentiment. A consistent nationalism is essential to civic life, and we are not dispensed from achieving consistent nationalism by the difficulties in our way. No multiplication of difficulties makes an impossibility. Upon what props did the Venetians build the fairest city of the world?

We cannot in this country hope for the compelling devotion which has animated Germany; still less for the supreme moral and intellectual force which is the staying power of France. Mrs. Wharton has best described the intelligence with which Frenchmen translate their ideals into doctrine. They know for what they stand in the civilized world, and the first "white heat of dedication" has hardened into steel-like endurance. To the simple emotions of men who are defending their homes from assault have been added the emotions of men who are defending the world's noblest inheritance from degradation. "It is the reasoned recognition of this peril which is making the most intelligent people in the world the most sublime."

The problems of England are so closely akin to our own problems, and her perplexities are so closely akin to our own perplexities, that we should regard them with insight and with sympathy. We too must pause in every keen emergency to cajole, to persuade, to placate, to reconcile conflicting interests, to humor conflicting opinions,—termed by those who hold them, "principles." We too must forever bear in mind the political party which is in power, and the political party which waits to get into power; and we must pick our way as best we can by the crosslights of their abiding hostility. We too must face and overcome the dough-like resistance of apathy.

I have been told—though I refuse to believe it on hearsay—that British laborers have asked what difference it would make to them whether they worked for British or for German masters. It is quite true that British pacifists and British radicals have not only put this question, but have answered it, greatly to their own satisfaction, in American periodicals; but American periodicals are not mouthpieces of the British workmen. I make no doubt that if we were fighting for our lives, there would be found American pacifists and American radicals writing in British periodicals that no great harm would come to America if she submitted passively to invasion; and that, whether their country's cause were right or wrong, the slaughter of her sons was a crime, and the wealth of her capitalists was a sufficient reason for refusing to do battle for her liberty. The painful certainty that we should never be free from the babbling of treason, any more than England is free from it now, makes Americanism (the Americanism which means civic loyalty founded on civic intelligence) shine like a far-off star on a very dim horizon.

At present, disloyalty founded upon ignorance meets with more attention than it deserves. Why, after all, should two thousand people assemble in New York to hear Miss Helen Keller say that, in the event of invasion, the American workman "has nothing to lose but his chains"? He has his manhood to lose, and it should mean as much to him as to any millionaire in the land. What new and debilitating doctrine is this which holds that personal honor is the exclusive attribute of wealth, and that a laborer has no more business with it than has a dog! The fact that Miss Keller has overcome the heavy disabilities which nature placed in her path, lends interest to her person, but no weight to her opinions, which give evidence of having been adopted wholesale, and of having never filtered through any reasoning process of her own. It is always agreeable to hear her speak about good and simple things. When she said in Philadelphia that happiness does not lie in pleasure, and that, although she did not expect to be always pleased, she did expect to be always happy, by doing what she could to make those about her happy, we gave our hearty concurrence to sentiments so unexceptionable. It was the way we ourselves should have liked to feel, and we knew it was our own fault that we did not. But when in New York she adjured workingmen never to enter the United States Army, and informed us that all we needed for adequate defense were shooting galleries "within reach of every family," so that we could all learn—like the old ladies in *Punch*—to fire a gun, there was something profoundly sad in words so ill-judged and so fatuous. It cannot be a matter of no moment that, in the hour of our danger and indecision, thousands of people stand ready to applaud the disloyal utterances which should affront every honorable man or woman who hears them.

The *Yale Review* quotes the remark of a "foreigner" that Americans are always saying, "I don't care." The phrase is popular, and sounds disheartening; but if we spare ourselves concern over trivial things (if, for example, we were not excited or inflamed by Captain von Papen's calling us "idiotic Yankees"), it does not follow that big issues leave us unmoved. If they did, if they ever should, the word Americanism might as well be obliterated from the language. The consistent nationalism for which it stands admits of no indifference. It is true that the possible peril of New York—as defenseless as a soft-shell crab, and as succulent—is not an ever-present care to San Francisco. It is true that San Francisco's deep anxiety over Japanese immigration and land ownership was lightly treated by New York. And it is true that Denver, sitting in the safety zone, looks down from her lofty heights without any pressing solicitude about either of her sister cities. But just as the San Francisco earthquake wrung the heart of New York, so the first gun fired at New York would arm the citizens of San Francisco. Only it might then be too late.

The Christmas cartoon of Uncle Sam holding a package marked "Peace and Prosperity," and saying with a broad smile, "Just what I wanted!" was complacent rather than comprehensive. We want peace and we want prosperity, but they are not all we want; partly because their permanency depends upon certain props which seem to many of us a bit unsteady, and partly because we do not, any more than other men, live by bread alone. The things of the spirit are for us, even as for heroic and suffering France, of vital worth and import. If we could say with certainty, "All is gained but honor," there are still some of us who would feel our blessings incomplete; but, as it chances, the contempt meted out to us has taken the palpable form of encroachment upon our common rights. Until we can protect our industries from assault and our citizens from butchery, until we can couple disavowal of past injuries with real assurance of safety in the future, peace limps, and prosperity is shadowed. With every fresh shock we have received, with every fresh sorrow we have endured, there has come to us more and more clearly the vision of a noble nationalism, purged of "comfort-mongering," and of perverted sentiment.

Cynical newspaper writers have begun to say that the best way to make Americans forget one injury is to inflict on them another. This is hardly a half truth. The sinking of the Ancona did not obliterate from our minds the names of the Falaba, the Gulflight, the Frye, the Hesperian, the Arabic, and the Lusitania. Neither has the sinking of the Persia buried the Ancona in oblivion. And it is not simple humanity which has burned these names into the tablets of our memories. The loss of American lives through the savage torpedoing of liners and merchant ships might be doubled and trebled any summer day by the sinking of an excursion steamer, and we should soon forget. A country which reports eight thousand murders in a single year is not wont to be deeply stirred by the perils which beset our munition workers. But when Americans have gone to their deaths through the violence of another government, or in the interests of another government, then the wrong done them is elevated to the importance of a national calamity, and redress becomes a national obligation. Because we do not wearily reiterate this patent truth does not mean that we have forgotten it. If words could save, if words could heal, we should have no fear, nor shame, nor sorrow. Nothing is less worth while than to go on prattling about a consistent foreign policy. The cornerstone of civilization is man's dependence for protection on the state which he has reared for his own safety and support.

The concern of Americans for America (I use the word to symbolize the United States) must be the deep and loyal sentiment which brooks no injustice and no insult. We have need of many things, but first and foremost of fidelity. It is a matter of pride and pleasure that some of our foreign-born citizens should excel in art and letters; that, under our tutelage, they should learn to design posters, model statuary, write poems, and make speeches. These things have their admitted place and value. The encouragement which is given them, the opportunities which are made for them, the praise which is lavished upon them, are proofs of our goodwill, and of our genuine delight in fostering ability. But the real significance of the "Americanization" movement, the summoning of conferences, the promoting of exhibitions, the bestowing of prizes, is the need we all feel of unification, the hope we all cherish that, through the influence of congenial work, immigrants and the children of immigrants will become one in spirit with the native born. We could make shift to do without the posters and the symbolic statuary; we could read fewer poems and listen to fewer speeches; but we cannot possibly do without the loyalty which we have a right to demand, and which is needful to the safety of the Republic.

For the main thing to be borne in mind is that Americanization does not mean only an increase of opportunity for the alien, an effort toward his permanent well-being. It means also service and sacrifice on his part. This is what citizenship entails, although voters and those who clamor for the vote seldom take into account such an inexorable truth. The process of assimilation must go deeper than the polling booth and the trade union can carry it. Democracy forever teases us with the contrast between its ideals and its realities, between its heroic possibilities and its sorry achievements. But it is our appointed road, and the stones over which we perpetually stumble deny us the drowsy perils of content. When we read Dr. Eliot's noble words in praise of free government and equal opportunities, we know that his amazing buoyancy does not imply ignorance of primaries, of party methods, and of graft. With these things he has been familiar all his life; but the creaking machinery of democracy has never dimmed his faith in its holiness. Remediable disorders, however grievous and deep seated, afford us the comfort of hope, and the privilege of unending exertion.

To no one ignorant of history can the right of citizenship assume any real significance. In our country the ballot is so carelessly guarded, so shamefully misused, that it has become to some men a subject of derision; to many, an unconsidered trifle; to all, or almost all, an expression of personal opinion, which, at its best, reflects a popular newspaper, and, at its worst, stands for nothing less hurtful than stupidity. A recent contributor to the *Unpopular Review* reminds us soberly that, as the democratic state cannot rise above the level of its voters, and as nationality means for us merely the will of the people, it might not be amiss to guard the franchise with reasonable solicitude, and to ask something more than unlimited ignorance, and the absence of a criminal record, as its price. If every man—alien or native born—who casts his ballot could be made to know and to feel that "all the political forces of his country were mainly occupied for a hundred years in making that act possible," and that the United States is, and has always been, the nation of those "who willed to be Americans," citizenship might become for us what it was to Rome, what it is to France,—the exponent of honor, the symbol of self-sacrifice.

A knowledge of history might also prove serviceable in enabling us to recognize our place and our responsibility among the nations of the world. No remoteness (geographical remoteness counts for little in the twentieth century) can sever our interests from the interests of Europe, or lift from our shoulders the burden of helping to sustain the collective rights of mankind. We know now that the menace of frightfulness has overshadowed us. We know that, however cautiously we picked our steps, we could not, and did not, escape molestation. But even if we had saved our own skin, if we had suffered no destruction of property, and if none of our dead lay under the water, the freedom of Europe, the future of democracy, and the rights of man would be to us matters of concern.

It is true, moreover, that friendship and alliance with those European states whose aspirations and ideals respond to our own aspirations and ideals, are as consistent with Americanism as are friendship and alliance with the states of South America, which we are now engaged in loving. It is not from Bolivia, or Chile, or Venezuela, or the Argentine that we have drawn our best traditions, our law, language, literature, and art. We extend to these "sister Republics" the arms of commercial affection; but they have no magic words like Magna Carta and *le Tiers État* to stir our souls an inch beyond self-profit. When we count up our assets, we must reckon heavily on the respect of those nations which we most respect, and whose goodwill in the past is a guarantee of goodwill in the future. It is worth our while, even from the standpoint of Americanism, to prove our fellowship with humanity, our care for other interests than our own. The civilization of the world is the business of all who live in the world. We cannot see it crashing down, as it crashed in the sinking of the Lusitania and the Ancona, and content ourselves with asking how many Americans were drowned. Noble standards, and noble sympathies, and noble sorrows have their driving power, their practical utility. They have counted heavily in the destinies of nations. Carthage had commerce. Rome had ideals.

7

Town and Suburb*

I prize civilization, being bred in towns, and liking to hear and see what new things people are up to. —George Santayana

When I was a child, and people lived in towns and read poetry about the country, American cities had sharply accentuated characteristics, which they sometimes pretended to disparage, but of which they were secretly and inordinately proud. Less rich in tradition and inheritance than the beautiful cities of Europe, they nevertheless possessed historic backgrounds which colored their communal life, and lent significance to social intercourse. The casual allusion of the Bostonian to his "Puritan conscience," the casual allusion of the Philadelphian to his "Quaker forbears," did not perhaps imply what they were meant to imply; but they indicated an outlook, and established an understanding. The nearness of friends in those days, the familiar, unchanging streets, the convivial clubs, the constant companionship helped to knit the strands of life into a close and well-defined pattern. Townsmen who made part of this pattern were sometimes complacent without much cause, and combative without any cause at all; but the kind of cynicism which breeds fatigue about human affairs was no part of their robust constitutions.

A vast deal of abuse has been leveled against cities; and the splendor of the parts they have played has been dimmed by a too

---

* From *Times and Tendencies*, 1931.

persistent contemplation of their sins and their suffering. Thomas Jefferson said that they were a sore on the body politic; but then Jefferson appears to have believed that farming was the only sin-less employment for man. When he found himself loving Paris, because he was an American and could not help it, he excused his weakness by reflecting that, after all, France was not England, and by admitting a little ruefully that in Paris "a man might pass his life without encountering a single rudeness." It was Jefferson's contemporary, Cobbett, who, more than a hundred years ago, started the denouncement of towns and town life which has come rumbling down to us through the century. London was the object of his supreme detestation. Jews and Quakers lived in London (so he said), also readers of the *Edinburgh Review;* and Jews, Quakers, and readers of the *Edinburgh Review* were alike to him anathema. "Cobbett," mused Hazlitt, "had no comfort in fixed principles"; and for persistent fixity of principles the *Review* ran a close third to the followers of Moses and of Fox.

It was pure wrong-headedness on the part of a proletarian fighting the cause of the proletariat to turn aside from the age-old spectacle of the townsman cradling his liberty, and rejoicing in his labor. There was not an untidy little mediaeval city in Europe that did not help to carry humanity on its way. The artisans scorned by Froissart, the "weavers, fullers, and other ill-intentioned people of the town," who gave so much trouble to their betters, battled unceasingly for communal rights, and very often got them. The guilds, proud, quarrelsome and defiant, gave to the world the pride and glory of good work, and the pride and glory of freedom. As for London, those "mettlesome Thames dwellers" held their own for centuries against every form of aggression. The silken cord which halts each king of England at Temple Bar on his way to coronation is a reminder of the ancient liberties of London. There stood the city's gates, which were opened only at the city's will. Charles I signed his own death warrant when he undertook to coerce that stubborn will. When George I asked Sir Robert Walpole how much it would cost to enclose Saint James's Park (long the delight of Londoners), and make it the private pleasure-ground of the king, the minister answered in four words, "Only three crowns, Sire," and the Hanoverian shrugged his shoulders in silent understanding. What a strange people he had come to rule!

We Americans think that we put up a brave fight against the stupid obstinacy of George III, and so we did for seven years. But London fought him all the years of his reign. "It was not for nothing," says Trevelyan, "that Londoners with their compact organization, and their habits of political discipline, proudly regarded themselves as the regular army of freedom." George, whose conception of kingship was singularly simple and primitive, regarded his hostile city pretty much as Victoria regarded her House of Commons. "Very unmanageable and troublesome," was her nursery governess's comment upon a body of men who were (though she did not like to think so) the lawmakers of Britain.

With all history to contradict us, it is hardly worth while to speak of city life as entailing "spiritual loss," because it is out of touch with Nature. It is in touch with humanity, and humanity is Nature's heaviest asset. Blake, for some reason which he never made plain (making things plain was not his long suit), considered Nature—"the vegetable universe," he phrased it—to be depraved. He also considered Wordsworth to be more or less depraved because of his too exclusive worship at her shrine. "I fear Wordsworth loves Nature," he wrote (proud of his penetration) to Crabbe Robinson; "and Nature is the work of the Devil. The Devil is in us all so far as we are natural." Yet, when Wordsworth the Nature-lover stood on Westminster Bridge at dawn, and looked upon the sleeping London, he wrote a noble sonnet to her beauty:

Earth has not anything to show more fair.

When Blake looked upon London, he saw only her sorrow and her sin, he heard only "the youthful harlot's curse" blighting her chartered streets. She was a trifle more depraved than Nature.

The present quarrel is not even between Nature and man, between the town and the country. It is between the town and the suburb, that midway habitation which fringes every American city, and which is imposing or squalid according to the incomes of suburbanites. This semi-rural life, though it has received a tremendous impetus in the present century, is not precisely new. Clerkenwell, London's oldest suburb, dates from the Plantagenets. John Stow, writing in the days of Elizabeth, says that rich men who dwelt in London town spent their money on hospitals for the sick and alms-houses for the poor; but that rich men who dwelt in Shoreditch and other suburbs spent their money on costly residences to gratify their vanity. Being an antiquarian, and a freeman of Merchant Taylors' Company, Stow naturally held by the town.

It is the all-prevailing motor which stands responsible for the vast increase of suburban life in the United States, just as it was the coming of the locomotive which stood responsible for the increased population of London in Cobbett's last days. "The facilities which now exist for moving human bodies from place to place," he wrote in 1827 (being then more distressed by the excellence of the coaching roads than by the invasion of steam), "are among the curses of the country, the destroyers of industry, of morals, and of happiness."

It sounds sour to people who are now being taught that to get about easily and quickly is ever and always a blessing. The motor, we are given to understand, is of inestimable service because it enables men and women to do their work in the city, and escape with ease and comfort to their country homes—pure air, green grass, and so on. Less stress is laid upon the fact that it is also the motor which has driven many of these men and women into the suburbs by rendering the city insupportable; by turning into an open-air Bedlam streets which were once peaceful, comely and secure. Mr. Henry Ford, who has added the trying role of prophet to his other avocations, proclaimed six years ago that American cities were doomed. They had had their day. They had abused their opportunities. They had become unbearably expensive. They had grown so congested that his cars could make no headway in their streets. Therefore they must go. "Delenda est Carthago; dum Ford deliberat."

If Dickens still has readers as well as buyers, they must be grimly diverted by the art with which, in *A Tale of Two Cities*, he works up the incident of the child run over and killed in the crowded streets of Paris. He makes this incident the key to all that follows. It justifies the murder by which it is avenged. It interprets the many murders that are on their way. It is an indictment of a class condemned to destruction for its wantonness. And to emphasize the dreadfulness of the deed, Dickens adds this damnatory sentence: "Carriages were often known to drive on, and leave their wounded behind them."

All this fire and fury over a child killed in the streets! Why, we Americans behold a yearly holocaust of children that would have glutted the bowels of Moloch. When thirty-two thousand people are slain by motors in twelve months, it is inevitable that a fair proportion of the dead should be little creatures too feeble and foolish to save themselves. As for driving on and leaving the wounded, that is a matter of such common occurrence that we have with our usual ingenuity invented a neat and expressive phrase for it, thus fitting it into the order of the day. The too-familiar headlines in the press, "Hit-and-run victim found unconscious in the street," "Hit-and-run victim dies in hospital," tell over and over again their story of callous cruelty. That such cruelty springs from fear is no palliation of the crime. Cowardice explains, but does not excuse, the most appalling brutalities. This particular form of ruffianism wins out (more's the pity!) in a majority of cases, and so it is likely to continue. In the year 1926, three hundred and sixty-one hit-and-run drivers remained unidentified, and escaped the penalty they deserved. Philippe de Comines cynically observed that he had known very few people who were clever enough to run away in time. The hit-and-runners of America could have given him points in this ignoble game.

The supposed blessedness of country life (see every anthology in the libraries) has been kindly extended to the suburbs. They are open to Whistler's objection that trees grow in them, and to Horace Walpole's objection that neighbors grow in them also. Rich men multiply their trees; poor men put up with the multiplication of neighbors. Rich men can conquer circumstances wherever they are. Poor men (and by this I mean men who are urbanely alluded to as in "moderate circumstances") do a deal of whistling to keep themselves warm. They talk with serious fervor about Nature, when the whole of their landed estate is less than one of the back yards in which the town dwellers of my youth grew giant rosebushes that bloomed brilliantly in the mild city air. Mowing a grass plot is to them equivalent to plowing the soil. Sometimes they have not even a plot to mow, not even the shelter of a porch, nor the dignity and distinction of their own front door; but live in gigantic suburban apartment houses, a whole community under one roof like a Bornean village. Yet this monstrous standardization leaves them happy in the belief that they are country dwellers, lovers of the open, and spiritual descendants of the pioneers.

And the city? The abandoned city whose sons have fled to suburbs, what is it but a chaotic jumble of skyscrapers, public institutions, and parked cars? A transition stage is an uncomely stage, and cities on the move have a melancholy air of degradation. Shops elbow their uneasy way, business soars up into the air, houses disappear from their familiar settings, tired men and women drop into their clubs on the twentieth story of an inhospitable building, streets are dug up, paved, and dug up again, apparently with a view to buried treasure; dirt, confusion, and piercing noise are permitted by citizens who find it easier to escape such evils than to control them. An impression prevails that museums, libraries, and imposing banks constitute what our American press delights in calling "the city beautiful." That there is no beauty without distinction, and that distinction is made or marred by the constant, not the casual, contact of humanity, is a truth impressed upon our minds by countless towns in Europe, and by a great many towns in the United States. They tell their tale as plainly as a printed page, and far more convincingly.

If this tale is at an end; if the city has nothing to give but dirt, disorder, and inhuman racket, then let its sons fly to the suburbs and mow their grass plots in content. If it has no longer a vehement communal life, if it is not, as it once was, the center of pleasure and of purpose, if it is a thoroughfare and nothing else, then let them pass through it and escape. One thing is sure. No rural community, no suburban community, can ever possess the distinctive qualities that city dwellers have for centuries given to the world.

The common interests, the keen and animated intercourse with its exchange of disputable convictions, the cherished friendships and hostilities—these things shaped townsmen into a compact, intimate society which left its impress upon each successive generation. The home gives character to the city; the man gives character to the home. If, when his day's work is over, he goes speeding off to a suburb, he breaks the link which binds him to his kind. He says that he has good and beautiful and health-giving relations with Nature—a tabloid Nature suited to his circumstances; but his relations with men are devitalized. Will Rogers indicated delicately this devitalization when he said: "League of Nations! No, Americans aren't bothering about the League of Nations. What they want is some place to park their cars."

Londoners, who have no cause to fear a semi-deserted London, grieve that even a single thoroughfare should change its aspect, should lose its old and rich association with humanity. So Mr. Street grieved over an altered Piccadilly, reconstructing the dramas it had witnessed, the history in which it had borne a part; wandering in fancy from house to house, where dwelt the great, the gay, and the undaunted. His book, he said, was an epitaph. Piccadilly still lived, and gave every day a clamorous demonstration of activity; but her two hundred years of social prominence were over, and her very distinguished ghosts would never have any successors.

This is what is known as progress, and from it the great cities of Europe have little or nothing to fear. London, Paris, and Rome remain august arbiters of fate. They may lose one set of associations, but it would take centuries to rob them of all. Only a mental revolution could persuade their inhabitants that they are not good places to live in; and the eloquence of an archangel would be powerless to convince men bred amid arresting traditions that they are less fit to control the destinies of a nation than are their bucolic neighbors.

It would be hard to say when or why the American mind acquired the conviction that the lonely farmhouse or the sacrosanct village was the proper breeding-place for great Americans. It can hardly be due to the fact that Washington was a gentleman farmer, and Lincoln a country boy. These circumstances are without significance.

The youthful Washington would have taken as naturally to fighting, and the youthful Lincoln to politics, if they had been born in Richmond and Louisville. But the notion holds good. It has been upheld by so keen an observer and commentator as Mr. Walter Lippmann, who has admitted that ex-Governor Smith, for whom he cherishes a profound and intelligent admiration, was debarred from the presidency by "the accident of birth." The opposition to him was based upon a sentiment "as authentic and as poignant as his support. It was inspired by the feeling that the clamorous life of the city should not be acknowledged as the American ideal."

This is, to say the least, bewildering. The qualities which Mr. Lippmann endorses in Mr. Smith, his "sure instinct for realities," his "supremely good-humored intelligence, and practical imagination about the ordinary run of affairs," are products of his environment. His name can be written in the book of state as one who knows his fellow men; and he knows them because he has rubbed elbows with them from boyhood. The American people, says Mr. Lippmann, resent this first-hand knowledge. They will not condone or sanction it.

> In spite of the mania for size and the delusions of grandeur which are known as progress, there is still an attachment to village life. The cities exist, but they are felt to be alien; and in this uncertainty men turn to the scenes from which the leaders they have always trusted have come. The farmhouse at Plymouth, with old Colonel Coolidge doing the chores, was an inestimable part of President Coolidge's strength. The older Americans feel that it is in such a place that American virtue is bred; a cool, calm, shrewd virtue, with none of the red sins of the sidewalks of New York.

There may be Americans who entertain this notion, but Mr. Lippmann, I am sure, is not of the number. He is well aware that sin does not belong to sidewalks. It has no predisposition towards pavements or mud roads. It is indigenous to man. Our first parents lived in the country, and they promptly committed the only sin they were given a chance to commit. Cain was brought up in the heart of the country, and he killed one of the small group of people upon whom he could lay his hands. That "great cities, with their violent contrasts of riches and poverty, have produced class hatred all the world over," is true—but a half-truth. The *Jacquerie,* most hideous illustration of well-earned class hatred, was a product of the countryside. So was the German *Bundschuh.* The French and the Russian Revolutionists lighted up wide landscapes with burning homes, and soaked the innocent soil with blood. The records of crime prove the universality of crime. Bastards and morons and paranoiacs and degenerates and the criminally insane may be found far from the sidewalks of New York.

To live in stable harmony with Nature should be as easy for the town dweller as for the countryman. As a matter of fact, it should be easier, inasmuch as "the brutal, innocent injustice of Nature" leaves the town dweller little the worse. Like authorship, Nature is a good stick but a bad crutch, and they love her best who are not dependent on her caprices:

> Bred in the town am I,
> So would I wish to be,
> Loving its glimpses of sky,
> Swayed by its human sea.

If Browning in his incomparable poem, "Up at a Villa—Down in the City," appears to mock at the street-loving lady, he nevertheless makes out a strong case in her favor. I have sympathized with her all my life; and it is worthy of note that the poet himself preferred to live in towns, and, like Santayana, see what people were up to. The exceptionally fortunate man was Montaigne who drew a threefold wisdom from the turbulent city of Bordeaux, which he ruled as mayor; from the distinction of Paris and the French court, where he was a gentleman of the king's chamber; and from the deep solitude of Auvergne, where stood his ancestral home. He knew the life of the politician, the life of the courtier, the life of the farmer. Therefore, being kindly disposed towards all the vanities of the world, he was balanced and moderate beyond the men of his day.

Lovers of the town have been content, for the most part, to say they loved it. They do not brag about its uplifting qualities. They have none of the infernal smugness which makes the lover of the country insupportable. "I gravitate to a capital by a primary law of nature," said Henry Adams, and was content to say no more. It did not seem to occur to him that the circumstance called for ardor or for apology. But when Mr. John Erskine turns his ungrateful back upon the city which loves him, he grows enthusiastic over the joy of regaining "the feel of the soil, the smell of earth and rain, the dramatic contact of the seasons, the companionship of the elements." It is a high note to strike; but if for drama we must fall back upon the seasons, and for companionship upon the elements, ours will be a dreary existence in a world which we have always deemed both dramatic and companionable. If, as Mr. Erskine asserts, spring, summer, autumn, and winter are "annihilated" in town, we lose their best, but we escape their worst, features. That harsh old axiom, "Nature hates a farmer," has a fund of experience behind it. A distinguished surgeon, having bought, in a Nature-loving mood, a really beautiful farm, asked an enlightened friend and neighbor: "What had I better do with my land?" To which the answer came with judicious speed: "Pave it."

There is a vast deal of make-believe in the carefully nurtured sentiment for country life, and the barefoot boy, and the mountain girl. I saw recently in an illustrated paper a picture of a particularly sordid slum in New York's unredeemed East Side, and beneath it the reproachful query: "Is this a place to breed supermen?" Assuredly not. Neither is a poverty-stricken, fallen-to-pieces farmhouse, with a hole in its screen door; or a grim little home in a grim little suburb, destitute of beauty and cheer. If we want supermen (and to say the truth Germany has put us out of conceit with the species), we shall have to breed them under concentrated violet rays. Sunshine and cloud refuse to sponsor the race.

When Dr. Johnson said, "The man who is tired of London is tired of life," he expressed only his own virile joy in humanity. When Lamb said, "That man must have a rare receipt for melancholy who can be dull in Fleet Street," he summed up the brimming delight afforded him by this epitome of civilization. When Sydney Smith wrote from the dignified seclusion of his rectory at Combe-Florey,

"I look forward eagerly to the return of the bad weather, coal fires, and good society in a crowded city," he put the pleasures of the mind above the pleasures of the senses. All these preferences are temperately and modestly stated. It was only when Lamb was banished from the thronged streets he loved that he grew petulant in his misery. It was only when he dreamed he was in Fleet Market, and woke to the torturing dullness of Enfield, that he cried out: "Give me old London at fire and plague times rather than this healthy air, these tepid gales, these purposeless exercises." Yet even then he claimed no moral superiority over the Nature-lovers who were beginning to make themselves heard in England. He knew only that London warmed his sad heart, and that it broke when he lost her.

Generally speaking, and leaving out of consideration the very poor to whom no choice in life is given, men and women who live in cities or in suburbs do so because they want to. Men and women who live in small towns do so because of their avocations, or for other practical reasons. They are right in affirming that they like it. I once said to a New York taxi driver: "I want to go to Brooklyn." To which he made answer: "You mean you have to." So with the small-town dwellers. They may or may not "want to," but the "have to" is sure. Professional men, doctors and dentists especially, delight in living in the suburbs, so that those who need their services cannot reach them. The doctor escapes from his patients, who may fall ill on Saturday, and die on Sunday, without troubling him. The dentist is happy in that he can play golf all Saturday and Sunday while his patients agonize in town. Only the undertaker, man's final servitor, stands staunchly by his guns.

It is not because the city is big, but because it draws to its heart all things that are gay and keen, that life in its streets is exhilarating. It is short of birds (even the friendly little sparrows are being killed off by the drip of oil into its gutters); but that is a matter of more concern to the city's cats than to the city's inhabitants. It is needlessly noisy; but the suburb is not without its sufferings on this score. Motors shriek defiance in the leafy lanes, dogs bark their refrain through the night, and the strange blended sounds of the radios, like lost souls wailing their perdition, float from piazza to piazza. These are remediable evils; but so are most of the city's evils, which are not remedied because Americans are born temporizers, who dislike nothing so much as abating a public nuisance. They will spend time and money on programs to outlaw war, because that is a purely speculative process; but they will not stir themselves to outlaw excessive noise or dangerous speeding, because such measures mean actual campaigning. "The city," says one clear-eyed and very courageous American, "is the flower of civilization. It gives to men the means to make their lives expressive. It offers a field of battle, and it could be made a livable place if its sons would stay and fight for it, instead of running away."

8

On a Certain Condescension in Americans*

Sixty-two years ago Mr. James Russell Lowell published in the *Atlantic Monthly* an urbanely caustic essay, "On a Certain Condescension in Foreigners." Despite discursiveness (it was a leisurely age), this *Apologia pro patria sua* is a model of good temper, good taste, and good feeling. Its author regretted England's dislike for our accent, France's distaste for our food, and Germany's contempt for our music; but he did not suffer himself to be cast down. With a modesty past all praise, he even admitted, what no good American will admit today, that popular government "is no better than any other form except as the virtue and wisdom of the people make it so"; and that self-made men "may not be divinely commissioned to fabricate the higher qualities of opinion on all possible topics of human interest." Nevertheless, he found both purpose and principle in the young nation, hammered into shape by four years of civil war. "One might be worse off than even in America," mused this son of Massachusetts; and we are instantly reminded of William James's softly breathed assurance: "A Yankee is also, in the last analysis, one of God's creatures."

Sixty-two years are but a small fragment of time. Not long enough surely for the civilization of Europe to decay, and the civilization of

* From *Times and Tendencies*, 1931.

the United States to reach a pinnacle of splendor. Yet the condescension which Mr. Lowell deprecated, and which was based upon superiority of culture, seems like respectful flattery compared to the condescension which Americans now daily display, and which is based upon superiority of wealth. There has been no startling decline of European institutions, no magnificent upbuilding of our own; only a flow of gold from the treasuries of London, Paris, and Rome into the treasury of Washington. Germany's belief in the economic value of war, fruit of the evil seed sown in 1870, has been realized in a fashion which Germans least expected. England is impoverished in money and men. The casualties in the British army were over three million; the killed numbered six hundred and fifty-eight thousand. France is impoverished in money, men, and resources. A conscientious destruction of everything that might prove profitable if spared marked the progress of the invading Teutons. But the tide of wealth did not flow to Berlin. It leaped the sea, and filled the coffers of the nation that had provided the sinews of war, and that had turned the tide of victory.

Under these circumstances the deep exhaustion of countries that have been struggling for life as a drowning man struggles for breath, is hardly a matter for surprise. Cause and effect are too closely linked to need elucidation. That such countries should have recovered some measure of order, of reason, of normal energy, and of a heaven-sent capacity for enjoyment, is the blessed miracle of our century. The superb conservation of force, which Mr. Galsworthy says makes it difficult to come to the end of an Englishman, has held him uncrushed under a load of taxation which would have broken the heart and hopes of any other people. The strength and invulnerability of France's creative instinct, her unfailing respect for individual distinction, have filled her national life with something besides care. Our admiration for such qualities in no wise lessens our liking for our own civilization, our preference for what is ours and for what suits us best; but it might save us from a blinding and naïvely spoken self-esteem.

A year or two ago Governor A. Harry Moore of New Jersey made an address to the congregation of the First Presbyterian Church of

Manasquan. It was a patriotic address, and, as such, followed the formula which invariably refers our goodness and greatness to the active partnership of God. "The world," said Governor Moore, "is waiting for America. It leaps to hear every blow America strikes. America shines among nations as the little child that shall lead them. Just as God gave humanity a new chance when He directed Noah to build the Ark, so He gave it a new chance when He put it into the head of an Italian navigator to discover America."

My excuse for quoting these words is that they were spoken by an official, printed by a representative newspaper, and read by the general public. They may therefore be considered as representing one layer of the American adult mind. The suggestion of an ex-governor of Iowa that we should expel from our country all foreigners who cannot recite the Constitution of the United States and Lincoln's "Gettysburg Address," represents a second layer. The ultimatum of a popular evangelist: "If I had my way there would be no language but English taught in the United States, and any immigrant coming here and not speaking our tongue would be immediately sent back," represents a third. Or perhaps they are one and the same. Now it is all very well for an ironical scientist, like Dr. Joseph Collins, to intimate that there is no such thing as an American adult mind, and that the great body of the people think like children until they reach senility, and cease thinking at all. The fact remains that nobody but a moron has any right to think like a child after he has ceased to be one. He may go on doing it because it is an easy, pleasant, and self-sufficient thing for him to do. But the value of our thinking is the test of our civilization. If we apprehend the exact nature of our offering to the great depositories of human thought, we know where we stand in the orderly progress of the ages.

There does not seem to be much doubt on this score in the mind (I must continue to use the word) of the average American. The *Atlantic Monthly* published in February, 1924, a paper by Mr. Langdon Mitchell on "The American Malady." The writer quoted a few lines from an editorial in the *Ladies' Home Journal*, August, 1923: "There is only one first-class civilization in the world today. It is right here in the United States and the Dominion of Canada.

Europe's is hardly second-class, and Asia's is about fourth- to sixth-class." I verified this quotation, finding it a little difficult to credit, and borrowed it for a lecture I was giving in New York. My audience took it at its face value, and cheerfully, I might say enthusiastically, applauded the sentiment. It was evident that to them it was a modest statement of an incontrovertible fact, and they registered their cordial agreement. They seemed—so far as I could apprehend them—to believe that we were, like the Jews, a chosen people, that our mission was the "uplift" of the human race, and that it behooved those who were to be uplifted to recognize their inferior altitude.

Is this an unusual frame of mind among educated Americans? Is it confined to Main Street, or to the film actress who told Paris reporters that the United States was forty years (why forty?) ahead of Europe "intellectually and morally"? Where can we find a better spokesman for the race than Mr. Walter Hines Page, a man to whom was given a hard and heartrending job, who did it superlatively well (even the animadversions of his critics are based upon the success of his activities), and who died in the doing of it, worn out, body and soul and mind, as if he had been shot to pieces in the trenches? Yet this able and representative American thought and said that Latin civilization was a negligible asset to the world. He could see little good in people who did not speak English, and no good at all in people who did not speak English or French. "Except the British and the French," he wrote to his son, Arthur Page, in December, 1917, "there's no nation in Europe worth a tinker's damn when you come to the real scratch. The whole continent is rotten, or tyrannical, or yellow dog. I wouldn't give Long Island or Moore County for the whole of continental Europe."

It was a curious estimate of values. Long Island is a charming place, and very rich. Moore County is, I doubt not, one of the most beautiful tracts in a supremely beautiful State. Nevertheless, there are those who would think them dearly bought at the price of Rome. No one can truly say that Switzerland, Denmark, and Holland are rotten, or tyrannical, or yellow dog. Indeed, Mr. Page admitted that the Danes were a free people, and that Switzerland was a true republic, but too small to count—a typically American point of view. To interpret life in terms of size and numbers rather than in terms of intellect, beauty, and goodness is natural for a patriot who has more than three million square miles of country, and over a hundred million countrymen. As Walt Whitman lustily sang:

> I dote on myself—there is that lot of me, and all so luscious.

That Mr. Page clearly foresaw the wealth and strength that would accrue to the United States from the World War proves the keenness of his vision. In 1914 he wrote to President Wilson: "From an economic point of view, we *are* the world; and from a political point of view also." That he was sure this wealth and strength were well placed proves the staunchness of his civic pride. "In all the humanities, we are a thousand years ahead of any people here," was his summing-up in a letter to Mr. Frank Doubleday, 1916. Even our reluctance to credit Prussia with militarism showed the immaculate innocence of our hearts. "There could be no better measure of the moral advance that the United States has made over Europe than the incredulity of our people." Finally, in a burst of enthusiasm, or sentiment, or perhaps homesickness, comes a magnificent affirmation and elucidation of our august preeminence: "God has as yet made nothing or nobody equal to the American people; and I don't think He ever will or can." Which is a trifle fettering to omnipotence.

Mr. Page's Americanism being what it was, I cannot help thinking that his countrymen might have more readily forgiven his admiration for the admittedly inferior qualities of Great Britain. His regard for England was not wholly unlike the regard of the English for the United States in Mr. Lowell's day: a friendly feeling, made friendlier by a definite and delightful consciousness of superiority. Ten months before the war, he wrote to President Wilson: "The future of the world belongs to us. . . . Now what are we going to do with this leadership when it falls into our hands? And how can we use the English for the highest purposes of democracy?"

The last sentence is a faultless expression of national condescension. It would have given Mr. Lowell as much entertainment as did the comments of his British acquaintances. I know nothing to put by its side, because it is so kindly meant. Our lordliness is, as a rule, a trifle more severe, tinged with reproof rather than sweetened with patronage. When the Locarno Conference progressed to its satisfactory conclusion without our help or hindrance, a leading American newspaper seized the opportunity (which was not a good opportunity) to assert our domination over Europe, and to remind her of the finality of our verdicts. If our president urged "international agreements," his words must be received outside the United States as "a warning that this government, as represented by Mr. Coolidge, will accept no excuse for war anywhere."

But why, in heaven's name, should any European nation have offered an excuse to Mr. Coolidge for anything it felt disposed to do? If it belonged to the League of Nations, and undertook, however lamely, to go to war on its own account, excuses were in order, but not to Washington. Even in the World Court we share our rights and responsibilities with other Governments, and accept or reject excuses in accordance with the will of the majority.

The Locarno Treaty does, in fact, give us food for thought. It in no way impairs our safety or our interests. We are as big and as strong and as rich as we were before. But it shows us that something can be accomplished without our controlling influence. Our help is needed in the reconstruction of battered Europe; but, while we can withhold it at pleasure, giving it does not warrant too sharp a tone of authority. A little boy, who has since grown into a distinguished man of letters, once stepped with deliberation into a pond, and stood there to the detriment of his health and of his shoes. An indignant aunt summoned him to dry land. The little boy, being well out of reach, remained waterlogged and defiant. The aunt, indisposed to pursuit, said sternly: "Do you know what I do when youngsters refuse to obey me! I whip them." The little boy, aware of moral as well as of physical immunity, replied with decision: "You don't vip other people's children, I pwesume." And neither, when it comes to the point, does the United States.

It is natural, though regrettable that inferior nations, crowded together in Europe which they have somehow contrived to make glorious and beautiful ("Thank God," cried Henry James, "for a world which holds so rich an England, so rare an Italy!"), should resent our presenting ourselves to them as an example. They have troubles and traditions of their own, inheritances great and grievous which reach back to

>   ... old, unhappy, far-off things,
> And battles long ago.

They cannot wipe the slate clean, and begin afresh after a new and improved model. We keep on telling them (I quote now from recent American utterances) that our "accumulated heritage of spiritual blessings" is theirs to command; that our idealism "has made itself felt as a great contributory force in the advancement of mankind," and that "the Stars and Stripes are a harbinger of a new and happier day for the lesser nations of the world." We explain to them that if we have demanded payment of their debts it was in order to maintain "the principle of the integrity of international obligations"; and that our connection with a World Court is in the nature of a public notice "that the enormous influences of our country are to be cast on the side of the enlightened processes of civilization." "Lord, gie us a guid conceit o' ourselves," is about the only prayer which the American has no need to utter.

If Europeans pay insufficient regard to our carefully catalogued virtues, Americans are far too deeply impressed by them. It is as demoralizing for a nation to feel itself an ethical exhibit as it is demoralizing for a young woman to win a beauty prize in an Atlantic City contest. The insult offered to our country by calling such a prize-winner "Miss America" is not greater than the insult offered to our country by calling every expansive wave of self-esteem "Americanism." If our civilization be "infinitely the best so far developed in the ages," we have all the less need to say so. If we are giving to the world "supreme grandeur in service," we can afford to be modest in calling attention to the fact. If we are, by virtue of precept and example, "working great changes in the spirit of international morality," it would be more self-respecting to give other nations a chance to express their unprodded appreciation and gratitude.

America has invested her religion as well as her morality in sound income-paying securities. She has adopted the unassailable position of a nation blessed because it deserves to be blessed; and her sons, whatever other theologies they may affect or disregard, subscribe unreservedly to this national creed. Scholars, men of letters, and the clergy lend it their seasonable support. Professor Thomas Nixon Carver of Harvard, who has written a clear, forceful, and eminently readable book on "The Present Economic Revolution in the United States," seems to have no shadow of doubt that our good fortune, which might be better, is due to our good behavior, which cannot be improved on. "Prosperity is coming to us," he says, "precisely because our ideals are not materialistic. It is coming to us because we are pursuing the exalted ideal of equality under liberty, as it must of necessity come to any nation that pursues that ideal whole-heartedly and enthusiastically. . . . All these things are being added to us precisely because we are seeking the Kingdom of God and His righteousness, as they are always added, and must of logical necessity always be added, unto any nation that seeks those ideals of justice which are the very essence of the Kingdom of God."

I wonder if righteousness can be linked so securely to the elements of success; and if food and raiment—all that is promised in the Gospel—can be magnified into the colossal fortunes of America. The American may not be materialistic; but he has certainly hallowed commercialism, and made of it both a romantic and a moral adventure. He sings its saga at banquets, and he relates its conquests to his sons in magazines and in much-read books. There is great satisfaction in doing this, and we are told it is well done. If something be lacking in such a philosophy, that something is not missed. It is easy to count up the value of the proprieties in a watchful world; but exceedingly hard to put the spiritual life on a paying basis. The Old Testament consistently taught that goodness and piety were rewarded with material well-being; but Christianity has committed itself to no such untenable proposition. "He that findeth his life shall lose it," sounds inconceivably remote from the contemplation of well-merited affluence.

A point of difference between the condescension of foreigners in 1869 and the condescension of Americans in 1931 is that the magniloquence which amused and ruffled Mr. Lowell was mainly spoken (he was in a position to hear it both at home and abroad), and the magniloquence which today ruffles, without amusing, sensitive foreigners and Americans is, as I have shown by liberal quotations, printed for all the reading world to see. An editorial in *Current Opinion* modestly suggests that "Europeans might learn a good deal if they would come over here, study the history of America since the war, and try to imitate our example. . . . We may be crass and uncultured; but at least we have been good sports, and have been honest enough, farsighted enough, and sagacious enough to render the United States the soundest and healthiest nation in the world today."

A "good sport" recognizes handicaps. He knows and he admits that poverty is not the equivalent of wealth, that dead men are not equal to live men, that ruined towns are less habitable than whole ones. A "good sport" may honestly believe that the one hope for mankind is "the Americanization of the world"; but he does not coarsely call on Europe to "clean up and pay up"; he does not write with comprehensive ignorance: "Europeans will have to abandon their national vanities, and get together, before they can expect to get together with us"; he does not second the Congressman from Ohio who informed the American Chamber of Commerce in London that "right now the United States wants to see Europe do some housecleaning without delay." He may have even ventured a doubt when the Honorable David F. Houston, writing ably and reasonably in *Harper's Magazine,* June, 1924, affirmed our superior spotlessness. "The United States," said Mr. Houston, "is in a position of leadership in all the fundamental idealistic, moral, and spiritual forces which make a nation great, and constitute a worthy civilization. It seeks as its highest aim to have a clean national household from cellar to attic."

Seeks it, yes. All civilized countries seek political integrity, and justice in the administration of law. Sufficiency, security, and freedom are not the exclusive ideals of the United States. We may be as good as we are great, but our distaste for sincere and searching criticism blurs our national vision. A blustering, filibustering, narrow-minded Senate is not a source of legitimate pride. To lead the world in crime should be a source of legitimate humiliation. President Coolidge called the attention of the state governors in January, 1926, to the fact that twenty-four thousand persons had met their deaths by highway fatalities within twelve months. He said it was too many for one country in one year, and he was right. Yet twenty-four thousand deaths by accidents—some of which were unavoidable—are less appalling than eleven thousand deaths by violence in the same length of time. The combined numbers are worth the consideration of peace-loving Americans who write eloquently about the sacredness of life.

The crime waves in every state of the union have now reached a stage of permanent inundation; and the ever-increasing youthfulness of criminals (the American Bar Association has called our attention to this point) promises more complete submergence in the future. It is gratifying to know that twenty-odd million American children go to our schools every day; but some of them appear to spare time from their studies for the more exciting pursuits of robbery, house-breaking, and pathetically premature attempts at banditry; to say nothing of such higher flights as firing their schools, and murdering their grandmothers. These lawless infants are the distinctive product of our age. Their years are few, but their delinquencies are many. If they keep on getting younger and younger, and more and more murderously inclined, we shall after a while be afraid to pass a baby in a perambulator.

The *Ladies' Home Journal* has recently told us that "everywhere in Europe the ambitious youngsters of the new generation are learning English, and studying American geography and political history. They want to get the spirit of what American democracy really is." We cannot but hope that these innocent offspring of effete civilizations will not extend their studies to American newspapers. If they do, they may give their backward countries a rude jolt. In 1926, Scotland, with a population of five millions, had only eleven murders, while Massachusetts, with a population of four millions, could boast of one hundred and seven. Mr. Francis B. Sayre, writing for the *Atlantic Monthly* in June, 1928, says that more robberies are committed every year in Cleveland (which used to be an innocent-looking town) than in England, Scotland, and Wales. Also that for every ten murders committed in London, one hundred and sixty are committed in New York; and that seven out of London's ten murderers are hanged, while one out of New York's hundred and sixty are electrocuted. It almost seems as though we could do a little housecleaning of our own.

The superiority complex is, however, as impervious to fact as to feeling. It denies the practical, it denies the intellectual, and it denies the spiritual. The Sorbonne and the Institut Pasteur make no more appeal to it than does the girl, Jeanne d'Arc, or the defenders of Verdun. France as the inspiration of the artist, the stimulus of the thinker, the home of those who seek to breathe the keen air of human intelligence, is lost in the France whose stabilized franc is worth four cents of "real" American money. She is, in our eyes, a nation reprehensible because she demands the security which two oceans guarantee to us, and contemptible because she has failed to readjust herself after such calamities as we have never known.

What the American likes and respects is what he is happy enough to possess: efficiency, moral uniformity, and a fairly good brand of standardized thought. Conventions are the life and soul of the country, and there is nothing like a convention (except perhaps a political campaign) for making us think well of ourselves. The importunate virtues of small communities are nourished by oratory, and by uplift-mongers on platforms, and in the editorial columns of widely circulated periodicals. Uplifting has become a vocation, and its practitioners enjoy the esteem and gratitude of the public. "Every American," says André Siegfried, "is at heart an evangelist." If he isn't, it is felt that he ought to be. There is a poignantly funny description in one of William James's letters of a lady, the wife of a Methodist minister whom he met at Chautauqua, who told him she had his portrait hanging in her bedroom, and underneath it these words: "I want to bring balm to human lives." "Supposed," said the horrified—and modest—philosopher, "to be a quotation from *me!*"

Americanism has been defined as "the more or less perfect expression of the common belief that American ideals realize themselves in American society." This belief is wholly disassociated from the austere creed of the patriot. It was not patriotism which made foreigners in Mr. Lowell's day so sure that they were conferring a favor on the United States by visiting our shores. It is not patriotism which makes Americans today so sure that they are conferring a benefit on Europe by advice and admonition, by bidding her study our methods and imitate our example. There is an intellectual humility which is another name for understanding. It enables us to measure the depths of tragedies which have brought us no personal pain, and the heights of supremacies which have failed to arouse our ambitions. It is the key to history, and the open-sesame to the hearts of men. It may even come as close to deciphering the mysterious ways of God as does the complete assurance that we are his deservedly favorite children.

Santayana says that goodwill is the great American virtue, but that it lacks direction. It should, if it be a veritable virtue, save us outright from the cruel pleasure of contrast, which we are too often bidden to enjoy, and which we confuse in our minds with gratitude for the gifts of heaven. The sorrowful burden of human knowledge is ours to bear. The dark places of the earth are not confined to other continents than ours. Efficiency is an asset; but without a well balanced emotional life it gets us no further than the door of happiness. Peace and wealth are serviceable possessions; but only intense personalities can create art and letters. It takes a great deal to make an enjoyable world. It takes all we have to give to make a world morally worthy of man.

Books and Education

9

Our Friends, The Books[*]

There is a short paragraph in Hazlitt's *Conduct of Life* that I read very often, and always with fresh delight. He is offering much good counsel to a little lad at school, and when he comes to a matter upon which most counselors are wont to be exceedingly didactic and diffuse—the choice of books—he condenses all he has to say into a few wise and gentle words that are well worth taking to heart:

> As to the works you will have to read by choice or for amusement, the best are the commonest. The names of many of them are already familiar to you. Read them as you grow up with all the satisfaction in your power, and make much of them. It is perhaps the greatest pleasure you will have in life, the one you will think of longest, and repent of least. If my life had been more full of calamity than it has been (much more than yours, I hope, will be) I would live it over again, my poor little boy, to have read the books I did in my youth.

In all literature there is nothing truer or better than this, and its sad sincerity contrasts strangely with the general tone of the essay, which is somewhat in the manner of Lord Chesterfield. But here, at least, Hazlitt speaks with the authority of one whose books had

---

[*] From *Essays in Miniature*, 1892.

ever been his friends; who had sat up all night as a child over *Paul and Virginia,* and to whom the mere sight of an odd volume of some good old English author, on a street stall, brought back with keen and sudden rapture the flavor of those early joys which he remembered longest, and repented least. His words ring consolingly in these different days, when we have not only ceased reading what is old, but when—a far greater misfortune—we have forgotten how to read "with all the satisfaction in our power," and with a simple surrendering of ourselves to the pleasure which has no peer. There are so many things to be considered now besides pleasure, that we have well-nigh abandoned the effort to be pleased. In the first place, it is necessary to "keep up" with a decent proportion of current literature, and this means perpetual labor and speed, whereas idleness and leisure are requisite for the true enjoyment of books. In the second place, few of us are brave enough to withstand the pressure which friends, mentors and critics bring to bear upon us, and which effectually crushes anything like the weak indulgence of our own tastes. The reading they recommend being generally in the nature of a corrective, it is urged upon us with little regard to personal inclination; in fact, the less we like it, the greater our apparent need. There are people in this world who always insist upon others remodeling their diet on a purely hygienic basis; who entreat us to avoid sweets or acids, or tea or coffee, or whatever we chance to particularly like; who tell us persuasively that cress and dandelions will purify our blood; that celery is an excellent febrifuge; that shaddocks should be eaten for the sake of their quinine, and fish for its phosphorus; that stewed fruit is more wholesome than raw; that rice is more nutritious than potatoes;—who deprive us, in a word, of that hearty human happiness which should be ours when dining. Like Mr. Woodhouse, they are capable of having the sweetbreads and asparagus carried off before our longing eyes, and baked apples provided as a substitute.

It is in the same benevolent spirit that kind-hearted critics are good enough to warn us against the books we love, and to prescribe for us the books we ought to read. With robust assurance they offer to give our tutelage their own personal supervision, and their disinterested zeal carries them occasionally beyond the limits of discretion. I have been both amazed and gratified by the lack of reserve with which these unknown friends have volunteered to guide my own footsteps through the perilous paths of literature. They are so urgent, too, not to say severe, in their manner of proffering assistance: "To Miss Repplier we would particularly recommend"—and then follows a list of books of which I dare say I stand in open need; but which I am naturally indisposed to consider with much kindness, thrust upon me, as they are, like paregoric or a porous plaster. If there be people who can take their pleasures medicinally, let them read by prescription and grow fat! But let me rather keep for my friends those dear and familiar volumes which have given me a large share of my life's happiness. If they are somewhat antiquated and out of date, I have no wish to flout their vigorous age. A book, Hazlitt reminds us, is not, like a woman, the worse for being old. If they are new, I do not scorn them for a fault which is common to all their kind. *Paradise Lost* was once new, and was regarded as a somewhat questionable novelty. If they come from afar, or are compatriots of my own, they are equally well-beloved. There can be no aliens in the ranks of literature, no national prejudice in an honest enjoyment of art. The book, after all, and not the date or birthplace of its author, is of material importance. "It seems ungracious to refuse to be a *terrae filius*," says Mr. Arnold; "but England is not all the world." Neither, for that matter, is America, nor even Russia. The universe is a little wider and a little older than we are pleased to think, and to have lived long and traveled far does not necessarily imply inferiority. The volume that has crossed the seas, the volume that has survived its generation, stand side by side with their newborn American brother, and there is no lack of harmony in such close companionship. Books of every age and of every nation show a charming adaptability in their daily intercourse; and, if left to themselves, will set off each other's merits in the most amiable and disinterested manner, each one growing better by contact with its excellent neighbor. It is only when the patriotic critic comes along, and stirs up dissensions in their midst, that this peaceful atmosphere is rent with sudden discord; that the English book grows disdainful and supercilious; the American, aggressive and sarcastic; the French, malicious and unkind. It is only when we apply to them a test which is neither wise nor worthy that they show all their bad qualities, and afford a wrangling ground for the ill-natured reviewers of two continents.

There is a story told of the Russian poet, Pushkin, which I like to think true, because it is so pretty. When he was carried home fatally wounded from the duel which cost him his life, his young wife, who had been the innocent cause of the tragedy, asked him whether there were no relatives or friends whom he wished to see summoned to his bedside. The dying man lifted his heavy eyes to the shelf where stood his favorite books, and murmured faintly in reply, "Farewell, my friends." When we remember that Pushkin lived before Russian literature had become a great and dispiriting power, when we realize that he had never been ordered by critics to read Turgenev, never commanded severely to worship Tolstoy or be an outcast in the land, never even reveled in the dreadful gloom of Dostoyevsky, it seems incredible to the well-instructed that he should have loved his books so much. It is absolutely afflicting to think that many of these same volumes were foreign, were romantic, perhaps even cheerful in their character; that they were not his mentors, his disciplinarians, his guides to a higher and sadder life, but only his "friends." Why, Hazlitt himself could have used no simpler term of endearment. Charles Lamb might have uttered the very words when he closed his patient eyes in the dull little cottage at Edmonton. Sir Walter Scott might have murmured them on that still September morn when the clear rippling of the Tweed hushed his tired heart to rest. I think that Shelley bade some swift, unconscious farewell to all the dear delights of reading, when he thrust into his pocket the little volume of Keats, with its cover bent hastily backward, and rose, still dreamy with fairyland, to face a sudden death. I think that Montaigne bade farewell to the fourscore "every-day books" that were his chosen companions, before turning serenely away from the temperate pleasures of life.

For all these men loved literature, not contentiously, nor austerely, but simply as their friend. All read with that devout sincerity which precludes petulance, or display, or lettered asceticism, the most dismal self-torment in the world. In that delicious dialogue of Landor's between Montaigne and Scaliger, the scholar intimates to the philosopher that his library is somewhat scantily furnished, and that he and his father between them have written nearly as many volumes as Montaigne possesses on his shelves. "Ah!" responds the sage with gentle malice, "to write them is quite another thing; but one reads books without a spur, or even a pat from our Lady Vanity."

Could anything be more charming, or more untrue than this? Montaigne, perched tranquilly on his Guyenne hill slope, may have escaped the goad; but we, the victims of our swifter day, know too well how remorselessly Lady Vanity pricks us round the course. Are we not perpetually showing our paces at her command, and under the sharp incentive of her heel? Yet Charles Lamb, in the heart of London, preserved by some fine instinct the same intellectual freedom that Montaigne cherished in sleepy Gascony. He too was fain to read for pleasure, and his unswerving sincerity is no less enviable than the clearness of his literary insight. Indeed, while many of his favorite authors may have no message for our ears, yet every line in which he writes his love is pregnant with enjoyment; every word expresses subtly a delicious sense of satisfaction. The soiled and torn copies of *Tom Jones* and *The Vicar of Wakefield* from the circulating library, which speak eloquently to him of the thousand thumbs that have turned over each well-worn page; the "kind-hearted play-book" which he reaches down from some easy shelf; the old *Town and Country Magazine* which he finds in the window seat of an inn; the "garrulous, pleasant history" of Burnet; the "beautiful, bare narrative" of *Robinson Crusoe;* the antiquated, time-stained edition of "that fantastic old great man," Robert Burton; the Folio Beaumont and Fletcher—all these and many more are Lamb's tried friends, and he writes of them with lingering affection. He is even able, through some fine choice of words, to convey to us the precise degree and quality of pleasure which they yield him, and which he wins us to share, not by exhortations or reproaches, but gently, with alluring smiles, and hinted promises of reward. How craftily he holds each treasured volume before our eyes! How apt the brief, caressing sentence in which he sings its praises!—"The sweetest names, and which carry a perfume in the mention, are Kit Marlowe, Drayton, Drummond of Hawthornden, and Cowley." "Milton almost requires a solemn service of music to be played before you enter upon him. Who listens, had need bring docile thoughts, and purged ears." "Winter evenings—the world shut out—with less of ceremony the gentle Shakespeare enters. At such a season, the *Tempest,* or his own *Winter's Tale.*"

In fact, the knowledge of when to read a book is almost as valuable as the knowledge of what book to read, and Lamb, as became a true lover of literature, realized instinctively that certain hours and certain places seem created expressly for the supreme enjoyment of an author, who yields to these harmonious surroundings his best and rarest gifts. To pick up *The Faerie Queene* as a stopgap in the five or six impatient minutes before dinner, to carry *Candide* into the "serious avenues" of a cathedral, to try and skim over Richardson when in the society of a lively girl—Lamb knew too well that these unholy feats are the accomplishments of an intellectual acrobat, not of a modest and simple-hearted reader. Hazlitt also was keenly alive to the influences of time and place. His greatest delight in poring over the books of his youth lay in the many recollections they aroused of scenes and moments rich in vanished joys. He opened a faded, dusty volume, and behold! the spot where first he read it, the day it was received, the feeling of the air, the fields, the sky, all returned to him with charming distinctness, and with them returned his first rapturous impression of that long-closed, long-neglected romance: "Twenty years are struck off the list, and I am a child again." Mr. Pater lays especial emphasis on the circumstances under which our favorite authors are read. "A book," he says, "like a person, has its fortunes with one; is lucky or unlucky in the precise moment of its falling in our way; and often, by some happy accident, ranks with us for something more than its independent value." Thus it is that Marius and Fabian, nestled in the ripened corn amid the cool brown shadows, receive from the *Golden Ass* of Apuleius a strange keen pleasure; each lad taking from the story that which he is best fitted to absorb; each lad as unmindful of the other's feelings as of the grosser elements in the tale. For without doubt a book has a separate message for every reader, and tells him, of good or evil, that which he is able to hear. Plato, indeed, complains of all books that they lack reticence or propriety toward different classes of persons, and his protest embodies the aversion of the flexible Greek mind for the precision of written literature. A poem or an oration which, crystallized into characters, speaks to all alike, and reveals itself indiscriminately to everybody, is of less value to the ancient scholar than the poem or oration which lingers in the master's mind, and maintains a delicate reserve toward the inferior portion of the community. Plato is so far removed from the modern spirit which seeks to persuade the multitude to read Shakespeare and Milton, that he practically resents their peering with rude, but pardonable curiosity, into the stately domains of genius. We have now grown so insistently generous in these matters that our unhappy brothers, harassed beyond endurance, may well envy the plebeian Greeks their merciful limitations; or wish, with the little girl in *Punch,* that they had lived in the time of Charles II, "for then education was very much neglected." But strive as we may, we cannot coerce great authors into universal complaisance. Plato himself, were he so unfortunate as to be living now, would recognize and applaud their manifest reserves. Even to the elect they speak with varying voices, and it is sometimes difficult to believe that all have read alike. When *Guy Mannering* was first given to the public, who awaited it with frantic eagerness, Wordsworth thoughtfully observed that it was a novel in the style of Mrs. Radcliffe. Murray, from whom one expects more discernment, wrote to Hogg that *Meg Merrilies* was worthy of Shakespeare; "but all the rest of the novel might have been written by Scott's brother, or any other body." Blackwood, about the same time, wrote to Murray: "If Walter Scott be the author of *Guy Mannering,* he stands far higher in this line than in his former walk." One of these verdicts has been ratified by time, but who could suppose that Julia Mannering and honest Dandy Dinmont would ever have whispered such different messages into listening ears!

And it is precisely because of the independence assumed by books, that we have need to cherish our own independence in return. They will not all be our friends, and not one of them will give itself freely to us at the dictation of a peremptory critic. Hazlitt says nobly of a few great writers, notably Milton and Burke, that "to have lived in the cultivation of an intimacy with such works, and to have familiarly relished such names, is not to have lived in vain." This is true, yet if we must seek for companionship in less august circles, there are many milder lights who shine with a steady radiance. It is not the privilege of every one to love so great a prose writer as Burke, so great a poet as Milton. "An appreciation of *Paradise Lost,*" says Mr. Mark Pattison, "is the reward of exquisite scholarship"; and the number of exquisite scholars is never very large. To march up to an author as to the cannon's mouth is at best but unprofitable heroism. To take our pleasures dutifully is the least likely way to enjoy them. The laws of Crete, it is said, were set to music, and sung as alluringly as possible after dinner; but I doubt if they afforded a really popular pastime. The well-fed guests who listened to such decorous chants applauded them probably from the standpoint of citizenship, rather than from any undisguised sentiment of enjoyment, and a few degenerate souls must have sighed occasionally over the joys of a rousing and unseemly chorus. We of today are so rich in laws, so amply disciplined at every turn, that we have no need to be reminded at dinner of our obligations. A kind-hearted English critic once said that reading was not a duty, and had therefore no business to be made disagreeable; and that no man was under any obligation to read what another man wrote. This is an old-fashioned point of view, which has lost favor of late years, but which is not without compensations of its own. If the office of literature be to make glad our lives, how shall we seek the joy in store for us save by following Hazlitt's simple suggestion, and reading "with all the satisfaction in our power"? And how shall we insure this satisfaction, save by ignoring the restrictions imposed upon us, and cultivating, as far as we can, a sincere and pleasurable intercourse with our friends, the books?

10

Reverend Mother's Feast*

"Mother's feast"—in other words the saint's day of the Superioress—was dawning upon our horizon, and its lights
and shadows flecked our checkered paths. Theoretically, it was an
occasion of pure joy, assuring us, as it did, a *congé*, and not a *congé*
only, but the additional delights of a candy fair in the morning,
and an operetta, "The Miracle of the Roses," at night. Such a round
of pleasures filled us with the happiest anticipations; but—on the
same principle that the Church always prefaces her feast days with
vigils and with fasts—the convent prefaced our *congé* with a competition in geography, and with the collection of a "spiritual bouquet,"
which was to be our offering to Reverend Mother on her fête.

A competition in anything was an unqualified calamity. It meant
hours of additional study, a frantic memorizing of facts, fit only
to be forgotten, and the bewildering ordeal of being interrogated
before the whole school. It meant for *me* two little legs that shook
like reeds, a heart that thumped like a hammer in my side, a sensa-
tion of sickening terror when the examiner—Madame Bouron—
bore down upon me, and a mind reduced to sudden blankness,
washed clean of any knowledge upon any subject, when the simplest
question was asked. Tried by this process, I was only one degree

---

* From *In Our Convent Days*, 1905.

removed from idiocy. Even Elizabeth, whose legs were as adamant, whose heartbeats had the regularity of a pendulum, and who, if she knew a thing, could say it, hated to bound states and locate capitals for all the school to hear. "There are to be prizes, too," she said mournfully. "Madame Duncan said so. I don't like going up for a prize. It's worse than a medal at Primes."

"Oh, well, maybe you won't get one," observed Tony consolingly. "You didn't, you know, last time."

"I did the time before last," said Elizabeth calmly. "It was 'La Corbeille de Fleurs.'"

There was an echo of resentment in her voice, and we all—even Tony—admitted that she had just cause for complaint. To reward successful scholarship with a French book was one of those black-hearted deeds for which we invariably held Madame Bouron responsible. She may have been blameless as the babe unborn; but it was our habit to attribute all our wrongs to her malign influence. We knew "La Corbeille de Fleurs." At least, we knew its shiny black cover, and its frontispiece, representing a sylphlike young lady in a floating veil bearing a hamper of provisions to a smiling and destitute old gentleman. There was nothing in this picture, nor in the accompanying lines, "Que vois-je? Mon Dieu! Un ange de Ciel, qui vient à mon secours," which tempted us to a perusal of the story, even had we been in the habit of voluntarily reading French.

As for the "spiritual bouquet," we felt that our failure to contribute to it on a generous scale was blackening our reputations forever. Every evening the roll was called, and girl after girl gave in her list of benefactions. Rosaries, so many. Litanies, so many. Aspirations, so many. Deeds of kindness, so many. Temptations resisted, so many. Trials offered up, so many. Acts, so many. A stranger, listening to the replies, might have imagined that the whole school was ripe for Heaven. These blossoms of virtue and piety were added every night to the bouquet; and the sum total, neatly written out in Madame Duncan's flowing hand, was to be presented, with an appropriate address, to Reverend Mother on her feast, as a proof of our respectful devotion.

It was a heavy tax. From what resources some girls drew their supplies remained ever a mystery to us. How could Ellie Plunkett have found the opportunity to perform four deeds of kindness, and resist seven temptations, in a day? We never had any temptations to resist. Perhaps when one came along, we yielded to it so quickly that it had ceased to tempt before its true character had been ascertained. And to whom was Ellie Plunkett so overweeningly kind? "Who wants Ellie Plunkett to be kind to her?" was Tony's scornful query. There was Adelaide Harrison, too, actually turning in twenty acts as one day's crop, and smiling modestly when Madame Duncan praised her self-denial. Yet, to our unwarped judgment, she seemed much the same as ever. We, at least, refused to accept her estimate of her own well-spent life.

"Making an act" was the convent phraseology for doing without something one wanted, for stopping short on the verge of an innocent gratification. If I gave up my place in the swing to Viola Milton, that was an act. If I walked to the woods with Annie Churchill, when I wanted to walk with Elizabeth, that was an act. If I ate my bread unbuttered, or drank my tea unsweetened, that was an act. It will be easily understood that the constant practice of acts deprived life of everything that made it worth the living. We were so trained in this system of renunciation that it was impossible to enjoy even the very simple pleasures that our convent table afforded. If there were anything we particularly liked, our nagging little consciences piped up with their intolerable "Make an act, make an act"; and it was only when the last mouthful was resolutely swallowed that we could feel sure we had triumphed over asceticism. There was something maddening in the example set us by our neighbors, by those virtuous and pious girls who hemmed us in at study time at our meals. When Mary Rawdon gently waved aside the chocolate custard—which was the very best chocolate custard it has ever been my good fortune to eat—and whispered to me as she did so, "An act for the bouquet"; I whispered back, "Take it, and give it to me," and held out my plate with defiant greed. Annie Churchill told us she hadn't eaten any butter for a week; whereat Tony called her an idiot, and Annie— usually the mildest of girls—said that "envy at another's spiritual good" was a very great sin, and that Tony had committed it. There is nothing so souring to the temper as abstinence.

What made it singularly hard to sacrifice our young lives for the swelling of a spiritual bouquet was that Reverend Mother, who was to profit by our piety, had so little significance in our eyes. She was as remote from the daily routine of the school as the Grand Lama is remote from the humble Tibetans whom he rules; and if we regarded her with a lively awe, it was only because of her aloofness, of the reserves that hedged her majestically round. She was an Englishwoman of good family, and of vast bulk. There was a tradition that she had been married and widowed before she became a nun; but this was a subject upon which we were not encouraged to talk. It was considered both disrespectful and indecorous. Reverend Mother's voice was slow and deep, a ponderous voice to suit her ponderous size; and she spoke with what seemed to us a strange and barbarous accent, pronouncing certain words in a manner which I have since learned was common in the days of Queen Elizabeth, and which a few ripe scholars are now endeavoring to reintroduce. She was nearsighted to the verge of blindness, and always at Mass used a large magnifying glass, like the one held by Leo the Tenth in Raphael's portrait. She was not without literary tastes of an insipid and obsolete order, the tastes of an English gentlewoman, reared in the days when young ladies read the "Female Spectator," and warbled "Oh, no, we never mention her." Had she not "entered religion," she might have taken Moore and Byron to her heart,—as did one little girl whose "Childe Harold" lay deeply hidden in a schoolroom desk,—but the rejection of these profane poets had left her stranded upon such feeble substitutes as Letitia Elizabeth Landon, whose mysterious death she was occasionally heard to deplore.

Twice on Sundays Reverend Mother crossed our orbit; in the morning, when she instructed the whole school in Christian doctrine, and at night, when she presided over Primes. During the week we saw her only at Mass. We should never even have known about Letitia Elizabeth Landon, had she not granted an occasional audience to the graduates, and discoursed to them sleepily upon the books she had read in her youth. Whatever may have been her qualifications for her post (she had surpassing dignity of carriage, and was probably a woman of intelligence and force), to us she was a mere embodiment of authority, as destitute of personal malice as of personal charm. I detested Madame Bouron, and loved Madame Rayburn. Elizabeth detested Madame Bouron, and loved Madame Dane. Emily detested Madame Bouron, and loved Madame Duncan. These were emotions, amply nourished, and easily understood. We were capable of going to great lengths to prove either our aversion or our love. But to give up chocolate custard for Reverend Mother was like suffering martyrdom for a creed we did not hold.

"It's because Reverend Mother is so fond of geography that we're going to have the competition," said Lilly. "Madame Duncan told me so."

"Why can't Reverend Mother, if she likes it so much, learn it for herself?" asked Tony sharply. "I'll lend her my atlas."

"Oh, she knows it all," said Lilly, rather scandalized. "Madame Duncan told me it was her favorite study, and that she knew the geography of the whole world."

"Then I don't see why she wants to hear us say it," observed Elizabeth, apparently under the impression that competitions, like gladiatorial shows, were gotten up solely for the amusement of an audience. It never occurred to her, nor indeed to any of us, to attach any educational value to the performance. We conceived that we were butchered to make a convent holiday.

"And it's because Reverend Mother is so fond of music that we are going to have an operetta instead of a play," went on Lilly, pleased to have information to impart.

I sighed heavily. How could anybody prefer anything to a play? I recognized an operetta as a form of diversion, and was grateful for it, as I should have been grateful for any entertainment, short of an organ recital. We were none of us surfeited with pleasures. But to me song was at best only an imperfect mode of speech; and the meaningless repetition of a phrase, which needed to be said but once, vexed my impatient spirit. We were already tolerably familiar with "The Miracle of the Roses." For two weeks past the strains had floated from every music room. We could hear, through the closed doors, Frances Fenton, who was to be St. Elizabeth of Hungary, quavering sweetly,—

> Unpretending and lowly,
> Like spirits pure and holy,
> I love the wild rose best,
> I love the wild rose best,
> I love the wi-i-ild rose best."

We could hear Ella Holrook announcing in her deep contralto,—

> "'Tis the privilege of a Landgrave
> To go where glory waits him,
> Glory waits him";

and the chorus trilling jubilantly,—

> Heaven has changed the bread to roses,
> Heaven has changed the bread to roses.

Why, I wondered, did they have to say everything two and three times over? Even when the Landgrave detects St. Elizabeth in the act of carrying the loaves to the poor, his anger finds a vent in iteration.

> Once again you've dared to brave my anger,
> Yes, once again you've dared to brave my anger;
> > My power you scorn,
> > My power you scorn.

To which the Saint replies gently, but tediously,—

> My lord they are,
> My lord they are
> But simple roses,
> But simple ro-o-oses,
> That I gathered in the garden even now.

"Suppose that bread hadn't been changed to roses," said Elizabeth speculatively, "I wonder what St. Elizabeth would have done."

"Oh, she knew it had been, because she prayed it would be," said Marie, who was something of a theologian.

"But suppose it hadn't."

"But it *had,* and she knew it had, because of her piety and faith," insisted Marie.

"I shouldn't have liked to risk it," murmured Elizabeth.

"*I* think her husband was a pig," said Tony. "Going off to the Crusade, and making all that fuss about a few loaves of bread. If I'd been St. Elizabeth"—

She paused, determining her course of action, and Marie ruthlessly interposed. "If you're not a saint, you can't tell what you would do if you were a saint. You would be different."

There was no doubt that Tony as a saint would have to be so very different from the Tony whom we knew, that Marie's dogmatism prevailed. Even Elizabeth was silenced; and, in the pause that followed, Lilly had a chance to impart her third piece of information. "It's because Reverend Mother's name is Elizabeth," she said, "that we're going to have an operetta about St. Elizabeth; and Bessie Treves is to make the address."

"Thank Heaven, there is another Elizabeth in the school, or I might have to do it," cried our Elizabeth, who coveted no barren honors; and—even as she spoke—the blow fell. Madame Rayburn appeared at the schoolroom door, a folded paper in her hand. "Elizabeth," she said, and, with a hurried glance of apprehension, the saint's unhappy namesake withdrew. We looked at one another meaningly. "It's like giving thanks before you're sure of dinner," chuckled Tony.

I had no chance to hear any particulars until night, when Elizabeth watched her opportunity, and sallied forth to brush her teeth while I was dawdling over mine. The strictest silence prevailed in the dormitories, and no child left her alcove except for the ceremony of tooth-brushing, which was performed at one of two large tubs, stationed in the middle of the floor. These tubs—blessed be their memory!—served as centers of gossip. Friend met friend, and smothered confidences were exchanged. Our gayest witticisms,— hastily choked by a toothbrush,—our oldest and dearest jests were whispered brokenly to the accompaniment of little splashes of water. It was the last social event of our long social day, and we welcomed it as freshly as if we had not been in close companionship since seven o'clock in the morning. Elizabeth, scrubbing her teeth with ostentatious vigor, found a chance to tell me, between scrubs, that Bessie Treves had been summoned home for a week, and that she, as the only other bearer of Reverend Mother's honored name, had been chosen to make the address. "It's the feast of St. Elizabeth," she whispered, "and the operetta is about St. Elizabeth, and they want an Elizabeth to speak. I wish I had been christened Melpomene."

"You couldn't have been christened Melpomene," I whispered back, keeping a watchful eye upon Madame Chapelle, who was walking up and down the dormitory, saying her beads. "It isn't a Christian name. There never was a St. Melpomene."

"It's nearly three pages long," said Elizabeth, alluding to the address, and not to the tragic Muse. "All about the duties of women, and how they ought to stay at home and be kind to the poor, like St. Elizabeth, and let their husbands go to the Crusades."

"But there are no Crusades any more for their husbands to go to," I objected.

Elizabeth looked at me restively. She did not like this fractious humor. "I mean let their husbands go to war," she said.

"But if there are no wars," I began, when Madame Chapelle, who had not been so inattentive as I supposed, intervened. "Elizabeth and Agnes, go back to your alcoves," she said. "You have been quite long enough brushing your teeth."

I flirted my last drops of water over Elizabeth, and she returned the favor with interest, having more left in her tumbler than I had. It was our customary good-night. Sometimes, when we were wittily disposed, we said *"Asperges me."* That was one of the traditional jests of the convent. Generations of girls had probably said it before us. Our language was enriched with scraps of Latin and apt quotations, borrowed from Church services, the Penitential Psalms, and the catechism.

For two days Elizabeth studied the address, and for two days more she rehearsed it continuously under Madame Rayburn's tutelage. At intervals she recited portions of it to us, and we favored her

with our candid criticisms. Tony objected vehemently to the very
first line:—

"A woman's path is ours to humbly tread."

She said she didn't intend to tread it humbly at all; that Elizabeth
might be as humble as she pleased (Elizabeth promptly disclaimed
any personal sympathy with the sentiment), and that Marie and
Agnes were welcome to all the humility they could practise (Marie
and Agnes rejected their share of the virtue), but that she—Tony—
was tired of behaving like an affable worm. To this, Emily, with
more courage than courtesy, replied that a worm Tony might be,
but an affable worm, never; and Elizabeth headed off any further
retort by hurrying on with the address.

A woman's path is ours to humbly tread,
And yet to lofty heights our hopes are led.
We may not share the Senate's stern debate,
Nor guide with faltering hand the helm of state;
Ours is the holier right to soften party hate,
And teach the lesson, lofty and divine,
Ambition's fairest flowers are laid at Virtue's shrine.

"Have you any idea what all that means?" asked Marie discon-
tentedly.

"Oh, I don't have to say what it means," returned Elizabeth, far
too sensible to try to understand anything she would not be called
upon to explain. "Reverend Mother makes that out for herself."

Not ours the right to guide the battle's storm,
Where strength and valor deathless deeds perform.
Not ours to bind the blood-stained laurel wreath
In mocking triumph round the brow of death.
No! 't is our lot to save the failing breath,
'T is ours to heal each wound, and hush each moan,
To take from other hearts the pain into our own.

"It seems to me," said Tony, "that we are expected to do all the work, and have none of the fun."

"It seems to *me*," said Marie, "that by the time we have filled ourselves up with other people's pains, we won't care much about fun. Did Reverend Mother, I wonder, heal wounds and hush up moans?"

"St. Elizabeth did," explained Elizabeth. "Her husband went to the Holy Land, and was killed, and then she became a nun. There are some lines at the end, that I don't know yet, about Reverend Mother,—

Seeking the shelter of the cloister gate,
Like the dear Saint whose name we venerate.

"Madame Rayburn wants me to make an act, and learn the rest of it at recreation this afternoon. That horrid old geography takes up all my study time."

"I've made three acts today," observed Lilly complacently, "and said a whole pair of beads this morning at Mass for the spiritual bouquet."

"I haven't made one act," I cried aghast. "I haven't done anything at all, and I don't know what to do."

"You might make one now," said Elizabeth thoughtfully, "and go talk to Adelaide Harrison."

I glanced at Adelaide, who was sitting on the edge of her desk, absorbed in a book. "Oh, I don't want to," I wailed.

"If you wanted to, it wouldn't be an act," said Elizabeth.

"But she doesn't want me to," I urged. "She is reading 'Fabiola.'"

"Then you'll give her the chance to make an act, too," said the relentless Elizabeth.

Argued into a corner, I turned at bay. "I won't," I said resolutely; to which Elizabeth replied: "Well, I wouldn't either, in your place," and the painful subject was dropped.

Four days before the feast the excitement had reached fever point, though the routine of school life went on with the same smooth precision. Every penny had been hoarded up for the candy fair. It was with the utmost reluctance that we bought even the stamps for our home letters, those weekly letters we were compelled to write, and which were such pale reflections of our eager and vehement selves. Perhaps this was because we knew that every line was read by Madame Bouron before it left the convent; perhaps the discipline of those days discouraged familiarity with our parents; perhaps the barrier which nature builds between the adult and the normal child was alone responsible for our lack of spontaneity. Certain it is that the stiffly written pages despatched to father or to mother every Sunday night gave no hint of our abundant and restless vitality, our zest for the little feast of life, our exaltations, our resentments, our thrice-blessed absurdities. Entrenched in the citadel of childhood, with laws of our own making, and passwords of our own devising, our souls bade defiance to the world.

If all our hopes centred in the *congé,* the candy fair, and the operetta,—which was to be produced on a scale of unwonted magnificence,—our time was sternly devoted to the unpitying exactions of geography. Every night we took our atlases to bed with us, under the impression that sleeping on a book would help us to remember its contents. As the atlases were big, and our pillows very small, this device was pregnant with discomfort. On the fourth night before the feast, something wonderful happened. It was the evening study hour, and I was wrestling sleepily with the mountains of Asia,— hideous excrescences with unpronounceable and unrememberable names,—when Madame Rayburn entered the room. As we rose to our feet, we saw that she looked very grave, and our minds took a backward leap over the day. Had we done anything unusually bad, anything that could call down upon us a public indictment, and was Madame Rayburn for once filling Madame Bouron's office? We could think of nothing; but life was full of pitfalls, and there was no sense of security in our souls. We waited anxiously.

"Children," said Madame Rayburn, "I have sorrowful news for you. Reverend Mother has been summoned to France. She sails on her feast day, and leaves for New York tomorrow."

We stared open-mouthed and aghast. The ground seemed sinking from under our feet, the walls crumbling about us. Reverend Mother sailing for France! And on her feast day, too,—the feast for which so many ardent preparations had been made. The *congé*, the competition, the address, the operetta, the spiritual bouquet, the candy fair,—were they, too, sailing away into the land of lost things? To have asked one of the questions that trembled on our lips would have been an unheard-of liberty. We listened in respectful silence, our eyes riveted on Madame Rayburn's face.

"You will all go to the chapel now," she said. "Tonight we begin a novena to *Mater Admirabilis* for Reverend Mother's safe voyage. She dreads it very much, and she is sad at leaving you. Pray for her devoutly. Madame Dane will bring you down to the chapel."

She turned to go. Our hearts beat violently. She knew, she could not fail to know, the thought that was uppermost in every mind. She was too experienced and too sympathetic to miss the significance of our strained and wistful gaze. A shadowy smile crossed her face. "Madame Bouron would have told you tomorrow," she said, "what I think I shall tell you tonight. It is Reverend Mother's express desire that you should have your *congé* on her feast, though she will not be here to enjoy it with you."

A sigh of relief, a sigh which we could not help permitting to be audible, shivered softly around the room. The day was saved; yet, as we marched to the chapel, there was a turmoil of agitation in our hearts. We knew that from far-away France—from a mysterious and all-powerful person who dwelt there, and who was called Mother General—came the mandates which governed our community. This was not the first sudden departure we had witnessed; but Reverend Mother seemed so august, so permanent, so immobile. Her very size protested mutely against upheaval. Should we never again see that familiar figure sitting in her stall, peering through her glass into a massive prayer book, a leviathan of prayer books, as imposing in its way as she was, or blinking sleepily at us as we filed by? Why, if somebody were needed in France, had it not pleased Mother General to send for Madame Bouron? Many a dry eye would have seen *her* go. But then, as Lilly whispered to me, suppose it had been Madame Rayburn. There was a tightening of my heartstrings at the thought, a sudden suffocating pang, dimly foreboding the grief of another year.

The consensus of opinion, as gathered that evening in the dormitory, was not unlike the old Jacobite epitaph on Frederick, Prince of Wales. Every one of us was sincerely sorry that Madame Bouron had not been summoned,—

Had it been his father,
We had much rather;

but glad that Madame Dane, or Madame Rayburn, or Madame Duncan, or some other favorite nun had escaped.

Since it's only Fred
Who was alive, and is dead,
There is no more to be said.

The loss of our Superioress was bewildering, but not, for us, a thing of deep concern. We should sleep as sweetly as usual that night.

The next morning we were all gathered into the big First Cours classroom, where Reverend Mother came to bid us good-bye. It was a solemn leave-taking. The address was no longer in order; but the spiritual bouquet had been made up the night before, and was presented in our name by Madame Bouron, who read out the generous sum-total of prayers, and acts, and offered-up trials, and resisted temptations, which constituted our feast-day gift. As Reverend Mother listened, I saw a large tear roll slowly down her cheek, and my heart smote me—my heart was always smiting me when it was too late—that I had contributed so meagerly to the donation. I remembered the chocolate custard, and thought—for one mistaken moment—that I should never want to taste of that beloved dish again. Perhaps if I had offered it up, Reverend Mother would cross the sea in safety. Perhaps, because I ate it, she would have storms, and be drowned. The doubtful justice of this arrangement was no more apparent to me than its unlikelihood. We were accustomed to think that the wide universe was planned and run for our reward and punishment. A rainy Sunday following the misdeeds of Saturday was to us a logical sequence of events.

When the bouquet had been presented, Reverend Mother said a few words of farewell. She said them as if she were sad at heart, not only at crossing the ocean, not only at parting from her community, but at leaving us, as well. I suppose she loved us collectively. She couldn't have loved us individually, knowing us only as two long rows of uniformed, curtsying schoolgirls, whose features she was too near-sighted to distinguish. On the other hand, if our charms and our virtues were lost to her, so were our less engaging qualities. Perhaps, taken collectively, we were rather lovable. Our uniforms were spotless, our hair superlatively smooth,—no blowsy, tossing locks, as in these days of libertinism, and our curtsies as graceful as hours of practice could make them. We sank and rose like the crest of a wave. On the whole, Reverend Mother had the best of us. Madame Bouron might have been pardoned for taking a less sentimental view of the situation.

That afternoon, while we were at French class, Reverend Mother departed. We heard the carriage roll away, but were not permitted to rush to the windows and look at it, which would have been a welcome distraction from our verbs. An hour later, at recreation, Madame Rayburn sent for Elizabeth. She was gone fifteen minutes, and came back, tense with suppressed excitement.

"Oh, what is it?" we cried. "The *congé* is all right?"

"All right," said Elízabeth.

"And the candy fair?" asked Lilly, whose father had given her a dollar to squander upon sweets.

"Oh, it's all right, too. The candy is here now; and Ella Holrook and Mary Denniston and Isabel Summers are to have charge of the tables. Madame Dane told me that yesterday."

Our faces lightened, and then fell, "Is it the competition?" I asked apprehensively.

Elizabeth looked disconcerted. It was plain she knew nothing about the competition, and hated to avow her ignorance. We always felt so important when we had news to tell. "Of course, after studying all that geography, we'll have to say it sooner or later," she said. "But"—a triumphant pause—"a new Reverend Mother is coming tomorrow."

"*Ciel!*" murmured Marie, relapsing into agitated French; while Tony whistled softly, and Emily and I stared at each other in silence.

The speed with which things were happening took our breath away.

"Coming tomorrow," repeated Elizabeth; "and I'm going to say the address as a welcome to her, on the night of the *congé,* before the operetta."

"Is her name Elizabeth, too?" I asked, bewildered.

"No, her name is Catherine. Madame Rayburn is going to leave out the lines about St. Elizabeth, and put in something about St. Catherine of Siena instead. That's why she wanted the address. And she is going to change the part about not sharing the Senate's stern debate, nor guiding with faltering hand the helm of state, because St. Catherine did guide the helm of state. At least, she went to Avignon, and argued with the Pope."

"Argued with the Pope!" echoed Marie, scandalized.

"She was a saint, Marie," said Elizabeth impatiently, and driving home an argument with which Marie herself had familiarized us. "She persuaded the Pope to go back to Rome. Madame Rayburn would like Kate Shaw to make the address; but she says there isn't time for another girl to study it."

"When is the feast of St. Catherine of Siena?" cried Tony, fired suddenly by a happy thought. "Maybe we'll have another *congé* then."

She rushed off to consult her prayerbook. Lilly followed her, and in a moment their two heads were pressed close together, as they scanned the Roman calendar hopefully. But before my eyes rose the image of Reverend Mother, our lost Reverend Mother, with the slow teardrop rolling down her cheek. Her operetta was to be sung to another. Her address was to be made to another. Her very saint was pushed aside in honor of another holy patroness. "The King is dead. Long live the King."

11

The Educator*

The Schoolmaster is abroad. —Lord Brougham

It is recorded that Boswell once said to Dr. Johnson, "If you had had children, would you have taught them anything?" and that Dr. Johnson, out of the fullness of his wisdom, made reply: "I hope that I should have willingly lived on bread and water to obtain instruction for them; but I would not have set their future friendship to hazard for the sake of thrusting into their heads knowledge of things for which they might have neither taste nor necessity. You teach your daughters the diameters of the planets, and wonder, when you have done it, that they do not delight in your company."

It is the irony of circumstance that Dr. Johnson and Charles Lamb should have been childless, for they were the two eminent Englishmen who, for the best part of a century, respected the independence of childhood. They were the two eminent Englishmen who could have been trusted to let their children alone. Lamb was nine years old when Dr. Johnson died. He was twenty-seven when he hurled his impotent anathemas at the heads of "the cursed Barbauld crew," "blights and blasts of all that is human in man and child." By that time the educator's hand lay heavy on schoolroom and nursery. In France, Rousseau and Mme. de Genlis had succeeded in interesting parents so profoundly in their children that French babies led a *vie de parade*. Their toilets and their meals were as open to the public as

* From *A Happy Half-Century and Other Essays*, 1908.

were the toilets and the meals of royalty. Their bassinettes appeared in salons, and in private boxes at the playhouse; and it was an inspiring sight to behold a French mother fulfilling her sacred office while she enjoyed the spectacle on the stage. In England, the Edgeworths and Mr. Day had projected a system of education which isolated children from common currents of life, placed them at variance with the accepted usages of society, and denied them that wholesome neglect which is an important factor in self-development. The Edgeworthian child became the pivot of the household, which revolved warily around him, instructing him whenever it had the ghost of a chance, and guarding him from the four winds of heaven. He was not permitted to remain ignorant upon any subject, however remote from his requirements; but all information came filtered through the parental mind, so that the one thing he never knew was the world of childish beliefs and happenings. Intercourse with servants was prohibited; and it is pleasant to record that Miss Edgeworth found even Mrs. Barbauld a dangerous guide, because little Charles of the "Early Lessons" asks his nurse to dress him in the mornings. Such a personal appeal, showing that Charles was on speaking terms with the domestics, was something which, in Miss Edgeworth's opinion, no child should ever read; and she praises the solicitude of a mother who blotted out this, and all similar passages, before confiding the book to her infant son. He might—who knows?—have been so far corrupted as to ask his own nurse to button him up the next day.

Another parent, still more highly commended, found something to erase in *all* her children's books; and Miss Edgeworth describes with grave complacency this pathetic little library, scored, blotted, and mutilated, before being placed on the nursery shelves. The volumes were, she admits, hopelessly disfigured; "but shall the education of a family be sacrificed to the beauty of a page? Few books can safely be given to children without the previous use of the pen, the pencil, and the scissors. These, in their corrected state, have sometimes a few words erased, sometimes half a page. Sometimes many pages are cut out."

Even now one feels a pang of pity for the little children who, more than a hundred years ago, were stopped midway in a story by the absence of half a dozen pages. Even now one wonders how much furtive curiosity was awakened by this process of elimination. To hover perpetually on the brink of the concealed and the forbidden does not seem a wholesome situation; and a careful perusal of that condemned classic, "Bluebeard," might have awakened this excellent mother to the risks she ran. There can be no heavier handicap to any child than a superhumanly wise and watchful custodian, whether the custody be parental, or relegated to some phoenix of a tutor like Mr. Barlow, or that cocksure experimentalist who mounts guard over "Émile," teaching him with elaborate artifice the simplest things of life. We know how Tommy Merton fell from grace when separated from Mr. Barlow; but what *would* have become of Émile if "Jean Jacques" had providentially broken his neck? What would have become of little Caroline and Mary in Mary Wollstonecraft's "Original Stories," if Mrs. Mason—who is Mr. Barlow in petticoats—had ceased for a short time "regulating the affections and forming the minds" of her helpless charges? All these young people are so scrutinized, directed, and controlled, that their personal responsibility has been minimized to the danger point. In the name of nature, in the name of democracy, in the name of morality, they are pushed aside from the blessed fellowship of childhood, and from the beaten paths of life.

That Mary Wollstonecraft should have written the most priggish little book of her day is one of those pleasant ironies which relieves the tenseness of our pity for her fate. Its publication is the only incident of her life which permits the shadow of a smile; and even here our amusement is tempered by sympathy for the poor innocents who were compelled to read the "Original Stories," and to whom even Blake's charming illustrations must have brought scant relief. The plan of the work is one common to most juvenile fiction of the period. Caroline and Mary, being motherless, are placed under the care of Mrs. Mason, a lady of obtrusive wisdom and goodness, who shadows their infant lives, moralizes over every insignificant episode, and praises herself with honest assiduity. If Caroline is afraid of thunderstorms, Mrs. Mason explains that *she* fears no tempest, because "a mind is never truly great until the love of virtue overcomes the fear of death." If Mary behaves rudely to a visitor, Mrs. Mason contrasts her pupil's conduct with her own. "I have accustomed myself to think of others, and what they will suffer on all occasions," she observes; "and this loathness to offend, or even to hurt the feelings of another, is an instantaneous spring which actuates my conduct, and makes me kindly affected to everything that breathes. . . . Perhaps the greatest pleasure I have ever received has arisen from the habitual exercise of charity in its various branches."

The stories with which this monitress illustrates her precepts are drawn from the edifying annals of the neighborhood, which is rich in examples of vice and virtue. On the one hand we have the pious Mrs. Trueman, the curate's wife, who lives in a rose-covered cottage, furnished with books and musical instruments; and on the other, we have "the profligate Lord Sly," and Miss Jane Fretful, who begins by kicking the furniture when she is in a temper, and ends by alienating all her friends (including her doctor), and dying unloved and unlamented. How far her mother should be held responsible for this excess of peevishness, when she rashly married a gentleman named Fretful, is not made clear; but all the characters in the book live nobly, or ignobly, up to their patronymics. When Mary neglects to wash her face—apparently that was all she ever washed—or brush her teeth in the mornings, Mrs. Mason for some time only hints her displeasure, "not wishing to burden her with precepts"; and waits for a "glaring example" to show the little girl the unloveliness of permanent dirt. This example is soon afforded by Mrs. Dowdy, who comes opportunely to visit them, and whose reluctance to perform even the simple ablutions common to the period is as resolute as Slovenly Peter's.

In the matter of tuition, Mrs. Mason is comparatively lenient. Caroline and Mary, though warned that "idleness must always be intolerable, because it is only an irksome consciousness of existence" (words which happily have no meaning for childhood), are, on the whole, less saturated with knowledge than Miss Edgeworth's Harry and Lucy; and Harry and Lucy lead rollicking lives by contrast with "Edwin and Henry," or "Anna and Louisa," or any other little pair of heroes and heroines. Edwin and Henry are particularly ill used, for they are supposed to be enjoying a holiday with their father, "the worthy Mr. Friendly," who makes "every domestic incident, the vegetable world, sickness and death, a real source of instruction to his beloved offspring." How glad those boys must have been to get back to school! Yet they court disaster by asking so many questions. All the children in our great-grandmothers' storybooks ask questions. All lay themselves open to attack. If they drink a cup of chocolate, they want to know what it is made of, and where coconuts grow. If they have a pudding for dinner, they are far more eager to learn about sago and the East Indies than to eat it. They put intelligent queries concerning the slave trade, and make remarks that might be quoted in Parliament; yet they are as ignorant of the common things of life as though newborn into the world. In a book called *Summer Rambles, or Conversations Instructive and Amusing, for the Use of Children*, published in 1801, a little girl says to her mother: "Vegetables? I do not know what they are. Will you tell me?" And the mother graciously responds: "Yes, with a great deal of pleasure. Peas, beans, potatoes, carrots, turnips, and cabbages are vegetables."

At least the good lady's information was correct as far as it went, which was not always the case. The talented governess in *Little Truths* warns her pupils not to swallow young frogs out of bravado, lest perchance they should mistake and swallow a toad, which would poison them; and in a *History of Birds and Beasts*, intended for very young children, we find, underneath a woodcut of a porcupine, this unwarranted and irrelevant assertion:—

> This creature shoots his pointed quills,
> And beasts destroys, and men;
> But more the ravenous lawyer kills
> With his half-quill, the pen.

It was thus that natural history was taught in the year 1767.

The publication in 1798 of Mr. Edgeworth's *Practical Education* (Miss Edgeworth was responsible for some of the chapters) gave a profound impetus to child study. Little boys and girls were dragged from the obscure haven of the nursery, from their hornbooks, and the casual slappings of nursery maids, to be taught and tested in the light of day. The process appears to have been deeply engrossing. Irregular instruction, object lessons, and experimental play afforded scant respite to parent or to child. "Square and circular bits of wood, balls, cubes, and triangles" were Mr. Edgeworth's first substitutes for toys; to be followed by "card, pasteboard, substantial but not sharp-pointed scissors, wire, gum, and wax." It took an active mother to superintend this home kindergarten, to see that the baby did not poke the triangle into its eye, and to relieve Tommy at intervals from his coating of gum and wax. When we read further that "children are very fond of attempting experiments in dyeing, and are very curious about vegetable dyes," we gain a fearful insight into parental pleasures and responsibilities a hundred years ago.

Textbook knowledge was frowned upon by the Edgeworths. We know how the "good French governess" laughs at her clever pupil who has studied the *Tablet of Memory*, and who can say when potatoes were first brought into England, and when hair powder was first used, and when the first white paper was made. The new theory of education banished the *Tablet of Memory*, and made it incumbent upon parent or teacher to impart in conversation such facts concerning potatoes, powder, and paper as she desired her pupils to know. If books were used, they were of the deceptive order, which purposed to be friendly and entertaining. A London bookseller actually proposed to Godwin "a delightful work for children," which was to be called *A Tour through Papa's House*. The object of this precious volume was to explain casually how and where Papa's furniture was made, his carpets were woven, his curtains dyed, his kitchen pots and pans called into existence. Even Godwin, who was not a bubbling fountain of humor, saw the absurdity of such a book; and recommended in its place *Robinson Crusoe*, "if weeded of its Methodism" (alas! poor Robinson!), *The Seven Champions of Christendom*, and *The Arabian Nights*.

The one great obstacle in the educator's path (it has not yet been wholly leveled) was the proper apportioning of knowledge between boys and girls. It was hard to speed the male child up the stony heights of erudition; but it was harder still to check the female child at the crucial point, and keep her tottering decorously behind her brother. In 1774 a few rash innovators conceived the project of an advanced school for girls; one that should approach from afar a college standard, and teach with thoroughness what it taught at all; one that might be trusted to broaden the intelligence of women, without lessening their much-prized femininity. It was even proposed that Mrs. Barbauld, who was esteemed a very learned lady, should take charge of such an establishment; but the plan met with no approbation at her hands. In the first place she held that fifteen was not an age for school life and study, because then "the empire of the passions is coming on"; and in the second place there was nothing she so strongly discountenanced as thoroughness in a girl's education. On this point she had no doubts, and no reserves. "Young ladies," she wrote, "ought to have only such a general tincture of knowledge as to make them agreeable companions to a man of sense, and to enable them to find rational entertainment for a solitary hour. They should gain these accomplishments in a quiet and unobserved manner. The thefts of knowledge in our sex are connived at, only while carefully concealed; and, if displayed, are punished with disgrace. The best way for women to acquire knowledge is from conversation with a father, a brother, or a friend; and by such a course of reading as they may recommend."

There was no danger that an education conducted on these lines would result in an undue development of intelligence, would lift the young lady above "her own mild and chastened sphere." In justice to Mrs. Barbauld we must admit that she but echoed the sentiments of her day. "Girls," said Miss Hannah More, "should be led to distrust their own judgments." They should be taught to give up their opinions, and to avoid disputes, "even if they know they are right." The one fact impressed upon the female child was her secondary place in the scheme of creation; the one virtue she was taught to affect was delicacy; the one vice permitted to her weakness was dissimulation. Even her play was not like her brother's play,—a reckless abandonment to high spirits; it was play within the conscious limits of propriety. In one of Mrs. Trimmer's books, a model mother hesitates to allow her eleven-year-old daughter to climb three rounds of a ladder, and look into a robin's nest, four feet from the ground. It was not a genteel thing for a little girl to do. Even her schoolbooks were not like her brother's schoolbooks. They were carefully adapted to her limitations. Mr. Thomas Gisborne, who wrote a much-admired work entitled *An Enquiry into the Duties of the Female Sex*, was of the opinion that geography might be taught to girls without reserve; but that they should learn only "select parts" of natural history, and, in the way of science, only a few "popular and amusing facts." *A Young Lady's Guide to Astronomy* was something vastly different from the comprehensive system imparted to her brother.

In a very able and subtle little book called *A Father's Legacy to his Daughters*, by Dr. John Gregory of Edinburgh,—

> He whom each virtue fired, each grace refined,
> Friend, teacher, pattern, darling of mankind! (Beattie's *Minstrel*)

—we find much earnest counsel on this subject. Dr. Gregory was an affectionate parent. He grudged his daughters no material and no intellectual advantage; but he was well aware that by too great liberality he imperiled their worldly prospects. Therefore, although he desired them to be well read and well informed, he bade them never to betray their knowledge to the world. Therefore, although he desired them to be strong and vigorous,—to walk, to ride, to live much in the open air,—he bade them never to make a boast of their endurance. Rude health, no less than scholarship, was the exclusive prerogative of men. His deliberate purpose was to make them rational creatures, taking clear and temperate views of life; but he warned them all the more earnestly against the dangerous indulgence of seeming wiser than their neighbors. "Be even cautious in displaying your good sense," writes this astute and anxious father. "It will be thought you assume a superiority over the rest of your company. But if you happen to have any learning, keep it a profound secret, especially from men, who are apt to look with a jealous and malignant eye on a woman of great parts and cultivated understanding."

This is plain speaking. And it must be remembered that "learning" was not in 1774, nor for many years afterwards, the comprehensive word it is today. A young lady who could translate a page of Cicero was held to be learned to the point of pedantry. What reader of *Coelebs*—if *Coelebs* still boasts a reader—can forget that agitating moment when, through the inadvertence of a child, it is revealed to the breakfast table that Lucilla Stanley studies Latin every morning with her father. Overpowered by the intelligence, Coelebs casts "a timid eye" upon his mistress, who is covered with confusion. She puts the sugar into the cream jug, and the tea into the sugar basin; and finally, unable to bear the mingled awe and admiration awakened by this disclosure of her scholarship, she slips out of the room, followed by her younger sister, and commiserated by her father, who knows what a shock her native delicacy has received. Had the fair Lucilla admitted herself to be an expert tight-rope dancer, she could hardly have created more consternation.

No wonder Dr. Gregory counseled his daughters to silence. Lovers less generous than Coelebs might well have been alienated by such disqualifications. "Oh, how lovely is a maid's ignorance!" sighs Rousseau, contemplating with rapture the many things that Sophie does not know. "Happy the man who is destined to teach her. She will never aspire to be the tutor of her husband, but will be content to remain his pupil. She will not endeavor to mold his tastes, but will relinquish her own. She will be more estimable to him than if she were learned. It will be his pleasure to enlighten her."

This was a well established point of view, and English Sophies were trained to meet it with becoming deference. They heard no idle prating about an equality which has never existed, and which never can exist. "Had a third order been necessary," said an eighteenth-century schoolmistress to her pupils, "doubtless one would have been created, a midway kind of being." In default of such a connecting link, any impious attempt to bridge the chasm between the sexes met with the failure it deserved. When Mrs. Knowles, a Quaker lady, not destitute of self-esteem, observed to Boswell that she hoped men and women would be equal in another world, that gentleman replied with spirit: "Madam, you are too ambitious. *We* might as well desire to be equal with the angels."

The dissimulation which Dr. Gregory urged upon his daughters, and which is the safeguard of all misplaced intelligence, extended to matters more vital than Latin and astronomy. He warned them, as they valued their earthly happiness, never to make a confidante of a married woman, "especially if she lives happily with her husband"; and never to reveal to their own husbands the excess of their wifely affection. "Do not discover to any man the full extent of your love, no, not although you marry him. *That* sufficiently shows your preference, which is all he is entitled to know. If he has delicacy, he will ask for no stronger proof of your affection, for your sake; if he has sense, he will not ask it, for his own. Violent love cannot subsist, at least cannot be expressed, for any time together on both sides. Nature in this case has laid the reserve on you." In the passivity of women, no less than in their refined duplicity, did this acute observer recognize the secret strength of sex.

A vastly different counselor of youth was Mrs. West, who wrote a volume of *Letters to a Young Lady* (the young lady was Miss Maunsell, and she died after reading them), which were held to embody the soundest morality of the day. Mrs. West is as dull as Dr. Gregory is penetrating, as verbose as he is laconic, as obvious as he is individual. She devotes many agitated pages to theology, and many more to irrefutable, though one hopes unnecessary, arguments in behalf of female virtue. But she also advises a careful submission, a belittling insincerity, as woman's best safeguards in life. It is not only a wife's duty to tolerate her husband's follies, but it is the part of wisdom to conceal from him any knowledge of his derelictions. Bad he may be; but it is necessary to his comfort to believe that his wife thinks him good. "The lordly nature of man so strongly revolts from the suspicion of inferiority," explains this excellent monitress, "that a susceptible husband can never feel easy in the society of his wife when he knows that she is acquainted with his vices, though he is well assured that her prudence, generosity, and affection will prevent her from being a severe accuser." One is reminded of the old French gentleman who said he was aware that he cheated at cards, but he disliked any allusion to the subject.

To be "easy" in a wife's society, to relax spiritually as well as mentally, and to be immune from criticism;—these were the privileges which men demanded, and which well-trained women were ready to accord. In 1808 the "Belle Assemblée" printed a model letter, which purported to come from a young wife whose husband had deserted her and her child for the more lively society of his mistress. It expressed in pathetic language the sentiments then deemed correct,—sentiments which embodied the patience of Griselda, without her acquiescence in fate. The wife tells her husband that she has retired to the country for economy, and to avoid scandalous gossip; that by careful management she is able to live on the pittance he has given her; that "little Emily" is working a pair of ruffles for him; that his presence would make their poor cottage seem a palace. "Pardon my interrupting you," she winds up with ostentatious meekness. "I mean to give you satisfaction. Though I am deeply wronged by your error, I am not resentful. I wish you all the happiness of which you are capable, and am your once loved and still affectionate, Emilia."

That last sentence is not without dignity, and certainly not without its sting. One doubts whether Emilia's husband, for all her promises and protestations, could ever again have felt perfectly "easy" in his wife's society. He probably therefore stayed away, and soothed his soul elsewhere. "We can with tranquility forgive in ourselves the sins of which no one accuses us."

12

Living in History*

Whater Mr. Bagehot spoke his luminous words about "a fatigued way of looking at great subjects," he gave us the key to a mental attitude which perhaps is not the modern thing it seems. There were, no doubt, Greeks and Romans in plenty to whom the "glory" and the "grandeur" of Greece and Rome were less exhilarating than they were to Edgar Poe—Greeks and Romans who were spiritually palsied by the great emotions which presumably accompany great events. They may have been philosophers, or humanitarians, or academists. They may have been conscientious objectors, or conscienceless shirkers, or perhaps plain men and women with a natural gift of indecision, a natural taste for compromise and awaiting developments. In the absence of newspapers and pamphlets, these peaceful pagans were compelled to express their sense of fatigue to their neighbors at the games, or in the marketplace; and their neighbors—if well chosen—sighed with them over the intensity of life, the formidable happenings of history.

Since August, 1914, the turmoil and anguish incidental to the world's greatest war have accentuated every human type—heroic, base, keen, and evasive. The strain of four years' fighting was borne with astounding fortitude, and Allied statesmen and publicists saw

* From *Points of Friction*, 1920.

to it that the clear outline of events should not be blurred by ignorance or misrepresentation. If history in the making be a fluid thing, it swiftly crystallizes. Men, "living between two eternities, and warring against oblivion," make their indelible record on its pages; and other men receive these pages as their best inheritance, their avenue to understanding, their key to life.

Therefore it is unwise to gibe at history because we do not chance to know it. It pleases us to gibe at anything we do not know, but the process is not enlightening. In the second year of the war, the English *Nation* commented approvingly on the words of an English novelist who strove to make clear that the only things which count for any of us, individually or collectively, are the unrecorded minutiae of our lives. "History," said this purveyor of fiction, "is concerned with the rather absurd and theatrical doings of a few people, which, after all, have never altered the fact that we do all of us live on from day to day, and only want to be let alone."

"These words," observed the *Nation* heavily,

> have a singular truth and force at the present time. The people of Europe want to go on living, not to be destroyed. To live is to pursue the activities proper to one's nature, to be unhindered and unthwarted in their exercise. It is not too much to say that the life of Europe is something which has persisted in spite of the history of Europe. There is nothing happy or fruitful anywhere but witnesses to the triumph of life over history.

Presuming that we are able to disentangle life from history, to sever the inseverable, is this a true statement, or merely the expression of mental and spiritual fatigue? Were the great historic episodes invariably fruitless, and had they no bearing upon the lives of ordinary men and women? The battles of Marathon and Thermopylae, the signing of the Magna Charta, the Triple Alliance, the Declaration of Independence, the birth of the National Assembly, the first Reform Bill, the recognition in Turin of the United Kingdom of Italy—these things may have been theatrical, inasmuch as they were certainly dramatic, but absurd is not a wise word to apply to them. Neither is it possible to believe that the life of Europe went on in spite of these historic incidents, triumphing over them as over so many obstacles to activity.

When the *Nation* contrasted the beneficent companies of strolling players who "represented and interpreted the world of life, the one thing which matters and remains," with the companies of soldiers who merely destroyed life at its roots, we could not but feel that this editorial point of view had its limitations. The strolling players of Elizabeth's day afforded many a merry hour; but Elizabeth's soldiers and sailors did their part in making possible this mirth. The strolling players who came to the old Southwark Theater in Philadelphia interpreted "the world of life," as they understood it; but the soldiers who froze at Valley Forge offered a different interpretation, and one which had considerably more stamina. The magnifying of small things, the belittling of great ones, indicate a mental exhaustion which would be more pardonable if it were less complacent. There are always men and women who prefer the triumph of evil, which is a thing they can forget, to prolonged resistance, which shatters their nerves. But the desire to escape an obligation, while very human, is not generally thought to be humanity's noblest asset.

Many smart things have been written to discredit history. Mr. Arnold called it "the vast Mississippi of falsehood," which was easily said, and has been said in a number of ways since the days of Herodotus, who amply illustrated the splendors of unreality. Mr. Edward Fitzgerald was wont to sigh that only lying histories were readable, and this point of view has many secret adherents. Mr. Henry Adams, who taught history for seven years at Harvard, and who built his intellectual dwelling place upon its firm foundations, pronounced it to be "in essence incoherent and immoral." Nevertheless, all that we know of man's unending efforts to adjust and readjust himself to the world about him we learn from history, and the tale is an enlightening one. "Events are wonderful things," said Lord Beaconsfield. Nothing, for example, can blot out, or obscure, the event of the French Revolution. We are free to discuss it until the end of time; but we can never alter it, and never get away from its consequences.

The lively contempt for history expressed by readers who would escape its weight, and the neglect of history practiced by educators who would escape its authority, stand responsible for much mental confusion. American boys and girls go to school six, eight, or ten years, as the case may be, and emerge with a misunderstanding of their own country, and a comprehensive ignorance of all others. They say, "I don't know any history," as casually and as unconcernedly as they might say, "I don't know any chemistry," or "I don't know metaphysics." A smiling young freshman in the most scholarly of women's colleges told me that she had been conditioned because she knew nothing about the Reformation.

"You mean—" I began questioningly.

"I mean just what I say," she interrupted. "I didn't know what it was, or where it was, or who had anything to do with it."

I said I didn't wonder she had come to grief. The Reformation was something of an episode. And I asked myself wistfully how it happened she had ever managed to escape it. When I was a little schoolgirl, a pious Roman Catholic child with a distaste for polemics, it seemed to me I was never done studying about the Reformation. If I escaped briefly from Wycliffe and Cranmer and Knox, it was only to be met by Luther and Calvin and Huss. Everywhere the great struggle confronted me, everywhere I was brought face to face with the inexorable logic of events. That more advanced and more intelligent students find pleasure in every phase of ecclesiastical strife is proved by Lord Broughton's pleasant story about a member of Parliament named Joliffe, who was sitting in his club reading Hume's *History of England*, a book which well deserves to be called dry. Charles Fox, glancing over his shoulder, observed, "I see you have come to the imprisonment of the seven bishops"; whereupon Joliffe, like a man engrossed in a thrilling detective story, cried desperately, "For God's sake, Fox, don't tell me what is coming!"

This was reading for human delight, for the interest and agitation which are inseparable from every human document. Mr. Henry James once told me that the only reading of which he never tired was history. "The least significant footnote of history," he said, "stirs me more than the most thrilling and passionate fiction. Nothing that has ever happened to the world finds me indifferent." I used to think that ignorance of history meant only a lack of cultivation and a loss of pleasure. Now I am sure that such ignorance impairs our judgment by impairing our understanding, by depriving us of standards, of the power to contrast and the right to estimate. We can know nothing of any nation unless we know its history; and we can know nothing of the history of any nation unless we know something of the history of all nations. The book of the world is full of knowledge we need to acquire, of lessons we need to learn, of wisdom we need to assimilate. Consider only this brief sentence of Polybius, quoted by Plutarch: "In Carthage no one is blamed, however he may have gained his wealth." A pleasant place, no doubt, for business enterprise; a place where young men were taught how to get on, and extravagance kept pace with shrewd finance. A self-satisfied, self-confident, money-getting, money-loving people, honoring success and hugging their fancied security, while in far-off Rome Cato pronounced their doom.

There are readers who can tolerate and even enjoy history, provided it is shorn of its high lights and heavy shadows, its heroic elements and strong impelling motives. They turn with relief to such calm commentators as Sir John Seeley, for years professor of modern history at Cambridge, who shrank as sensitively as an eighteenth-century divine from that fell word "enthusiasm," and from all the agitation it evoked. He was a firm upholder of the British Empire, hating compromise and guiltless of pacifism; but, having a natural gift for aridity, he saw no reason why the world should not be content to know things without feeling them, should not keep its eyes turned to legal institutions, its mind fixed upon political economy and international law. The force that lay back of Parliament annoyed him by the simple primitive way in which it beat drums, fired guns, and died to uphold the institutions which he prized; also because by doing these things it evoked in others certain simple and primitive sensations which he strove always to keep at bay. "We are rather disposed to laugh," he said, "when poets and orators try to conjure us with the name of England." Had he lived a few years longer, he would have known that England's salvation lies in the fact that her name is, to her sons, a thing to conjure by. We may not wisely ignore the value of emotions, nor underestimate the power of human impulses which charge the souls of men.

The long years of neutrality engendered in the minds of Americans a natural but ignoble weariness. The war was not our war, yet there was no escaping from it. By day and night it haunted us, a ghost that would not be laid. Over and over again we were told that it was not possible to place the burden of blame on any nation's shoulders. Once at least we were told that the causes and objects of the contest, the obscure fountains from which had burst this stupendous and desolating flood, were no concern of ours. But this proffered release from serious thinking brought us scant peace of mind. Every honest man and woman knew that we had no intellectual right to be ignorant when information lay at our hand, and no spiritual right to be unconcerned when great moral issues were at stake. We could not in either case evade the duty we owed to reason. The Vatican Library would not hold the books that have been written about the war; but the famous five-foot shelf would be too roomy for the evidence in the case, the documents which are the foundation of knowledge. They, at least, are neither too profuse for our patience, nor too complex for our understanding. "The inquiry into the truth or falsehood of a matter of history," said Huxley, "is just as much an affair of pure science as is the inquiry into the truth or falsehood of a matter of geology; and the value of the evidence in the two cases must be tested in the same way."

The resentment of American pacifists, who, being more human than they thought themselves, were no better able than the rest of us to forget the state of Europe, found expression in petulant complaints. They kept reminding us at inopportune moments that war is not the important and heroic thing it is assumed to be. They asked that, if it is to figure in history at all (which seems, on the whole, inevitable), the truth should be told, and its brutalities, as well as its heroisms, exposed. They professed a languid amusement at the "rainbow of official documents" which proved every nation in the right. They inveighed bitterly against the "false patriotism" taught by American schoolbooks, with their absurd emphasis on the "embattled farmers" of the Revolution, and the volunteers of the Civil War. They assured us, in and out of season, that a doctor who came to his death looking after poor patients in an epidemic was as much of a hero as any soldier whose grave is yearly decorated with flowers.

All this was the clearest possible exposition of the lassitude induced in faint-hearted men by the pressure of great events. It was the wail of people who wanted, as the *Nation* feelingly expressed it, to be let alone, and who could not shut themselves away from the world's great tragedy. None of us are prepared to say that a doctor and a nurse who perform their perilous duties in an epidemic are not as heroic as a doctor and a nurse who perform their perilous duties in war. There is glory enough to go around. Only he that loveth his life shall lose it. But to put a flower on a soldier's grave is a not too exuberant recognition of his service, for he, too, in his humble way made the great sacrifice.

As for the brutalities of war, who can charge that history smoothes them over? Certain horrors may be withheld from children, whose privilege it is to be spared the knowledge of uttermost depravity; but to the adult no such mercy is shown. Motley, for example, describes cruelties committed three hundred and fifty years ago in the Netherlands, which equal, if they do not surpass, the cruelties committed six years ago in Belgium. Men heard such tales more calmly then than now, and seldom sought the coward's refuge—incredulity. The Dutch, like other nations, did better things than fight. They painted glorious pictures, they bred great statesmen and good doctors. They traded with extraordinary success. They raised the most beautiful tulips in the world. But to do these things peacefully and efficiently, they had been compelled to struggle for their national existence. The East India trade and the freedom of the seas did not drop into their laps. And because their security, and the comeliness of life which they so highly prized, had been bought by stubborn resistance to tyranny, they added to material well-being the "luxury of self-respect."

To overestimate the part played by war in a nation's development is as crude as to ignore its alternate menace and support. It is with the help of history that we balance our mental accounts. Voltaire was disposed to think that battles and treaties were matters of small moment; and Mr. John Richard Green pleaded, not unreasonably, that more space should be given in our chronicles to the missionary, the poet, the painter, the merchant, and the philosopher. They are not, and they never have been, excluded from any narrative comprehensive enough to admit them; but the scope of their authority is not always sufficiently defined. Man, as the representative of his age, and the events in which he plays his vigorous part—these are the warp and woof of history. We can no more leave John Wesley or Ignatius Loyola out of the canvas than we can leave out Marlborough or Pitt. We know now that the philosophy of Nietzsche is one with Bernhardi's militarism.

As for the merchant—Froissart was as well aware of his prestige as was Mr. Green. "Trade, my lord," said Dinde Desponde, the great Lombard banker, to the Duke of Burgundy, "finds its way everywhere, and rules the world." As for commercial honor—a thing as fine as the honor of the aristocrat or of the soldier—what can be better for England than to remember that after the great fire of 1666 not a single London shopkeeper evaded his liabilities; and that this fact was long the boast of a city proud of its shopkeeping? As for jurisprudence—Sully was infinitely more concerned with it than he was with combat or controversy. It is with stern satisfaction that he recounts the statutes passed in his day for the punishment of fraudulent bankrupts, whom we treat so leniently; for the annulment of their gifts and assignments, which we guard so zealously; and for the conviction of those to whom such property had been assigned. It was almost as dangerous to steal on a large scale as on a small one under the leveling laws of Henry of Navarre.

In this vast and varied chronicle, war plays its appointed part. "We cannot," says Walter Savage Landor, "push valiant men out of history." We cannot escape from the truths interpreted, and the conditions established by their valor. What has been slightingly called the "drum-and-trumpet narrative" holds its own with the records of art and science. "It cost Europe a thousand years of barbarism," said Macaulay, "to escape the fate of China."

The endless endeavor of states to control their own destinies, the ebb and flow of the sea of combat, the "recurrent liturgy of war," enabled the old historians to perceive with amazing distinctness the traits of nations, etched as sharply then as now on the imperishable pages of history. We read Froissart for human delight rather than for solid information; yet Froissart's observations—the observations of a keen-eyed student of the world—are worth recording five hundred years after he set them down.

"In England," he says, "strangers are well received"; yet are the English "affable to no other nation than their own." Ireland, he holds to have had "too many kings"; and the Scotch, like the English, "are excellent men-at-arms, nor is there any check to their courage as long as their weapons endure." France is the pride of his heart, as it is the pride of the world's heart today. "In France also is found good chivalry, strong of spirit, and in great abundance; for the kingdom of France has never been brought so low as to lack men ready for the combat." Even Germany does not escape his regard. "The Germans are a rude, unmannered race, but active and expert where their own personal advantage is concerned." If history be "philosophy teaching by example," we are wise to admit the old historians into our counsels.

To withhold from a child some knowledge—apportioned to his understanding—of the world's sorrows and wrongs is to cheat him of his kinship with humanity. We would not, if we could, bruise his soul as our souls are bruised; but we would save him from a callous content which is alien to his immaturity. The little American, like the little Austrian and the little Serb, is a son of the sorrowing earth. His security—of which no man can forecast the future—is a legacy bequeathed him by predecessors who bought it with sweat and with blood; and with sweat and with blood his descendants may be called on to guard it. Alone among educators, Mr. G. Stanley Hall finds neutrality, a "high and ideal neutrality," to be an attribute of youth. He was so gratified by this discovery during the years of the war, so sure that American boys and girls followed "impartially" the great struggle in Europe, and that this judicial attitude would, in the years to come, enable them to pronounce "the true verdict of history," that he "thrilled and tingled" with patriotic—if premature—pride.

"The true verdict of history" will be pronounced according to the documentary evidence in the case. There is no need to vex our souls over the possible extinction of this evidence, for closer observers than our impartial young Americans have placed it permanently on record. But I doubt if the equanimity which escapes the ordeal of partisanship is to be found in the mind of youth, or in the heart of a child. Can we not remember a time when the Wars of the Roses were not—to us—a matter for neutrality? Our little school histories, those vivacious, anecdotal histories, banished long ago by rigorous educators, were in some measure responsible for our Lancastrian fervor. They fed it with stories of high courage and the sorrows of princes. We wasted our sympathies on "a mere struggle for power"; but Hume's laconic verdict is not, and never can be, the measure of a child's solicitude. The lost cause fills him with pity, the cause which is saved by man's heroic sacrifice fires him to generous applause. The round world and the tale of those who have lived upon it are his legitimate inheritance.

Mr. Bagehot said, and said wisely after his wont, that if you catch an intelligent, uneducated man of thirty, and tell him about the battle of Marathon, he will calculate the chances, and estimate the results; but he will not really care. You cannot make the word "Marathon" sound in his ears as it sounded in the ears of Byron, to whom it had been sacred in boyhood. You cannot make the word "freedom" sound in untutored ears as it sounds in the ears of men who have counted the cost by which it has been preserved through the centuries. Unless children are permitted to know the utmost peril which has threatened, and which still threatens, the freedom of nations, how can they conceive of its value? And what is the worth of teaching which does not rate the gift of freedom above all earthly benefactions? How can justice live save by the will of freemen? Of what avail are civic virtues that are not the virtues of the free? Pericles bade the Athenians to bear reverently in mind the Greeks who had died for Greece. "Make these men your examples, and be well assured that happiness comes by freedom, and freedom by stoutness of heart." Perhaps if American boys bear reverently in mind the men who died for America, it will help them too to be stout of heart, and "worthy patriots, dear to God."

In the remote years of my childhood, the study of current events, that most interesting and valuable form of tuition, which, nevertheless, is unintelligible without some knowledge of the past, was left out of our limited curriculum. We seldom read the newspapers (which I remember as of an appalling dullness), and we knew little of what was happening in our day. But we did study history, and we knew something of what had happened in other days than ours; we knew and deeply cared. Therefore we reacted with fair intelligence and no lack of fervor when circumstances were forced upon our vision. It was not possible for a child who had lived in spirit with Saint Genevieve to be indifferent to the siege of Paris in 1870. It was not possible for a child who had lived in spirit with Jeanne d'Arc to be indifferent to the destruction of Rheims Cathedral in 1914. If we were often left in ignorance, we were never despoiled of childhood's generous ardor. Nobody told us that "courage is a sublime form of hypocrisy." Nobody fed our young minds on stale paradoxes, or taught us to discount the foolish impulsiveness of adults. Our parents, as Mr. Henry James rejoicingly observed, "had no desire to see us inoculated with importunate virtues." The Honorable Bertrand Russell had not then proposed that all teaching of history shall be submitted to an "international commission," "which shall produce neutral textbooks, free from patriotic bias." There was something profoundly fearless in our approach to life, in the exposure of our unarmored souls to the assaults of enthusiasms and regrets. "Events are wonderful things," and we were stimulated by them to believe with Froissart that "the most profitable thing in the world for the institution of human life is history."

13

The American Credo*

The United States is a country of diverse theologies and one creed, of many churches and one temple, of a thousand theories and one conviction. The creed is education, the temple is the schoolhouse, the conviction is the healing power of knowledge. Rich and poor, pretentious and plain, revivalist and atheist, all share this supreme and touching confidence. Our belief in education is unbounded, our reverence for it is unfaltering, our loyalty to it is unshaken by reverses. Our passionate desire, not so much to acquire it as to bestow it, is the most animated of American traits. The ideal democracy is an educated democracy; and our naïve faith in the moral intelligibility of an established order makes clear the path of progress. Of all the money expended by the Government, the billions it pays for the instruction of youth seems to us the most profitable outlay.

Mr. William Allen White stands convicted of saying that America is "the paradise of capital." It appears so to the casual observer; but, after all, the wide world is the paradise of capital, and has been since the stone age, when capital was a bit bulkier than it is now, and was the reward of muscle rather than of acuteness. America is really the paradise of education, which is a word to conjure by. The

---

* From *Times and Tendencies*, 1931.

capitalist may be consistently courted; but he is also consistently disliked. It is not in human nature to regard him otherwise than with hostility. While he flourishes, we quote Sidney Smith's witticism, and laugh—a trifle hollowly. When trouble comes to him (as to other men), we begin to think that maybe there is something after all in Emerson's doctrine of compensation.

Aware of this universal enmity, the capitalist seeks to buy his way into favor by gratifying his country's ruling passion, by smoothing and decorating those academic paths which he honors all the more if he has never trod them. He hurls millions at wealthy colleges, having been given to understand that it is no longer worth his while to proffer paltrier sums. Should he be temperamentally unfitted for such high flights, he seeks some humble byway where he can do the trick on a modest scale. He buys, refurnishes, and opens a country schoolhouse, where a little girl who never lived was never followed by a non-existent little lamb. This is felt to be at once a tribute to American education and to American letters.

A somewhat similar idea must have possessed the minds of the enthusiasts who bought and preserved the small frame building in which Walt Whitman once taught school. The teaching was a brief and negligible episode in Whitman's life. Without training, and without any burden of knowledge, the most that can be recalled of him as a pedagogue is that he dressed neatly and wore a black coat. But the association of a poet and a schoolhouse is sacred to all good Americans. What is really striking about Whitman's youth—the fact that at thirteen he could set up type rapidly and accurately—interests nobody. We do not approve of thirteen-year-old boys being able to do anything remunerative.

If we compare the modest and deprecatory tone in which the capitalist speaks of himself, and of the business of money-getting, with the grave appreciation shown by the educator for the cause which he represents, we realize that both these experts understand and conform to their country's prejudices. I say educator as apart from teacher. The teacher may be an untrained, ill-paid girl, valiantly striving to impart what she does not know to a handful of reluctant rustics. The educator is high up in the scale, and, while as ill-paid as ever, has the proud consciousness that he is the exponent of his country's creed, of what Barrett Wendell in a petulant moment once called the great American superstition. The addresses made every year on schools and schooling are weighted with laudations. A solemn self-sufficiency marks their periods. They deal in abstractions; but abstractions of a sacred and elevating character. Possibly they revive our fainting spirits. Certainly they please an acquiescent public which naturally likes to feel it has the right idol on its altar.

Over twenty million children attend the public schools in the United States. Their numbers are stupendous, and so are the sums spent in educating them. We can rightly claim to have the most comprehensive school equipment in the world. Is it not the plain duty of a democracy to extend to every boy or girl as much knowledge as he or she can assimilate? To extend it, moreover, on the easiest possible terms, in the pleasantest possible manner. The American child has, we are told, a right to demand that "at every level of his instruction he will have a teacher especially trained to meet the peculiar problems of that particular period"—which is a large order. The American youth has an equal right to demand that every state college shall furnish him the higher education on a low enough level to meet his moderate mental equipment. It is not so much a question of scholarly standards as of what the taxpayer wants for his money.

The pride and boast of our country (and it is a laudable pride and boast) is the costliness of our high schools. The rivalry is keen, and no money is begrudged to these spacious and stately edifices. Four years ago a contributor to the *Atlantic Monthly* summed up the "great American secret"—the secret of our wealth, power, and leadership—in this telling sentence: "The grandchildren of a Finlander who trailed reindeer over the snow are able to acquire their education in a $4,000,000 high school, in a mining town in Minnesota, equipped with electric stoves to do their cooking lessons on, and with everything else in proportion."

This is a magnificent truth, and affords the writer, editor, and reader proud thrills of satisfaction. Moreover, there is nothing the country has to give to which the Minnesota-born Finnish boy may not aspire when he leaves the $4,000,000 high school, and faces life. He may become a party boss, he may be appointed to represent the United States in foreign lands, he may appoint himself counselor at large to the people in general, like Senator Borah. On the other hand, there is just a possibility that, with wild blood flowing in his veins, this child of the North may look unfavorably upon his textbooks, and regard his educational palace as a prison. Through the plateglass windows he may glimpse in fancy the frozen wastes his eyes have never seen; and the image of the reindeer may appear to him more beautiful than the rattling, gasping flivver his rich acquaintance drives. That passionate cry of Andrew Lang's to the gypsy vagabonds who were his sires, and who bequeathed to him unsuitable instincts forever pulling at his heartstrings, has found an echo in other hearts too young and strange to worship at the shrine of production.

It is because of our unassailable enthusiasm, our profound reverence for education, that we habitually demand of it the impossible. The teacher is expected to perform a choice and varied series of miracles. The school day should hold two days' work without crowding and without fatigue. The child must wander at ease, yet with close and gratified attention, through diverse paths of learning. The world of art, no less than the world of scholarship, invites participation. One educational expert proves beyond a shadow of doubt that all children can sketch, and that what they need and should have are courses of "observation and representation." They must be taught to look at things, and to reproduce what they have seen, whether its outlines are as simple as a pig's, or as complicated as a lobster's. Musicians are no less certain that a child's salvation lies in music, which, it seems, he can not only enjoy, but compose in tender youth, just as he can write stories and draw pictures. Dramatists are well aware that all children can act, and conceive that acting is the only art which can give them the coveted power of self-expression. Rhythmic dancing and nature study demand attention. Play leaders, lifting their voices high above the din, assert that play and play alone can develop in young Americans those qualities of wisdom, understanding, counsel, and fortitude which our fathers ascribed to religion.

Meanwhile there are things to be taught which arouse no semblance of enthusiasm. The harassed teacher must see to it that her (it is pretty sure to be "her") artistic, athletic, dramatic, and musical little prodigies master the multiplication table. The multiplication table is a practical asset, and practical assets rank high, although we are seriously told, and evidently expected to believe, that the old, narrow purpose of fitting a boy to make a success of his life is no longer a factor in education. Today the school prepares both boy and girl for citizenship, for the service of their country. This preparation begins with kindergarten, and ends with the last day and hour of college. President Lowell has gone so far as to say that we can give the world neither scholars nor leaders unless we arouse in the heart of youth "a love and desire for the things it has no use for now." A brave word which will not perceptibly affect the horde of American undergraduates, taking their leadership for granted, and eager only to get on.

While one set of educational experts are urging a diversity of occupations, another set, equally importunate, are demanding that more time and attention be given to studies of their selection. I read in *Education* an amazing article on the teaching of history to high-school students. Now history, while undeniably the greatest of all studies, has had a hard time of it; partly because it "discourages and antagonizes children"—so, at least, we are told—and partly because it has been crowded out by more highly favored work. Dr. Arnold thought himself liberal when he deducted one hour a week from the all-pervading Greek and Latin of Rugby, and devoted it to modern history. He seemed quite unable to understand why, in that ample provision of time, the students made so little progress. American schools subordinate history to mathematics and rudimentary physics, which are to them what the classics were to England.

In no wise discouraged by this somewhat cloudy outlook, the writer of the *Education* paper demands the impossible as seriously and as determinedly as though he were drawing upon the resources of Helicon. In the first place, the pupils must be given a satisfactory motive for studying history; they must be convinced that it is worth their while to bestow on it their time and attention. This done, the teacher should quicken their acquiescence into enthusiasm by arousing in their minds an appreciation of noble lives and high achievements. He should make them sympathetic on the one hand and judicial on the other. He should avoid textbooks and reiterated questions. If he desires to find out what his class knows (which is but natural), "he should adapt his interrogations to the especial need and character of each student, and in this fashion cultivate the pupil's powers of oral description." Indeed, "to make the recitation really vital, the teacher should see to it that the students do most of the talking, questioning, and criticizing." The use of the blackboard is kindly permitted him; but only that he may cover it with "drawings and diagrams to illustrate the routes of armies, *or the plan of a medieval manor.*"

Artist, actor, and orator, as well as instructor, this versatile genius is expected to be "brilliant, enthusiastic, fair-minded, sympathetic, firm, and skilful in narration." "His lessons should be constantly enlivened by anecdotes, illustrations, stories, and dramatic postures." He should joke with his classes "in clean harmless fashion." "He should make the ancient Greeks live again in their minds." Above all, he should have a large stock of historic details always ready for use; and, to ensure this supply, "he must do wide outside reading, especially in memoirs and biographies." Why, with such capacity and equipment, and with all the educational institutions of the country competing for his services (for, if such a paragon exists, there can be but one), he should content himself with the modest post and less than modest salary of a high-school teacher (even in a four-million-dollar schoolhouse), is a point left to the reader's consideration.

What, after all, is a creed without miracles, and why exalt the educator unless he can accomplish the miraculous? The need of limit, the feasibility of performance, belong to less hallowed things. Thousands of people all over the country are now asking that children should be "educated for peace"; not in a normal way, but intensively. Dr. Abraham Flexner, it will be remembered, said definitely that children should be educated for life, and life embraces all eventualities. A director of the department of child guidance in New Jersey asks that children should be taught to enjoy life, a matter which, when I was a child, was remote from jurisdiction. The teacher's job then was to keep our enjoyment within bounds. We needed no incentive at her hands. A supervising principal of schools, who is also a sunny optimist, believes and says that students in high schools should be taught how to marry wisely and well. They should have especial courses designed to eliminate sentiment, and substitute common-sense; courses which will enable them to do for themselves what French parents are in the habit of doing for their children.

Cities that pay a third of their incomes for the support of their schools are naturally unreasonable in their demands. "The teacher," says Mr. Guedalla, "is the chief executive of the American future." His or her business is to fit the child to become a satisfactory member of the community. It is with this thought in our minds that we turn our hopeful attention from what is called the "formal" system of teaching to the "progressive" system, which promises a more open outlook, and a keener interest in all that appertains to life. In our exalted moments we see in the development of initiative, in the "humanizing" of education, a new and friendly link between instructor and instructed; we visualize the unfettered intelligence as a product of mutual trust and understanding. At the same time we are aware that such a gain is neutralized by a corresponding loss of mental and moral discipline. The most to be hoped for is that the intelligent child, freed from obstructive shackles, will in time acquire a habit of systematic thinking, and a just standard of taste and conduct. The least that we can ask is that he should be defended from the assault of chance desires, and saved, as a high-school student, from slipping overnight into a boy bandit and the leader of a gang.

What is called the individual trend of education, encouraging a pupil to decide which studies he likes best, or dislikes least, is a great economy of effort. Only in so far as he is attracted by, or sees the use of a given subject, will that subject be satisfactorily mastered. The enthusiastic "progressive" sees the modern schoolroom as the happy hunting-ground of children engaged in working out for themselves their chosen problems, while the teacher remains inconspicuously in the background, "like a breathing book of reference, able to turn its own pages, and to give an answer to every question." Just where such children and such teachers are to be found no one is bold enough to say. Doubtless they exist. I realize the progress that has been made in the conciliating science of pedagogy when I am told that the successful educator is the one who is able to take "the child's point of view," and recall Barrett Wendell's dark saying, "no normal boy ever learned anything he could avoid." Had my teachers taken my point of view concerning, let us say, the French irregular verbs, I should have been a better and a happier child; but I should not have acquired the polite language of France.

Because the interest of the nation is focused on education, we hear much censure and much laudation on every side; but little that is to the purpose, or that deserves serious consideration. There are critics who object to warlike pictures ("Washington Crossing the Delaware") on schoolroom walls. There are critics who object to warlike verse ("Sheridan's Ride") in school readers. There are critics who object every year to Christmas carols, because a number of taxpayers do not hold with Christianity. There are critics who think that "a light coat of moral disinfectant" is an insufficient substitute for religious instruction. There are critics who complain bitterly that our public schools are turning out a race of young mutineers who have no regard for the established order. There are critics who pour molten waves of wrath upon the same public schools because of their slavish subservience to the established order. "Education," they say, "is the propaganda department of the state, and of the existing social system." And there are critics who now and then speak a word of truth and wisdom, as did a writer in the *New Republic* who remarked that what we ask of our schools is education, and what we get is literacy.

One thing is sure. The literate can always become the educated if they are so minded. Franklin had two years' schooling, Lincoln less than twelve months. It is as impossible to withhold education from the receptive mind, as it is impossible to force it upon the unreasoning. Certain shreds of information can be transmitted under the most adverse circumstances; but not accurate knowledge upon any subject, and certainly not the intellectual tradition which is the glory of scholarship. Every year some malcontent rushes into print with a list of queries to which high-school students have given unexpected and very ingenious answers. They have opined that De Valera was a Mexican bandit, Lloyd George the king of England, and Henry Cabot Lodge a place where societies meet. These erroneous statements have been accredited to ignorance rather than to a general incapacity for thinking. The students, at some period of their young lives, had probably heard of the three contentious gentlemen; but they had never opened the pores of their minds to even a languid interest in their contentions, and were liable to be betrayed by the misleading sound of syllables.

A young Englishman, teaching in an American school, said that what struck him most sharply about American boys was their docility. He did not mean by this their readiness to do what they were told, but their readiness to think as they were told; in other words, to permit him to do their thinking for them. This mental attitude is not confined to youth, nor to the United States. "There is no expedient," said Sir Joshua Reynolds, "to which men will not resort to avoid the necessity of thinking." The common method of escape is to choose a newspaper and stick to it; to pin our faith in matters social, political, foreign, and domestic, upon its solemn dictum; to read the books it praises most conspicuously (the chances are it praises all), to see the plays it recommends.

If the disaffected and dissatisfied are perpetually reminding us that our schools are inadequate and our system slack, there are not wanting modernists to whom all that is old is outworn, and all that is untried is reassuring. They provide the hopeful element of which we no doubt stand in need. Very recently a professor of Teachers College, Columbia University, startled an audience of high-school teachers with the assurance that they had the wrong "dope" on the classics. "Literature," he said, "must be studied at the time and under the conditions in which it is produced. Once beyond that stage, its sole interest is to those who like antiques." The professor's list of antiques included the *Iliad*, which is undeniably old, and Gray's "Elegy," which is comparatively new. In their place he recommended the contents of the *Saturday Evening Post,* as comparing favorably in merit, and capable of being studied in the very process of production.

An equally optimistic professor of philosophy at the University of New York told the New York Advertising Club that in the matter of culture the American of today could bear comparison with the Athenian in the days of Pericles. He based this happy conviction on the sale of books in drug stores. The Athenians, it is well known, had no drug stores, few drugs (Hippocrates put scant faith in them), and not a great many books. "In all our walks of life," said the triumphant preceptor, "we see the evidences of an education that was not known in the past. In the newspapers, in the magazines, and on the radio are to be found the signs and tokens of the new culture."

Another evidence of an education which was not known in the past is the all-pervading woman teacher. She has her enemies—who has not?—but she is with us to stay. Whether, as Sir Andrew Macphail vehemently asserted, "Men of character are essential to the formation of character in boys"; or whether, as Susan B. Anthony said (and doubtless believed), "The God-given responsibility of women is to be the educators of the race"; the fact remains that American men won't teach school, and American women will.

Perhaps some dim survival of Miss Anthony's creed may account for the average politician's notion that one woman is as good as another for the job. If the responsibility be God-given, she can safely assume it. In April, 1931, a state senator of Pennsylvania introduced into the Harrisburg legislature a bill prohibiting the employment of married women as teachers or principals in Philadelphia and Pittsburgh schools. No word was said in this bill concerning the greater leisure or the freer mind that a spinster might possibly give to her task. The senator simply stated that there were upwards of two thousand young women in line for positions which could not be found for them; and that under these circumstances the employment of married women was an injustice. He held that a wife who was unlucky enough to be the sole support of her family should keep her post, or be appointed to a new one; but women whose husbands had work should be ineligible.

It was a perfectly sound proposition from the standpoint of economy; but what about the children? No one will seriously say that the primary purpose of our schools is to give employment to deserving young women. They are not even maintained for the benefit of publishers who have succeeded in getting the books they publish into the curriculum. The taxpayer supports them at a great expense that the children of the nation may be educated; and the only thing to be considered in a teacher is his or her capacity to teach. There must be a difference in this regard. Teachers are not like Mr. Ford's workmen, forever repeating an uncomplicated action that awakens no interest and requires no thought. Mr. Ford can give preference to a married man for the good of the country; but a state cannot give preference to an unmarried woman unless it be for the good of the children. The patrimony of a liberal education is their best inheritance. It does not necessarily mean four years in one of the great colleges which have been unkindly designated as charitable institutions for the rich. It means contract with a liberating mind.

On Storytelling, Writing,
and the Literary Way of Life

14

The Royal Road of Fiction*

"A tale," says that charming scholar and critic, M. Jusserand, "is
the first key to the heart of a child, the last utterance to penetrate the fastnesses of age." And what is true of the individual is true
also of the race. The earliest voice listened to by the nations in their
infancy was the voice of the storyteller. Whether he spoke in rude
prose or in ruder rhyme, his was the eloquence which won a hearing
everywhere. All through the young world's vigorous, ill-spent manhood it found time mid wars, and pestilence, and far migrations to
cherish and cultivate the first wild art of fiction. We, in our chastened, wise, and melancholy middle age, find still our natural solace
in this kind and joyous friend. And when mankind grows old, so
old we shall have mastered all the knowledge we are seeking now,
and shall have found ourselves as far from happiness as ever, I doubt
not we shall be comforted in the twilight of existence with the same
cheerful and deceptive tales we hearkened to in childhood. Facts
surround us from the cradle to the grave. Truth stares us coldly in
the face, and checks our unmeaning gayety of heart. What wonder
that we turn for pleasure and distraction to those charming dreams
with which the storyteller, now grown to be a novelist, is ever ready
to lure us away from everything that it is comfortable to forget.

And it was always thus. From the very beginning of civiliza-

---

* From *Varia*, 1897.

tion, and before civilization was well begun, the royal road of fiction ran straight to the hearts of men, and along it traveled the gay and prosperous spinners of wondrous tales which the world loved well to hear. When I was a little girl, studying literature in the hard and dry fashion then common in all schools, and which was not without its solid advantages after all, I was taught, first that *Pamela* was the earliest English novel; then that *Robinson Crusoe* was the earliest English novel; then that Lodge's *Rosalynde* was the earliest English novel. By the time I got that far back, I began to see for myself, what I dare say all little girls are learning now, that the earliest English novel dates mistily from the earliest English history, and that there is no such thing as a firm starting-point for their uncertain feet to gain. Long, long before Lodge's *Rosalynde* led the way for Shakespeare's "Rosalind" to follow, romantic tales were held in such high esteem that people who were fortunate enough to possess them in manuscript—the art of printing not having yet cheapened such precious treasures—left them solemnly by will to their equally fortunate heirs. In 1315, Guy, Earl of Warwick, bequeathed to Bordesley Abbey in Warwickshire his entire library of thirty-nine volumes, which consisted almost exclusively, like the library of a modern young lady, of stories, such as the *Romaunce de Troies*, and the *Romaunce d'Alisaundre*. In 1426, Thomas, Duke of Exeter, left to his sister Joan a single book, perhaps the only one he possessed, and this too was a romance on that immortal knight and lover, Tristan.

Earlier even than Thomas of Exeter's day, the hardy barons of England had discovered that when they were "fested and fed," they were ready to be amused, and that there was nothing so amusing as a story. In the twelfth century, before St. Thomas à Becket gave up his life in Canterbury cloisters, English knights and ladies had grown familiar with the tragic history of King Lear, the exploits of Jack the Giant Killer, the story of King Arthur and of the enchanter Merlin. The earliest of these tales came from Brittany, and were translated from Armorican into Latin by Geoffrey of Monmouth, a Benedictine monk, and a benefactor to the world; but, by the following century, Robin Hood, Tom-a-Lincoln, and a host of sturdy English-born heroes shared in the popular attention. It must have been inexpressibly helpful to the writers and compilers of early fiction that the uncritical age in which they lived had not yet been vitiated by the principles of realistic art. The modern maxims about sinning against the probabilities, and the novelist's bondage to truth, had not then been invented; and the man who told a story was free to tell it as he pleased. His readers or his hearers were seldom disposed to question his assertions. A knight did not go to the great and unnecessary trouble of learning his letters in order to doubt what he read. Merlin was as real to him as Robin Hood. He believed Sir John Mandeville, when that accomplished traveler told him of a race of men who had eyes in the middle of their foreheads. It was a curious fact, but the unknown world was full of greater mysteries than this. He believed in Prester John, with his red and white lions, his giants and pigmies, his salamanders that built cocoons like silk-worms, his river of stones that rolled perpetually with a mighty reverberation into a sandy sea. Why, indeed, should these wonders be doubted; for in that thrice famous letter sent by Prester John to Manuel Comnenus, Emperor of Constantinople, did he not distinctly say, "No vice is tolerated in our land; and, with us, no one lies."

This broad-minded, liberal credulity made smooth the novelist's path. He always located his romances in far and unknown countries, where anything or everything might reasonably be expected to happen. Scythia, Parthia, Abyssinia, were favorite latitudes; Bohemia could always serve at a pinch; and Arcadia, that blessed haven of romance, remained for centuries his happy hunting ground, where shepherds piped, and nymphs danced sweetly in the shade, and brave knights met in glorious combat, and lovers dallied all day long under the whispering boughs. In Elizabeth's day, Arcadia had reached the zenith of its popularity. Robert Green had peopled its dewy fields with amorous swains, and Sir Philip Sidney had described its hills and dales in the four hundred and eighty folio pages of his imperishable romance. A golden land, it lies before us still, brilliant with sunshine that shall never fade. Knights and noble ladies ride through it on prancing steeds. Well-bred shepherds, deeply versed in love, sing charming songs, and extend open-hearted hospitality. Shepherdesses, chaste and fair, lead their snowy flocks by meadows and rippling streams. There is always plenty of fighting for the knights when they weary of plighting their vows, and noble palaces spring up for their entertainment when they have had enough of pastoral pleasures and sylvan fare. Ah, me! We who have passed by Arcadia, and dwell in the sad haunts of men, know well what we have lost. Yet was there not a day when the inhabitants of the strange new world, a world not yet familiar with commercial depression and the stock exchange, were thus touchingly described in English verse?

> Guiltless men who danced away their time,
> Fresh as their groves, and happy as their clime.

And what gayer irresponsibility could be found even in the fields of Arcadia?

"In Elizabeth's day," says M. Jusserand, "adventurous narratives were loved for adventure's sake. Probability was only a secondary consideration." Geographical knowledge being in its innocent infancy, people were curious about foreign countries, and decently grateful for information, true or false. When a wandering knight of romance "sailed to Bohemia," nobody saw any reason why he should not, and readers were merely anxious to know what happened to him when he got there. So great, indeed, was the demand for fiction in the reign of the virgin queen that writers actually succeeded in supporting themselves by this species of composition, a test equally applicable today; and it is worth while to remember that the prose tales of Nash, Green, and Sidney were translated into French more than a century before that distinction was conferred on any play of Shakespeare's.

It need not be supposed, however, that Romance, in her triumphant progress through the land, met with no bitter and sustained hostility. From the very beginning she took the world by storm, and from the very beginning the godly denounced and reviled her. The jesters and gleemen and minstrels who relieved the insufferable ennui of our rude forefathers in those odd moments when they were neither fighting nor eating, were all branded as "Satan's children" by that

relentless accuser, "Piers Plowman." In vain the simple story-spin-
ners who narrated the exploits of Robin Hood and Tom-a-Lincoln
claimed that their merry legends were "not altogether unprofitable,
nor in any way hurtful, but very fitte to passe away the tediousness
of the long winter evenings." It was not in this cheerful fashion that
the "unco gude"—a race as old as humanity itself—considered the
long winter evenings should be passed. Roger Ascham can find no
word strong enough in which to condemn "certaine bookes of Chiv-
alrie, the whole pleasure of whiche standeth in two speciall poyntes,
in open manslaughter and bolde bawdrye." The beautiful old stories, so simply and reverently handled by Sir Thomas Malory in the
Morte d'Arthur, were regarded with horror and aversion by this gentle
ascetic; yet the lessons that they taught were mainly "curtosye, huma-
nyte, friendlynesse, hardynesse and love." The valorous deeds of Guy
of Warwick and Thomas of Reading lent cheer to many a hearth, and
sent many a man with brave and joyous heart to battle; yet the saintly
Stubbes, who loved not joyousness, lamented loudly that the unregenerate persisted in reading such "toys, fantasies and babbleries," in
place of that more dolorous fiction, Fox's *Book of Martyrs*. Even Sir
Philip Sidney's innocent *Arcadia* was pronounced by Milton a "vain,
amatorious" book; and the great poet who wrote "Comus" and "L'
Allegro" harshly and bitterly censured King Charles because that
unhappy monarch beguiled the sad hours of prison with its charming pages, and even, oh! crowning offense against Puritanism! copied for spiritual comfort, when condemned to die, the beautiful and
reverent invocation of its young heroine, Pamela. "The king hath, as
it were, unhallowed and unchristened the very duty of prayer itself,"
wrote Milton mercilessly. "Who would have imagined so little fear in
him of the true all-seeing deity, so little care of truth in his last words,
or honor to himself or to his friends, as, immediately before his death,
to pop into the hand of that grave bishop who attended him, for a
special relique of his saintly exercises, a prayer stolen word by word
from the mouth of a heathen woman praying to a heathen god."

But not even the mighty voice of Milton could check the resistless progress of romantic fiction. Not even dominant Puritanism
could stamp it ruthlessly down. When *Pilgrim's Progress*, the great

pioneer of religious novels, was given to the world, England read it with devout delight; but she read too, with admirable inconsistency, those endless tales, those "romances de longue haleine," which crossed the channel from France, and replaced the less decorous Italian stories so popular in the preceding century. Some of these prolix and ponderous volumes, as relentless in dullness as in length, held their own stoutly for centuries, and won allegiance where it seemed least due. There is an incredible story narrated of Racine, that, when a student at Port Royal, his favorite reading was an ancient prose epic entitled *Ethiopica; The History of Theagenes and Chariclea*. This guileless work, being too bulky for concealment, was discovered by his director and promptly burned, notwithstanding its having been written by a bishop, which ought to have saved it from the flames. Racine, undaunted, procured another copy, and fearing it would meet with the same cruel fate, he actually committed large portions of it to memory, so that nothing should deprive him of his enjoyment. Yet *Ethiopica* would seem as absolutely unreadable a book as even a bishop ever wrote. The heroine, though chaste as she is beautiful, has so many lovers, all with equally unpronounceable names, and so many battles are fought in her behalf, that no other memory than Racine's could have made any sort of headway with them; while, just in the middle of the story, an old gentleman is suddenly introduced, who, without provocation, starts to work and tells all *his* life's adventures, two hundred pages long.

The real promoters and encouragers of romance, however,—the real promoters and encouragers of fiction in every age—were women, and this is more than enough to account for its continued triumphs. There was little use in the stubborn old Puritan, Powell, protesting against the idle folly of females who wasted their time over Sidney's *Arcadia*, when they ought to have been studying the household recipe books. Long before Cromwell the mighty revolutionized England, women had wearied of recipes as steady reading, and had turned their wanton minds to matters more seductive. Wise and wary was the writer who kept these fair patronesses well in view. When John Lyly gave to the world his amazing *Euphues*, he dexterously announced that it was written for the amusement and the edification of women, and that he asked for it no better fate than to be read by them in idle moments, when they were weary of playing with their lap-dogs. For a young man of twenty-five, Lyly showed an admirable knowledge of feminine inconsistency. By alternately flattering and upbraiding the subtle creatures he hoped to please, now sweetly praising their incomparable perfections, now fiercely reviling their follies and their sins, he succeeded in making *Euphues* the best-read book in England, and he chained with affectations and foolish conceits the free and noble current of English speech.

It was the abundance of leisure enjoyed by women that gave the ten-volumed French romance its marvelous popularity; and one sympathizes a little with Mr. Pepys, though he was such a chronic grumbler, when he laments in his diary that Mrs. Pepys would not only read *Le Grand Cyrus* all night, but would talk about it all day, "though nothing to the purpose, nor in any good manner," remarks this censorious husband and critic. More melancholy still to contemplate is the early appearance on the scene of female novelists who wrote vicious twaddle for other women to read. We may fancy that this particular plague is a development of the nineteenth century; but twenty years before the virtuous Pamela saw the light, Eliza Heywood was doing her little best to demoralize the minds and manners of her countrywomen. Eliza Heywood was, in Mr. Gosse's opinion,—and he is one of the few critics who has expressed *any* opinion on the subject,—the Ouida of her period. The very names of her heroines, Lassellia, Idalia, and Douxmoure, are ouidesque, and their behavior would warrant their immediate presentation to that society which the authoress of "Strathmore" has so sympathetically portrayed. These "lovely Inconsiderates," though bad enough for a reformatory, are all as sensitive as nuns. They "sink fainting on a Bank" if they so much as receive letters from their lovers. Their "Limbs forget their Functions" on the most trifling provocation. "Stormy Passions" and "deadly Melancholy" succeed each other with monotonous vehemence in their "tortured Bosoms," and when they fly repentant to some remote Italian convent, whole cities mourn their loss.

Eliza Heywood's stories are probably as imbecile and as depraved as any fiction we possess today, but the women of England read them eagerly. They read too the iniquitous rubbish of Mrs. Aphra Behn; and no incident can better illustrate the tremendous change that swept over public sentiment with the introduction of good and decent novels than the well-known tale of Sir Walter Scott's aunt, Mrs. Keith of Ravelston. This sprightly old lady took a fancy, when in her eightieth year, to re-read Mrs. Behn's books, and persuaded Sir Walter to send them to her. A hasty glance at them was more than enough, and back they came to Scott with an entreaty that he would put them in the fire. The ancient gentlewoman confessed herself unable to linger over pages which she had not been ashamed nor abashed to hear read aloud to large parties in her youth.

It must be remembered, however, that Aphra Behn, uncompromisingly bad though she was, wrote the first English didactic novel, *Oroonoka*, the *Uncle Tom's Cabin* of its day. It has the advantage of "Uncle Tom" in being a true tale, Mrs. Behn having seen the slave, Oroonoka, and his wife, Imoinda, in the West Indies, and having witnessed his tragic fate. It was written at the solicitation of Charles II., and was a popular anti-slavery novel, with certain points of resemblance to Mrs. Stowe's famous book; in the grace and beauty of its Africans, for example; in the strength and constancy of their affections, and in the lavish nobility of their sentiments. Mrs. Behn knew as well as Mrs. Stowe that, if you want to produce a strong effect, you must not be too chary of your colors.

When the time came for the great flowering of English fiction, when Fielding and Richardson took England by storm, and France confessed herself beaten in the field ("Who would have thought," wrote the Marquis d'Argenson, "that the English would write novels, and better ones than ours?"), then it was that women asserted themselves distinctly as patronesses well worth the pleasing. To Smollett and Defoe they had never given whole-hearted approbation. Such robustly masculine writing was scarcely in their way. But Fielding, infinitely greater than these, met with no warmer favor at their hands. It is easy to account for the present unpopularity of Tom Joneses in decorous households by saying that modest women do not consider it fit for them to read. That covers the ground now to perfection. But the fact remains that, when *Tom Jones* was written, everybody *did* consider it fit to read. Why not, when all that it contained was seen about them day by day? Its author, like every other great novelist, described life as he found it. Arcadia had passed away, and big libertine London offered a scant assortment of Arcadian virtues. Fielding had nothing to tell that might not have been heard any day at one of Sir Robert Walpole's dinner-parties. He had the merit—not too common now—of never confusing vice with virtue; though it must be confessed that, like Dumas and Scott and Thackeray, he took very kindly to his scamps; and we all know how angry a recent critic permits himself to be because Thackeray calls Rawdon Crawley "honest Rawdon." As far as can be seen, Fielding never realized the grossness of his books. He prefaced *Tom Jones* with a beautiful little sermon about "the solid inward comfort of mind which is the sure companion of innocence and virtue;" and he took immense credit to himself for having written "nothing prejudicial to the cause of religion and virtue, nothing inconsistent with the strictest rules of decency, nor which can offend even the chastest eye in the perusal." What more than this could be claimed by the authors of *The Old Homestead* and *Little Lord Fauntleroy*?

I do not for one moment believe that it was the blithe and brutal coarseness of Fielding's novels that exiled them from the female heart, that inconsistent heart which never fluttered over the more repellent indecency of *Pamela*. Insidious influences were at work within the dovecotes. The eighteenth-century woman, while less given to self-analysis and self-assertion than her successor today, was just as conscious of her own nature, its resistless force, its inalienable laws, its permanent limitations; and in Richardson she recognized the artist who had divined her subtleties, and had given them form and color. His correspondence with women is unlike anything else the period has to show. To him they had an independence of thought and action which it took the rest of mankind a hundred years longer to concede; and it is not surprising to see the fervent homage this stout little tradesman of sixty received from his female flatterers, when we remember that he and he alone in all his century had looked into the rebellious secrets of their hearts with understanding and with reverence.

To any other man than Richardson, the devout attentions of so many women would have been a trifle fatiguing. They wrote him letters as long as Clarissa Harlowe's. They poured out their sentiments on endless reams of paper. They told him how they walked up and down their rooms, shedding torrents of tears over his heroine's distress, unable to either go on with the book, or to put it resolutely down. They told him how, when *Clarissa* was being read aloud in a bedchamber, the maid who was curling her mistress's hair wept so bitterly she could not go on with her work, so was given a crown for her sensibility, and sent out of the room. They implored and entreated him to end his story happily; "a turn," wrote one fair enthusiast, "that will make your almost despairing readers mad with joy." Richardson purred complacently over these letters, like a sleek old cat, and he answered every one of them, instead of pitching them unread into the fire. Yet, nevertheless, true and great artist that he was, in spite of all his vanity, these passionate solicitations moved him not one hair's breadth from his path. "As well," says Mr. Birrell, "hope for a happy ending for King Lear as for Clarissa Harlowe." She died, and England dissolved herself in tears, and gay, sentimental France lifted up her voice and wept aloud, and Germany joined in the sad chorus of lamentations, and even phlegmatic Holland was heard bewailing from afar the great tragedy of the literary world. This is no fancy statement. Men swore while women wept. Good Dr. Johnson hung his despondent head, and ribald Colley Cibber vowed with a great oath that this incomparable heroine should not die. Years afterwards, when Napoleon was first consul, an English gentleman named Lovelace was presented to him, whereupon the consul brightened visibly, and remarked, "Why, that is the name of Clarissa Harlowe's lover!"—an incident which won, and won deservedly for Bonaparte, the lifelong loyalty of Hazlitt.

Meanwhile Richardson, writing quietly away in his little summer-house, produced Sir Charles Grandison, a hero who is perhaps as famous for his priggishness as Lovelace is famous for his villainy. I think, myself, that poor Sir Charles has been unfairly handled. He is not half such a prig as Daniel Deronda; but he develops his priggishness with such ample detail through so many leisurely volumes. Richardson loved him, and tried hard to make his host of female readers love him too, which they did in a somewhat perfunctory and lukewarm fashion. Indeed, it should in justice be remembered that this eighteenth-century novelist intended all his books to be didactic. They seem now at times too painful, too detestable for endurance; but when *Pamela*, with all its loathsome details, was published, it was actually commended from the pulpit, declared to be better than twenty sermons, and placed by the side of the Bible for its moral influence. Richardson himself tells us a curiously significant anecdote of his childhood. When he was a little boy, eleven years old, he heard his mother and some gossips complaining of a quarrelsome and acrimonious neighbor. He promptly wrote her a long letter of remonstrance, quoting freely from the scriptures to prove to her the evil of her ways. The woman, being naturally very angry, complained to his mother of his impertinence, whereupon she, with true maternal pride, commended his principles, while gently censuring the liberty he had taken.

With Richardson's splendid triumph to spur them on, the passion of Englishwomen for novel-reading reached its height. Young girls, hitherto debarred from this diversion, began more and more to taste the forbidden sweets, and wise men, like Dr. Johnson, meekly acknowledged that there was no stopping them. When Frances Chamberlayne Sheridan told him that she never allowed her little daughter to read anything but the *Rambler*, or matters equally instructive, he answered with all his customary candor: "Then, madam, you are a fool! Turn your daughter's wits loose in your library. If she be well inclined, she will choose only good food. If otherwise, all your precautions will amount to nothing." Both Charles Lamb and Ruskin cherished similar opinions, but the sentiment was more uncommon in Dr. Johnson's day, and we know how even he reproached good Hannah More for quoting from *Tom Jones*.

With or without permission, however, the girls read gayly on. In Garrick's epilogue to Colman's farce, *Polly Honeycombe*, the wayward young heroine confesses her lively gratitude for all the dangerous knowledge she has gleaned from novels.

> So much these dear instructors change and win us,
> Without their light we ne'er should know what's in us.
> Here we at once supply our childish wants,
> Novels are hotbeds for your forward plants.

Later on, Sheridan gave us the immortal Lydia Languish feeding her sentimentality upon that "evergreen tree of diabolical knowledge," the circulating library. Lydia's taste in books is catholic, but not altogether free from reproach. "Fling 'Peregrine Pickle' under the toilet," she cries to Lucy, when surprised by a visit from Mrs. Malaprop and Sir Anthony. "Throw *Roderick Random* into the closet. Put *The Innocent Adultery* into *The Whole Duty of Man*. Thrust *Lord Aimworth* under the sofa. Cram Ovid behind the bolster. Put *The Man of Feeling* into your pocket. There—now for them!"

How *The Man of Feeling* ever went into Lucy's pocket remains a mystery, for it takes many volumes to hold that discursive romance, where everything from character to clothes is described with relentless minuteness. If a lady goes to a ball, we are not merely told that she looked radiant in "white and gold," or in "scarlet tulle," after the present slipshod fashion; but we are carefully informed that "a scarf of cerulean tint flew between her right shoulder and her left hip, being buttoned at each end by a row of rubies. A coronet of diamonds, through which there passed a white branch of the feathers of the ostrich, was inserted on the left decline of her lovely head." And so on, until the costume is complete.

By this time women had regularly enrolled themselves in the victorious army of novel-writers, and had won fame and fortune in the field. Consider the brilliant and instantaneous success of Frances Burney. Think of the excitement she aroused, and the honors heaped thick and fast upon her. A woman of twenty-six when she wrote *Evelina*, she was able, by dint of short stature and childish ways, to pass for a girl of seventeen, which increased amazingly the popular interest in her novel. Sheridan swore he could not believe so young a thing could manifest such genius, and begged her to write him a comedy on the spot. Sir Joshua Reynolds professed actual fear of such keen wit and relentless observation. Dr. Johnson vowed that Richardson had written nothing finer, and Fielding nothing so fine as *Evelina*; and playfully protested he was too proud to eat cold mutton for dinner when he sat by Miss Burney's side. Posterity, it is true, while preserving *Evelina* with great pride, has declined to place it by the side of *Tom Jones* or *Clarissa Harlowe*; but if we had our choice between the praise of posterity which was Miss Austen's portion, and the praise of contemporaries which was Miss Burney's lot, I doubt not we should be wise enough to take our applause off-hand,—"dashed in our faces, sounded in our ears," as Johnson said of Garrick, and leave the future to look after itself.

It is pleasant, however, to think that the first good woman novelist had her work over rather than under estimated. It is pleasant also to contemplate the really bewildering career of Maria Edgeworth. Miss Edgeworth's books are agreeable reading, and her children's stories are among the very best ever written; but it is not altogether easy to understand why France and England contended to do her honor. When she went to London or to Paris she became the idol of brilliant and fashionable people. Peers and poets united in her praise. Like Mrs. Jarley, she was the delight of the nobility and gentry. The Duke of Wellington wrote verses to her. Lord Byron, whom she detested, extolled her generously. Moore pronounced her "delightful." Macaulay compared the return of the Absentee to the return of Ulysses in the *Odyssey*. Sir Walter Scott took forcible possession of her, and carried her away to Abbotsford,—a too generous reward, it would seem, for all she ever did. Sydney Smith delighted in her. Mrs. Somerville, the learned, and Mrs. Fry, the benignant, sought her friendship; and finally, Mme. de Staël, who considered Jane Austen's novels "vulgar," protested that Miss Edgeworth was "worthy of enthusiasm."

Now this was all very charming, and very enjoyable; but with such rewards following thick and fast upon successful story-writing, it is hardly surprising that every year saw the band of literary aspirants increase and multiply amazingly. People were beginning to learn how easy it was to write a book. Already Hannah More had bewailed the ever increasing number of novelists, "their unparalleled fecundity," and "the frightful facility of this species of composition." What would she think if she were living now, and could see over a thousand novels published every year in England? Already Mrs. Radcliffe had woven around English hearths the spell of her rather feeble terrors, and young and old shuddered and quaked in the subterranean corridors of castles amid the gloomy Apennines. Why a quiet, cheerful, retiring woman like Mrs. Radcliffe, who hated notoriety, and who loved country life, and afternoon drives, and all that was comfortable and commonplace, should have written *The Mysteries of Udolpho* passes our comprehension; but write it she did, and England received it with a mad delight she has never manifested for any triumph of modern realism. The volume, we are assured, was too often torn asunder by frantic members of a household so that it might pass from hand to hand more rapidly than if it held together.

Mrs. Radcliffe not only won fame and amassed a considerable fortune—she received five hundred pounds for *Udolpho* and eight hundred for *The Italian*—but she gave such impetus to the novel of horrors, which had been set going by Horace Walpole's *Castle of Otranto*, that for years England was oppressed and excited by these dreadful literary nightmares. Matthew—otherwise "Monk"—Lewis, Robert Charles Matarin, and a host of feebler imitators, wrote grisly stories of ghosts, and murders, and nameless crimes, and supernatural visitations. Horrors are piled on horrors in these dismal and sulphurous tales. Blue fire envelops us, and persevering specters, who have striven a hundred years for burial rites, sit by their victims' bedsides and recite dolorous verses, which is more than any self-respecting specter ought to do. Compacts with Satan are as numerous as bargain counters in our city shops. Suicides alternate briskly with assassinations. In one melancholy story, the despairing heroine agrees to meet her lover in a lonely church, where they intend stabbing themselves sociably together. Unhappily, it rains hard all the afternoon, and—with an unexpected touch of realism—she is miserably afraid the bad weather will keep her indoors. "The storm was so violent," we are told, "that Augusta often feared she could not go out at the appointed time. Frequently did she throw up the sash, and view with anxious looks the convulsed elements. At half past five the weather cleared, and Augusta felt a fearful joy."

It might have been supposed that the gay, good-humored satire of *Northanger Abbey* would have laughed these tragic absurdities from the land. But Miss Austen alone, of all the great novelists of England, won less than her due share of profit and renown. Her sisters in the field were loaded down with honors. When the excellent Mrs. Opie became a Friend, and refused to write any more fiction, except, indeed, those moral but unlikely tales about the awful consequences of lying, her contemporaries spoke gravely of the genius she had sacrificed at the shrine of religion. Charlotte Brontë's masterpiece gained instant recognition throughout the length and breadth of England. Of George Eliot's sustained success there is no need to speak. But Jane Austen, whose incomparable art is now the theme of every critic's pen, was practically ignored while she lived, and perhaps never suspected, herself, how admirable, how perfect was her work. Sir Walter Scott, it is true, with the intuition of a great storyteller, instantly recognized this perfection; and so did Lord Holland and a few others, among whom let us always gladly remember George IV, who was wise enough to keep a set of Miss Austen's novels in every one of his houses, and who was happy enough to receive the dedication of *Emma*. Nevertheless, it cannot be forgotten that fifteen years elapsed between the writing of *Pride and Prejudice* and its publication; that Cadell refused it unread—a dreadful warning to publishers—and that all Miss Austen ever realized from her books in her lifetime was seven hundred pounds—one hundred pounds less than Mrs. Radcliffe received for a single story, and nearly two thousand pounds less than Frances Burney was paid for her absolutely unreadable *Camilla*. High-priced novels are by no means a modern innovation, though we hear so much more about them now than formerly. Blackwood gave Lockhart one thousand pounds for the manuscript of *Reginald Dalton*, and *Woodstock* brought to Scott's creditors the fabulous sum of eight thousand pounds.

For with Sir Walter flowered the golden age of English fiction. Fortune and fame came smiling at his beck, and the great reading world confessed itself better and happier for his genius. Then it was that the bookshops were besieged by clamorous crowds when a new Waverly novel was promised to the public. Then Lord Holland sat up all night to finish *Old Mortality*. Then the excitement over the Great Unknown reached fever heat, and the art of the novelist gained its absolute ascendancy, an ascendancy unbroken in our day, and likely to remain unbroken for many years to come. At present, every child that learns its letters makes one more story-reader in the world, and the chances are it will make one more story-writer to help deluge the world with fiction. Novels, it has been truly said, are the only things that can never be too dear or too cheap for the market. The beautiful and costly editions of Miss Austen and Scott and Thackeray compete for favor with marvelously cheap editions of Dickens, that true and abiding idol of people who have no money to spend on hand-made paper and broad margins. It is the same with living novelists. Rare and limited editions for the rich; cheap and unlimited editions for the poor; all bought, all read, and the novelist waxing more proud and prosperous every day. So prosperous, indeed, so proud, he is getting too great a man to amuse us as of yore. He spins fewer stories now, and his glittering web has grown a trifle gray and dusty with the sweepings from back outlets and mean streets. He preaches occasionally in the market-place, and he says acrimonious things anent other novelists whose ways of thinking differ from his own. These new, sad fashions of speech are often very grievous to his readers, but nothing can rob him of our friendship; for always we hope that he will take us by the hand, and lead us smilingly away from the relentless realities of life to the golden regions of romance where the immortal are.

15

The Condescension of Borrowers[*]

*Il n'est si riche qui quelquefois ne doibve. Il n'est si pauvre de qui
quelquefois on ne puisse emprunter.* —Pantagruel

"I lent my umbrella," said my friend, to my cousin, Maria.
I was compelled to lend it to her because she could not, or
would not, leave my house in the rain without it. I had need of that
umbrella, and I tried to make it as plain as the amenities of language
permitted that I expected to have it returned. Maria said superciliously that she hated to see other people's umbrellas littering the
house, which gave me a gleam of hope. Two months later I found my
property in the hands of her ten-year-old son, who was being mar-
shaled with his brothers and sisters to dancing school. In the first
joyful flash of recognition I cried, 'Oswald, that is my umbrella you
are carrying!' whereupon Maria said still more superciliously than
before, 'Oh, yes, don't you remember?' (as if reproaching me for my
forgetfulness)—'you gave it to me that Saturday I lunched with you,
and it rained so heavily. The boys carry it to school. Where there are
children, you can't have too many old umbrellas at hand. They lose
them so fast.' She spoke," continued my friend impressively, "as if

* From *Americans and Others*, 1912.

she were harboring my umbrella from pure kindness, and because she did not like to wound my feelings by sending it back to me. She made a virtue of giving it shelter."

This is the arrogance which places the borrower, as Charles Lamb discovered long ago, among the great ones of the earth, among those whom their brethren serve. Lamb loved to contrast the "instinctive sovereignity," the frank and open bearing of the man who borrows with the "lean and suspicious" aspect of the man who lends. He stood lost in admiration before the great borrowers of the world— Alcibiades, Falstaff, Steele, and Sheridan; an incomparable quartette, to which might be added the shining names of William Godwin and Leigh Hunt. All the characteristic qualities of the class were united, indeed, in Leigh Hunt, as in no other single representative. Sheridan was an unrivaled companion—could talk seven hours without making even Byron yawn. Steele was the most lovable of spendthrifts. Lending to these men was but a form of investment. They paid in a coinage of their own. But Leigh Hunt combined in the happiest manner a readiness to extract favors with a confirmed habit of never acknowledging the smallest obligation for them. He is a perfect example of the condescending borrower, of the man who permits his friends, as a pleasure to themselves, to relieve his necessities, and who knows nothing of gratitude or loyalty.

It would be interesting to calculate the amount of money which Hunt's friends and acquaintances contributed to his support in life. Shelley gave him at one time fourteen hundred pounds, an amount which the poet could ill spare; and, when he had no more to give, wrote in misery of spirit to Byron, begging a loan for his friend, and promising to repay it, as he feels tolerably sure that Hunt never will. Byron, generous at first, wearied after a time of his position in Hunt's commissariat (it was like pulling a man out of a river, he wrote to Moore, only to see him jump in again), and coldly withdrew. His withdrawal occasioned inconvenience, and has been sharply criticized. Hunt, says Sir Leslie Stephen, loved a cheerful giver, and Byron's obvious reluctance struck him as being in bad taste. His biographers, one and all, have sympathized with this point of view. Even Mr. Frederick Locker, from whom one would have expected a

different verdict, has recorded his conviction that Hunt had probably been "sorely tried" by Byron.

It is characteristic of the preordained borrower, of the man who
simply fulfils his destiny in life, that not his obligations only, but his
anxieties and mortifications are shouldered by other men. Hunt was
care-free and light-hearted; but there is a note akin to anguish in
Shelley's petition to Byron, and in his shamefaced admission that he
is himself too poor to relieve his friend's necessities. The correspondence of William Godwin's eminent contemporaries teem with proj-
ects to alleviate Godwin's needs. His debts were everybody's affair
but his own. Sir James Mackintosh wrote to Rogers in the autumn of
1815, suggesting that Byron might be the proper person to pay them.
Rogers, enchanted with the idea, wrote to Byron, proposing that the
purchase money of "The Siege of Corinth" be devoted to this good
purpose. Byron, with less enthusiasm, but resigned, wrote to Murray, directing him to forward the six hundred pounds to Godwin;
and Murray, having always the courage of his convictions, wrote
back, flatly refusing to do anything of the kind. In the end, Byron
used the money to pay his own debts, thereby disgusting everybody
but his creditors.

Six years later, however, we find him contributing to a fund which
tireless philanthropists were raising for Godwin's relief. On this
occasion all men of letters, poor as well as rich, were pressed into
active service. Even Lamb, who had nothing of his own, wrote to
the painter, Haydon, who had not a penny in the world, and begged
him to beg Mrs. Coutts to pay Godwin's rent. He also confessed that
he had sent "a very respectful letter"—on behalf of the rent—to Sir
Walter Scott; and he explained naïvely that Godwin did not concern
himself personally in the matter, because he "left all to his Committee"—a peaceful thing to do.

But how did Godwin come to have a "committee" to raise money
for him, when other poor devils had to raise it for themselves, or
do without? He was not well-beloved. On the contrary, he bored all
whom he did not affront. He was not grateful. On the contrary, he
held gratitude to be a vice, as tending to make men "grossly partial" to those who have befriended them. His condescension kept

pace with his demands. After his daughter's flight with Shelley, he expressed his just resentment by refusing to accept Shelley's cheque for a thousand pounds unless it were made payable to a third party, unless he could have the money without the formality of an acceptance. Like the great lords of Picardy, who had the "right of credit" from their loyal subjects, Godwin claimed his dues from every chance acquaintance. Crabb Robinson introduced him one evening to a gentleman named Rough. The next day both Godwin and Rough called upon their host, each man expressing his regard for the other, and each asking Robinson if he thought the other would be a likely person to lend him fifty pounds.

There are critics who hold that Haydon excelled all other borrowers known to fame; but his is not a career upon which an admirer of the art can look with pleasure. Haydon's debts hunted him like hounds, and if he pursued borrowing as a means of livelihood—more lucrative than painting pictures which nobody would buy—it was only because no third avocation presented itself as a possibility. He is not to be compared for a moment with a true expert like Sheridan, who borrowed for borrowing's sake, and without any sordid motive connected with rents or butcher's bills. Haydon would, indeed, part with his money as readily as if it belonged to him. He would hear an "inward voice" in church, urging him to give his last sovereign; and, having obeyed this voice "with as pure a feeling as ever animated a human heart," he had no resource but immediately to borrow another. It would have been well for him if he could have followed on such occasions the memorable example of Lady Cook, who was so impressed by a begging sermon that she borrowed a sovereign from Sydney Smith to put into the offertory; and—the gold once between her fingers—found herself equally unable to give it or to return it, so went home, a pound richer for her charitable impulse.

Haydon, too, would rob Peter to pay Paul, and rob Paul without paying Peter; but it was all after an intricate and troubled fashion of his own. On one occasion he borrowed ten pounds from Webb. Seven pounds he used to satisfy another creditor, from whom, on the strength of this payment, he borrowed ten pounds more to meet an impending bill. It sounds like a particularly confusing game; but it was a game played in dead earnest, and without the humorous touch which makes the charm of Lady Cook's, or of Sheridan's methods. Haydon would have been deeply grateful to his benefactors, had he not always stood in need of favors to come. Sheridan might perchance have been grateful, could he have remembered who his benefactors were. He laid the world under tribute; and because he had an aversion to opening his mail—an aversion with which it is impossible not to sympathize—he frequently made no use of the tribute when it was paid. Moore tells us that James Wesley once saw among a pile of papers on Sheridan's desk an unopened letter of his own, containing a ten-pound note, which he had lent Sheridan some weeks before. Wesley quietly took possession of the letter and the money, thereby raising a delicate, and as yet unsettled, question of morality. Had he a right to those ten pounds because they had once been his, or were they not rather Sheridan's property, destined in the natural and proper order of things never to be returned?

Yet men, even men of letters, have been known to pay their debts, and to restore borrowed property. Moore paid Lord Lansdowne every penny of the generous sum advanced by that nobleman after the defalcation of Moore's deputy in Bermuda. Doctor Johnson paid back ten pounds after a lapse of twenty years—a pleasant shock to the lender—and on his death-bed (having fewer sins than most of us to recall) begged Sir Joshua Reynolds to forgive him a trifling loan. It was the too honest return of a pair of borrowed sheets (unwashed) which first chilled Pope's friendship for Lady Mary Wortley Montagu. That excellent gossip, Miss Letitia Matilda Hawkins, who stands responsible for this anecdote, lamented all her life that her father, Sir John Hawkins, could never remember which of the friends borrowed and which lent the offending sheets; but it is a point easily settled in our minds. Pope was probably the last man in Christendom to have been guilty of such a misdemeanor, and Lady Mary was certainly the last woman in Christendom to have been affronted by it. Like Doctor Johnson, she had "no passion for clean linen."

Coleridge, though he went through life leaning his inert weight on other men's shoulders, did remember in some mysterious fashion to return the books he borrowed, enriched often, as Lamb proudly records, with marginal notes which tripled their value. His conduct in this regard was all the more praiseworthy inasmuch as the cobweb statutes which define books as personal property have never met with literal acceptance. Lamb's theory that books belong with the highest propriety to those who understand them best (a theory often advanced in defense of depredations which Lamb would have scorned to commit), was popular before the lamentable invention of printing. The library of Lucullus was, we are told, "open to all," and it would be interesting to know how many precious manuscripts remained ultimately in the great patrician's villa.

Richard Heber, that most princely of collectors, so well understood the perils of his position that he met them bravely by buying three copies of every book—one for show, one for use, and one for the service of his friends. The position of the show-book seems rather melancholy, but perhaps, in time, it replaced the borrowed volume. Heber's generosity has been nobly praised by Scott, who contrasts the hard-heartedness of other bibliophiles, those "gripple niggards" who preferred holding on to their treasures, with his friend's careless liberality.

> Thy volumes, open as thy heart,
> Delight, amusement, science, art,
> To every ear and eye impart.
> Yet who, of all who thus employ them,
> Can, like the owner's self, enjoy them?

The "gripple niggards" might have pleaded feebly in their own behalf that they could not all afford to spend, like Heber, a hundred thousand pounds in the purchase of books; and that an occasional reluctance to part with some hard-earned, hard-won volume might be pardonable in one who could not hope to replace it. Lamb's books were the shabbiest in Christendom; yet how keen was his pang when Charles Kemble carried off the letters of "that princely woman, the thrice noble Margaret Newcastle," an "illustrious folio" which he well knew Kemble would never read. How bitterly he bewailed his rashness in extolling the beauties of Sir Thomas Browne's *Urn Burial* to a guest who was so moved by this eloquence that he promptly borrowed the volume. "But so," sighed Lamb "have I known a foolish lover to praise his mistress in the presence of a rival more qualified to carry her off than himself."

Johnson cherished a dim conviction that because he read, and Garrick did not, the proper place for Garrick's books was on his—Johnson's—bookshelves; a point which could never be settled between the two friends, and which came near to wrecking their friendship. Garrick loved books with the chilly yet imperative love of the collector. Johnson loved them as he loved his soul. Garrick took pride in their sumptuousness, in their immaculate, virginal splendor. Johnson gathered them to his heart with scant regard for outward magnificence, for the glories of calf and vellum. Garrick bought books. Johnson borrowed them. Each considered that he had a prior right to the objects of his legitimate affection. We, looking back with softened hearts, are fain to think that we should have held our volumes doubly dear if they had lain for a time by Johnson's humble hearth, if he had pored over them at three o'clock in the morning, and had left sundry tokens—grease-spots and spatterings of snuff—upon many a spotless page. But it is hardly fair to censure Garrick for not dilating with these emotions.

Johnson's habit of flinging the volumes which displeased him into remote and dusty corners of the room was ill calculated to inspire confidence, and his powers of procrastination were never more marked than in the matter of restoring borrowed books. We know from Cradock's *Memoirs* how that gentleman, having induced Lord Harborough to lend him a superb volume of manuscripts, containing poems of James I, proceeded to re-lend this priceless treasure to Johnson. When it was not returned—as of course it was not—he wrote an urgent letter, and heard to his dismay that Johnson was not only unable to find the book, but that he could not remember having ever received it. The despairing Cradock applied to all his friends for help; and George Steevens, who had a useful habit of looking about him, suggested that a sealed packet, which he had several times observed lying under Johnson's ponderous inkstand, might possibly contain the lost manuscripts. Even with this ray of hope for guidance, it never seemed to occur to anyone to storm Johnson's fortress and rescue the imprisoned volume; but after the Doctor's death, two years later, Cradock made a formal application to the executors; and Lord Harborough's property was discovered under the inkstand, unopened, unread, and consequently, as by a happy miracle, uninjured.

Such an incident must needs win pardon for Garrick's churlishness in defending his possessions. "The history of book-collecting," says a caustic critic, "is a history relieved but rarely by acts of pure and undiluted unselfishness." This is true, but are there not virtues so heroic that plain human nature can ill aspire to compass them?

There is something piteous in the futile efforts of reluctant lenders to save their property from depredation They place their reliance upon artless devices which never yet were known to stay the marauder's hand. They have their names and addresses engraved on foolish little plates, which, riveted to their umbrellas, will, they think, suffice to insure the safety of these useful articles. As well might the border farmer have engraved his name and address on the collars of his grazing herds, in the hope that the riever would respect this symbol of authority. The history of book-plates is largely the history of borrower versus lender. The orderly mind is wont to believe that a distinctive mark, irrevocably attached to every volume, will insure permanent possession. Sir Edmund Gosse, for example, expressed a touching faith in the efficacy of the book-plate. He had but to explain that he "made it a rule" never to lend a volume thus decorated, and the would-be borrower bowed to this rule as to a decree of fate. "To have a book-plate," he joyfully observed, "gives a collector great serenity and confidence."

Is it possible that the world has grown virtuous without our observing it? Can it be that the old stalwart race of book-borrowers, those "spoilers of the symmetry of shelves," are foiled by so childish an expedient? Imagine Doctor Johnson daunted by a scrap of pasted paper! Or Coleridge, who seldom went through the formality of asking leave, but borrowed armfuls of books in the absence of their legitimate owners! How are we to account for the presence of book-plates—quite a pretty collection at times—on the shelves of men who possess no such toys of their own? When I was a girl I had access to a small and well-chosen library (not greatly exceeding Montaigne's fourscore volumes), each book enriched with an appropriate device of scaly dragon guarding the apples of Hesperides. Beneath the dragon was the motto (Johnsonian in form if not in substance), "Honor and Obligation demand the prompt return of borrowed Books." These words ate into my innocent soul, and lent a pang to the sweetness of possession. Doubts as to the exact nature of "prompt return" made me painfully uncertain as to whether a month, a week, or a day were the limit which Honor and Obligation had set for me. But other and older borrowers were less sensitive, and I have reason to believe that—books being a rarity in that little Southern town—most of the volumes were eventually absorbed by the gaping shelves of neighbors. Perhaps even now (their generous owner long since dead) these worn copies of Boswell, of Elia, of Herrick, and Moore, may still stand forgotten in dark and dusty corners, like gems that magpies hide.

It is vain to struggle with fate, with the elements, and with the borrower; it is folly to claim immunity from a fundamental law, to boast of our brief exemption from the common lot. "Lend therefore cheerfully, O man ordained to lend. When thou seest the proper authority coming, meet it smilingly, as it were halfway." Resistance to an appointed force is but a futile waste of strength.

16

Strayed Sympathies*

It is probably more instructive to entertain a sneaking kindness
for any unpopular person than to give way to perfect raptures of
moral indignation against his abstract vices.
—Robert Louis Stevenson

It is not only more instructive—it is more enlivening. The con-
ventionalities of criticism (moral, not literary, criticism) pass
from mouth to mouth, and from pen to pen, until the iterations
of the press are crystallized in encyclopedias and biographical dic-
tionaries. And from such verdicts there is no appeal. Their labored
impartiality, their systematic adjustments, their careful avoidance
of intuition, produce in the public mind a level sameness of misunderstanding. Many sensible people think this a good result. Even a
man who did his own thinking, and maintained his own intellectual freehold, like Mr. Bagehot, knew and upheld the value of ruts.
He was well aware how far a little intelligence can be made to go,
unless it aspires to originality. Therefore he grumbled at the paradoxes which were somewhat of a novelty in his day, but which are
outworn in ours, at the making over of virtue into vice, and of vice
into something more inspiriting than virtue. "We have palliations

* From *Under Dispute*, 1924.

of Tiberius, eulogies on Henry the Eighth, devotional exercises to Cromwell, and fulsome adulations of the first Napoleon."

That was a half-century ago. Today, Tiberius is not so much out of favor as out of mind; Mr. Froude was the last man really interested in the moral status of Henry VIII; Mr. Wells has given us his word for it that Napoleon was a very ordinary person; and the English people have erected a statue of Cromwell close to the Houses of Parliament, by way of reminding him (in his appointed place) of the survival of representative government. The twentieth century does not lean to extravagant partialities. Its trend is to disparagement, to searchlights, to that lavish and ironic candor which no man's reputation can survive.

When Mr. Lytton Strachey reversed Mr. Stevenson's suggestion, and chose, as subject-matter of a book, four people of whom the world had heard little but good, who had been praised and reverenced beyond their deserts, but for whom he cherished a secret and cold hostility, he experimented successfully with the latent uncharitableness of men's minds. The brilliancy with which the four essays were written, the keenness of each assault, the charm and persuasiveness of the style, delighted even the uncensorious. The business of a biographer, said the author in a very engaging preface, is to maintain his own freedom of spirit, and lay bare events as he understands them, "dispassionately, impartially, and without ulterior intentions."

It sounds fair and square; but the fact remains that Mr. Strachey disliked Manning, despised Arnold, had little sympathy with Gordon, and no great fancy for Florence Nightingale. It must be remembered also that in three cases out of four he was dealing with persons of stubborn character and compelling will, as far removed from irreproachable excellence as from criminality. Of such, much criticism may be offered; but the only way to keep an open outlook is to ask, "What was their life's job?" "How well did they do it?" Men and women who have a pressing job on hand (Florence Nightingale was *all* job) cannot afford to cultivate the minor virtues. They move with an irresistible impulse to their goal. It is a curious fact that Mr. Strachey is never so illuminating as when he turns his back upon these forceful and disconcerting personages, and dallies with their more amenable contemporaries. What he writes about Gordon we should be glad to forget; what he writes about Sir Evelyn Baring and Lord Hartington we hope to remember while we live.

The popularity of *Eminent Victorians* inspired a host of followers. Critics began to look about them for other vulnerable reputations. Mr. J. A. Strahan, stepping back from Victoria to Anne, made the happy discovery that Addison had been systematically over praised, and that every side of his character was open to assault. The result of this perspicuity is a damning denunciation of a man whom his contemporaries liked and esteemed, and concerning whom we have been content to take the word of those who knew him. He may have been, as Mr. Strahan asserts, a sot, a time-server, a toad-eater, a bad official and a worse friend; but he managed to give a different impression. Addison's friends and neighbors found him a modest, honorable, sweet-tempered gentleman; and Steele, whom he had affronted, wrote these generous words: "You can seldom get him to the tavern; but when once he is arrived to his pint, and begins to look about him, you admire a thousand things in him which before lay buried."

This seems to me a singularly pleasant thing to say about anybody. Were I coveting praise, this is the form I'd like the praise to take.

The pressure of disparagement, which is one result of the cooling of our blood after the fever-heat of war, is lowering our enthusiasms, thinning our sympathies, and giving us nothing very dazzling in the way of enlightenment. Americans are less critical than Englishmen, who so value their birthright of free speech that censure of public men has become a habit, a game of hazard (pulling planks out of the ship of state), at which long practice has made them perfect. "The editor of the *Morning Post*," observed Mr. Maurice Hewlett wearily, "begins his day by wondering whom he shall denounce"; and opposing editors, as nimble at the fray, match outcry against outcry, and malice against malignity.

I doubt if any other than an Englishman could have written *The Mirrors of Downing Street*, and I am sure that, were an American able to write such a book (which is problematic), it would never occur to him to think of it, or to brag of it, as a duty. The public actions of public men are open to discussion; but Mr. Balfour's personal selfishness, his parsimony, his indifference to his domestics, are not matters of general moment. To gossip about these things is to gossip with tradesmen and servants. To deny to Lord Kitchener "greatness of mind, greatness of character, and greatness of heart," is harsh speaking of the dead; but to tell a gaping world that the woman "whom he loved hungrily and doggedly, and to whom he proposed several times, could never bring herself to marry him," is a personality which *Town Topics* would scorn. *The Mirrors of Downing Street* aspired to a moral purpose; but taste is the guardian of morality. Its delicate and severe dictates define the terms upon which we may improve the world at the expense of our neighbor's character.

The sneaking kindness recommended by Mr. Stevenson is much harder to come by than the "raptures of moral indignation," of which he heard more than he wanted, and which are reverberating through the world today. The pages of history are heavy with moral indignation. We teach it in our schools, and there are historians like Macaulay who thunder it rapturously, with never a moment of misgiving. But here and there, as we step apprehensively into historic bypaths, we are cheered by patches of sunshine, straight glimpses into truths which put a more credible, because a more merciful, construction upon men's actions, and lighten our burden of dispraise.

I have often wondered why, with Philippe de Commines as an avenue of approach, all writers except Scott should deal with Louis XI as with a moral monstrosity. Commines is no apologist. He has a natural desire to speak well of his master; but he reviews every side of Louis's character with dispassionate sincerity.

First, as a Catholic:

The king was very liberal to the Church, and, in some respects, more so than was necessary, for he robbed the poor to give to the rich. But in this world no one can arrive at perfection.

Next, as a husband:

> As for ladies, he never meddled with them in my time; for when
> I came to his court he lost a son, at whose death he was greatly
> afflicted; and he made a vow to God in my presence never to have
> intercourse with any other woman than the queen. And though
> this was no more than he was bound to do by the canons of the
> Church, yet it was much that he should have such self-command
> as to persevere firmly in his resolution, considering that the queen
> (though an excellent lady in other respects) was not a princess in
> whom a man could take any great delight.

Finally, as a ruler:

> The king was naturally kind and indulgent to persons of mean
> estate, and hostile to all great men who had no need of him. . . .
> But this I say boldly in his commendation, that in my whole life I
> never knew any man so wise in his misfortunes.

To be brave in misfortune is to be worthy of manhood; to be
wise in misfortune is to conquer fate. We cannot easily or advan-
tageously regard Louis with affection; but when Commines epitomizes history in an ejaculation, "Our good master, Louis, whom
God pardon!" it rests our souls to say, "Amen!"

We cannot easily love Swift. The great "professional hater" fright-
ens us out of the timid regard which we should like—in honor of
English literature—to cherish for his memory. But there is a noble
sentence of Thackeray's which, if it does not soften our hearts, cannot fail to clarify our minds, to free us from the stupid, clogging
misapprehension which we confuse with moral distaste. "Through
the storms and tempests of his [Swift's] furious mind the stars of
religion and love break out in the blue, shining serenely, though
hidden by the driving clouds and maddening hurricane of his life."
One clear and penetrating note ("Childe Roland to the Dark Tower
came") is worth much careful auditing of accounts.

The picture of John Wilkes drawn by Sir George Otto Trevelyan
in his *Early History of Charles James Fox*, and the picture of Aaron

Burr drawn by Mr. Albert J. Beveridge in his *Life of John Marshall*, are happy illustrations of unpopular subjects treated with illuminating kindness. Wilkes was a demagogue and Burr a troublemaker (the terms are not necessarily synonymous), and neither of them is a man whose history is widely or accurately known. Both historians are swayed by their political passions. An historian without political passions is as rare as a wasp without a sting. To Trevelyan all Conservatives were in fault, and all Liberals in the right. Opposition to George III is the acid test he applies to separate gold from dross. Mr. Beveridge regards the Federalists as the strength, and the Republicans as the weakness, of the young nation. Thomas Jefferson is *his* test, and a man hated and hounded by Jefferson necessarily wins his support.

Nevertheless, Wilkes and Burr are presented to us by their sympathizers in a cold north light which softens and conceals nothing. Men of positive quality, they look best when clearly seen. "Research and fact are ever in collision with fancy and legend," observes Mr. Beveridge soberly; and it is to research and fact that he trusts to rescue his accomplished filibuster from those unproved charges which live by virtue of their vagueness. Writers of American school histories, remembering the duty of moral indignation, have played havoc with the reputation of Aaron Burr; and American school-children, if they know him at all, know him as a duelist and a traitor. They are sure about the duel (it was one of the few facts firmly established in my own mind after a severe struggle with American history); but concerning the treason, they are at least as ill-informed as their elders.

British children do better, perhaps, with John Wilkes. Little Londoners can gaze at the obelisk which commemorates his mayoralty, and think of him as a catless Whittington. The slogan "Wilkes and Liberty" has an attractive ring to all who are not of Madame Roland's way of thinking. No man ever gave his partisans more to defend, or his opponents better chances to attack; and friends and foes rose repeatedly and fervently to their opportunities. A century later, Sir George Trevelyan, a friend well worth the having, reviews the case with wise sincerity, undaunted confidence, a careful art in the arrangement of his high lights, and a niceness of touch which wins halfway all readers who love the English language. Wilkes was as naturally and inevitably in debt as was William Godwin, and Wilkes's debts were as naturally and inevitably paid by some one else as were Godwin's; but when Trevelyan alludes softly to his "unambitious standard of solvency," this sordid detail becomes unexpectedly pleasurable. So easily are transgressions pardoned, if they provoke the shadow of a smile.

Lord Rosebery's *Napoleon: The Last Phase* is a work nobly conceived and admirably executed; but its impelling motive is an austere resolve to make what amends a single Englishman can make for an ungenerous episode in English history. Its sympathy for a fallen foe bears no likeness to the sympathy which impelled Théodore de Banville, broken in health and hope by the siege of Paris, to write a lyric in memory of a young Prussian officer, a mere boy, who was found dead on the field, with a blood-stained volume of Pindar in his tunic. Lord Rosebery's book is written with a proud sadness, a stern indignation, eminently fitted to its subject; but he is not so much kind as just. Napoleon is too vast a figure to be approached with benevolence. It is true, as Mr. Wells asserts, that, had he been unselfish and conscientious, he would never have conquered Europe; but only Mr. Wells is prepared to say that a lack of these qualities won him renown. He shares the lack with Wilhelm the Second, who has had neither an Austerlitz nor a Waterloo.

There is a wide assortment of unpopular characters whose company it would be very instructive to keep. They belong to all ages, countries and creeds. Spain alone offers us three splendid examples—the Duke of Alva, Cardinal Ximenez, and Philip II. Alva, like the Corsair, possessed one virtue, which was a more valuable virtue than the Corsair's, but brings him in less credit, because the object of his unswerving loyalty and devotion was not a guileless lady, but a sovereign, less popular, if possible, than himself. Cardinal Ximenez, soldier, statesman, scholar, priest, ascetic, author and educator, was also Grand Inquisitor, and this fact alone seems to linger in the minds of men. That, for this day, he was a moderate, avails him little. That he made a point of protecting scholars and professors from the pernicious interference of the Inquisition ought to avail him a great deal. It might were it better known. There is a play of Sardou's in which he is represented as concentrating all the deadly powers of his office against the knowledge which he most esteemed. This is the way the drama educates.

And Philip? It would be a big piece of work to win for Philip even a partial recognition of his moderate merits. The hand of history has dealt heavily with him, and romance has preyed upon his vitals. In fact, history and romance are undistinguishable when they give free play to the moral indignation he inspires. It is not enough to accuse him of the murder of the son whom he hated (though not more heartily than George II hated the Prince of Wales): they would have us understand that he probably poisoned the brother whom he loved. "Don John's ambitions had become troublesome, and he ceased to live at an opportune moment for Philip's peace of mind," is the fashion in which Gayarré insinuates his suspicions; and Gayarré's narrative—very popular in my youth—was recommended to the American public by Bancroft, who, I am convinced, never read it. Had he penetrated to the eleventh page, where Philip is alluded to as the Christian Tiberius, or to the twentieth, where he is compared to an Indian idol, he would have known that, whatever the book might be, it was not history, and that, as an historian, it ill became him to tell innocent Americans to read it.

But how were they to be better informed? Motley will not even allow that Philip's fanatical devotion to his Church was a sincere devotion. He accuses him of hypocrisy, which is like accusing Cromwell of levity, or Burke of Jacobinism. Prescott has a fashion of turning the King's few amiabilities, as, for example, his tenderness for his third wife, Isabella of France, into a suggestion of reproach. "Well would it be for the memory of Philip, could the historian find no heavier sin to lay to his charge than his treatment of Isabella." Well would it be for all of us, could the recording angel lay no heavier charge to our account than our legitimate affections. The Prince of Orange, it is true, charged Philip with murdering both wife and son; but that was merely a political argument. He would as soon have charged him with the murder of his father, had the Emperor not been safely isolated at Yuste; and Philip, in return, banned the Prince of Orange—a brave and wise ruler—as "an enemy of the human race."

Twenty-five years ago, an Englishman who was by nature distrustful of popular verdicts, and who had made careful studies of certain epochs of Spanish history, ventured to paint Philip in fresh colors. Mr. Martin Hume's monograph shows us a cultivated gentleman, with a correct taste in architecture and art, sober, abstemious, kind to petitioners, loyal and affectionate to his friends, generous to his soldiers and sailors; a man beloved by his own household, and reverenced by his subjects, to whom he brought nothing but misfortune. The book makes melancholy reading, because Philip's political sins were also political blunders; his mad intolerance was a distortion, rather than a rejection, of conscience; and his inconceivable rigidity left him helpless to face the essential readjustments of life. "I could not do otherwise than I have done," he said with piercing sincerity, "though the world should fall in ruins around me."

Now what befell Mr. Hume who wrote history in this fashion, with no more liking for Philip than for Elizabeth or the Prince of Orange, but with a natural desire to get within the purlieus of truth? Certain empty honors were conferred upon him: a degree from Cambridge, membership in a few societies, the privilege of having some letters printed after his name. But the University of Glasgow and the University of Liverpool stoutly refused to give him the chairs of history and Spanish. He might know more than most men on these subjects; but they did not want their students exposed to new impressions. The good old way for them. Mr. Hume, being a reader, may have recalled in bitterness of spirit the words of the acute and unemotional Sully, who had scant regard for Catholicism (though the Huguenots tried him sorely), and none at all for Spain; but who said, in his balanced, impersonal way, that Philip's finer qualities, his patience, piety, fortitude and single-mindedness, were all alike "lost on the vulgar."

Lucrezia Borgia is less available for our purpose, because the imaginary Lucrezia, though not precisely beloved, is more popular in her way than the real Lucrezia could ever hope to be. "In the mat-

ter of pleasantness," says Lucian, "truth is far surpassed by falsehood"; and never has it been more agreeably overshadowed than in
this fragment of Italian history. We really could not bear to lose the
Lucrezia of romance. She has done fatigue duty along every line of
iniquity. She has specialized in all of the seven deadly sins. On Ros-
setti's canvas, in Donizetti's opera, in Victor Hugo's play, in countless poems and stories and novels, she has erred exhaustively for our
entertainment. The image of an attractive young woman poisoning
her supper guests is one which the world will not lightly let go.

And what is offered in return? Only the dull statements of people
who chanced to know the lady, and who considered her a model wife
and duchess, a little over-anxious about the education of her numerous children, but kind to the poor, generous to artists, and pitiful to
Jews. "She is graceful, modest, lovable, decorous and devout," wrote
Johannes Lucas from Rome to Ercole, the old Duke of Ferrara. "She
is beautiful and good, gentle and amiable," echoed the Chevalier
Bayard years later. Were we less avid for thrills, we might like to
think of this young creature, snatched at twenty-one from the mael-
strom of Rome, where she had been a pawn in the game of politics,
and placed in a secure and splendid home. The Lucrezia of romance
would have found the court of Ferrara intolerably dull. The Lucrezia
of history took to dullness as a duck to water. She was a sensible,
rather than a brilliant woman, fully alive to the duties and dignities
of her position, and well aware that respectability is a strong card to
play in a vastly disreputable world.

There was a time when Robespierre and Marat made a high bid
for unpopularity. Even those who clearly understood the rehabili-
tation of man in the French Revolution found little to say for its
chosen instruments, whose purposes were high, but whose methods were open to reproach. Of late, however, a certain weariness
has been observable in men's minds when these reformers are in
question, a reluctance to expand with *any* emotion where they are
concerned. M. Lauzanne is, indeed, by way of thinking that the
elemental Clemenceau closely resembles the elemental Robespierre;
but this is not a serious valuation; it is letting picturesqueness run
away with reason—a habit incidental to editorship.

The thoroughly modern point of view is that Robespierre and Marat were ineffective; not without ability in their respective lines, but unfitted for the parts they played. Marat's turn of mind was scientific (our own Benjamin Franklin found him full of promise). Robespierre's turn of mind was legal; he would have made an acute and successful lawyer. The Revolution came along and ruined both these lives, for which we are expected to be sorry. M. Lauzanne does not go so far as to say that the Great War ruined Clemenceau's life. The "Tiger" was seventy-three when the Germans marched into Belgium. Had he been content to spend all his years teaching in a girls' school, he might (though I am none too sure of it) have been a gentler and a better man. But France was surely worth the price he paid. A lifeboat is not expected to have the graceful lines of a gondola.

"Almost everybody," says Stevenson, "can understand and sympathize with an admiral, or a prize-fighter"; which genial sentiment is less contagious now than when it was uttered, thirty years ago. A new type of admiral has presented itself to the troubled consciousness of men, a type unknown to Nelson, unsuspected by Farragut, unsung by Newbolt. In robbing the word of its ancient glory, Tirpitz has robbed us of an emotion we can ill-afford to lose. "The traditions of sailors," says Mr. Shane Leslie, "have been untouched by the lowering of ideals which has invaded every other class and profession." The truth of his words was brought home to readers by the behavior of the British merchant marine, peaceful, poorly paid men, who in the years of peril went out unflinchingly, and as a matter of course, to meet "their duty and their death." Many and varied are the transgressions of seafaring men; but we have hitherto been able to believe them sound in their nobler parts. We should like to cherish this simple faith, and, though alienated from prize fighters by the narrowness of our civic and social code, to retain our sympathy for admirals. It cannot be that their fair fame will be forever smirched by the tactics of a man who ruined the government he served.

The function of criticism is to clear our mental horizon, to get us within close range of the criticized. It recognizes moral as well as intellectual issues; but it differentiates them. When Emerson said,

"Goethe can never be dear to men. His is not even the devotion to pure truth, but to truth for the sake of culture," he implied that truth, besides being a better thing than culture, was also a more lovable thing, which is not the case. It takes temerity to love Goethe; but there are always men—young, keen, speculative, beauty-loving men—to whom he is inexpressibly dear because of the vistas he opens, the thoughts he releases, the "inward freedom" which is all he claimed to give. It takes no less temerity to love Emerson, and he meant that it should be so, that we should climb high to reach him. He is not lovable as Lamb is lovable, and he would not have wanted to be. A man who all his life repelled unwelcome intimacies had no desire to surrender his memory to the affection of every idle reader.

It is such a sure thing to appeal from intelligence to the moral sense, from the trouble involved in understanding to the ease with which judgment is passed, that critics may be pardoned their frequent misapprehensions. Problems of conduct are just as puzzling as problems of intellect. That is why Mr. Stevenson pronounced a sneaking kindness to be "instructive." He offered it as a road to knowledge rather than as a means of enjoyment. Not that he was unaware of the pleasures which follow in its wake. He knew the world up and down well enough to be thankful that he had never lost his taste for bad company.

17

Note to *A Book of Drawings**

If Thackeray's pride lay in authorship, his pleasure lay in artistry. The path of letters was for him an uphill climb; and he escaped from it when he could to dally in the debatable land of palette and easel. He had not been a precocious child, and, beyond a few school-boy rhymes, he showed no disposition to write; but he drew as soon as his little fingers could grasp a pencil. It is characteristic of his boyhood that when Dr. Cornish, vicar of Ottery St. Mary, lent him Cary's translation of the *Birds of Aristophanes*, the only proofs he gave of having read it were three comic drawings in watercolors. It is characteristic of his youth that, having attended Pryme's lectures on political economy at Cambridge, the only proofs he gave of having listened to them were the pen and ink sketches which decorated his syllabus. It is characteristic of his early manhood that the most interesting experience he had to relate of his stay in Germany was the negligible fact that Goethe had glanced at his caricatures.

James Payn, the novelist, used to say that his early love for the classics was little more than hatred of mathematics. Thackeray hated mathematics without ever laying himself open to the imputation of loving the classics; and he hated law with a heartiness which brought his legal studies to a safe and speedy end. On the other

---

* From *A Book of Drawings*, William Makepeace Thackeray, A Series of Metamorphoses made in Philadelphia, 1853, for the children of William B. Reed, The Pennell Club, with a Note by Agnes Repplier, 1925.

hand, the life of an art student in Paris, "the easiest, merriest, dirtiest existence possible," enchanted him. He would have liked to be an artist by profession, and an author for recreation; but destiny and genius were too much for him. *Punch* afforded the best field for his dual gifts, and to *Punch* he clung for years, disliking its politics very often, but loving its fun always. When destiny and genius had won their way, and he stood on the highest reaches of fame, he turned for rest and amusement to his drawing board. Long hours of writing, even after he had nobly mastered his medium, left him spent and weary; but sketching and painting were a pure delight. The fact that he was never known to frame his sketches shows his modest estimate of their worth. He labored strenuously, yet with intense delight, over the illustrations of his stories and novels; and, when he was not so engaged, he drew pictures for his little daughters and for his little daughters' playmates; he enriched his letters with appropriate caricatures; and he made for the children of an American friend the clever, ironic and elaborate drawings which are reproduced for the first time in this little book.

It was an engaging trait of Thackeray's that habits of reserve and a taste for solitude never prevented him from strewing his pathway with friends. During his first visit to the United States in the winter of 1853 he made the acquaintance of Mr. William B. Reed of Philadelphia. An easy intimacy marked their intercourse. Thackeray appears to have felt at home in Mr. Reed's house, and to have greatly fancied his little children. It probably never occurred to him that Reed would print the story of their friendship, which lasted, with interruptions, until the Civil War, in a booklet bearing the dignified title, *Haud Immemor,* which is now rarest of the rare, and a much valued prize for collectors. To read this booklet, a copy of which is in Mr. Geo. J. C. Grasberger's possession, is to see Thackeray through the eyes of a genuinely simple and sentimental man who drew from the great novelist opinions, the like of which he was seldom known to express. When urged, for example, to say what he truly thought of this country, he replied that he delighted in it because, morally, it resembled England. "Firesides like ours, domestic virtues as gentle and as pure."

On the strength of this family likeness, which would have gratified the upholders of Nordic civilization, had the phrase been as current then as now, Reed hoped that Thackeray would accept the post
of British consul in Philadelphia. But the Englishman wanted something besides domestic virtues, however gentle and pure, to vivify
his life. He explained as urbanely as possible that he liked living in
London, and that he also liked the nearness of England to the Continent which enabled him to escape for brief holidays to Switzerland
and Italy. It was from Switzerland that he wrote to Reed three pages
of a letter before discovering that a "rubbishing picture," sketched
carelessly in pen and ink, decorated the fourth page. He apologized
for its presence, and mailed the letter. Pen and ink sketches were
sure to be found if a sheet of paper and a quill lay within Thackeray's
reach. Perhaps some vague recollection of Reed's proposal induced
him a year or two later to seek the secretaryship of the British Lega-
tion in Washington. Happily he did not get it. He was always trying
to sidetrack his genius, and rob the world; and this in spite of the
fact that fortune as well as fame lay waiting for his hand.

When Reed lost his brother, Henry Reed, in the shipwreck of
the "Arctic," September, 1854, Thackeray wrote to him with great
feeling and compassion. A presentation copy of *Esmond* (and the
novelist was chary of presentation copies) found its way to Mrs.
Reed. The two men saw each other familiarly when Thackeray made
his second visit to the United States, and when Reed was in London, after serving as Minister to China, in 1859. This little book
of "sliced" or "combination" drawings[1] (a device very popular seventy-five years ago) survives as a curious token of friendship. The
sketches are worked out with a care and precision which must have
cost both time and trouble. Their satiric quality (noticeable especially in the sickbed picture) was doubtless lost on the children for
whom they were made, and who, in all likelihood, were never permitted to handle anything so precious. Their history since that first
presentation has been a chequered one. Passing from hand to hand,
they were finally given by Mr. George W. Childs to Dr. Charles Fred-

---

1. Drawings of this sort are called by Thackeray *metamorphoses* and this is the technical
name by which they are known. J.P.

erick DaCosta, at the sale of whose books they were purchased by Mr. Grasberger for Mr. William M. Elkins, in whose possession they are now, and who has sanctioned their reproduction.

It has been well said of Thackeray's drawings that they are "literary compositions." They tell their part of the story with sympathetic accuracy, and they have moreover a pleasant fashion of taking the public into their confidence. Becky Sharpe fairly winks at us out of the page, as if to say, "You know the part I play." And we do know it to our inextinguishable delight. The worst in life being compatible with the best in art, Becky has become to her true lovers a solace and a refreshment in the arid wastes of fiction. We only wish that the great moralist who gave her to us had had a more genuine pleasure in her company.

It was true wisdom on Thackeray's part to refrain from illustrating ESMOND. He was able, being a great literary artist, to keep his humor under stern control when writing this masterpiece, because he chose that Esmond should tell the tale, and Esmond is gravity personified. But he could never have been serious and dignified with his pencil. Like Richard Doyle, who so admirably illustrated *The Newcomes*, he was dominated by a spirit of adventurous whimsicality. The flowing lines and stately grouping of George du Maurier are as well adapted to the somber tragedy of *Esmond* as the incurable humor of the *Vanity Fair* illustrations are adapted to that great social satire. If once or twice a type is badly presented—why, for example, should Lord Steyne look like a grocer?—we cannot conceive of Pitt Crawley, or Joseph Osborne, or Miss Pinkerton—of whom but a single satisfying glimpse is vouchsafed us—or the interesting Miss Swartz, as differing by a hairbreadth from their veracious portraits. And the little tail piece of the author sitting cross-legged with mask and jester's bauble at the end of chapter eight is a very demure and perfect embodiment of the spirit of comedy.

For to Thackeray, humor was a moral emancipation, and cynicism a delicate adjustment of reflection to experience. In him the heart of England beat sanely and steadily. He loved great cities, and complex civilizations, and crowded canvases, and the supreme irony of truth. There is a hint of this last conception in his most careless caricatures, and in the toy drawings he made, like these now printed, for the amusement of children. He never heard the aphorism of Santayana: "Everything in nature is lyrical in its ideal essence, tragic in its fate, and comic in its existence"; but he knew these things in his day as well as the philosopher knows them in ours. The knowledge lent wisdom to his pen and gaiety to his pencil. We learn and we laugh, and what better things are there in the world for us to do?

18

Horace*

That a poet should survive two thousand years is not remarkable. Whatever changes two thousand more may bring about, they will not affect the standing of Homer or of Virgil. "*Ce n'est que le premier pas qui coûte.*" If you survive your first thousand, the others will fall into line. But that a poet writing two thousand years ago should today be the helpmate and spokesman of humanity is in the nature of a miracle. It can be accounted for only by the fact that Horace was a man wholly disillusioned, and wholly good-tempered.

No word in our language has been so misused in the past nineteen years as the word "disillusionment." It has come to mean the perpetual grouch of men still deeply resentful that the World War was not in the nature of a garden party, and that the World Peace was not a highway to Utopia. Every crime and every folly have been excused on this ground. Even the kaleidoscopic divorces of Reno, the suspension of privacy, the repeal of reticence, have been accounted for by the disillusionment of youth at the way the world was run when it was too young to run it, as the natural result of a war which saw greater acts of heroism and of supreme self-sacrifice than had ever before purified the souls of men.

---

* From *Eight Decades, Essays and Episodes*, 1937.

The disillusionment of Horace was not of this order. It meant that he had awakened from the noble dreams of youth to the equally noble realities of manhood. He saw life as a whole, and this educational process taught him that it is not easy to find happiness in ourselves, and that it is not possible to find it elsewhere. Reason, moderation, content, a wide mental horizon, a firm foundation of principle—these were the gifts of the gods (and Horace reverenced his gods) to men of good purpose and sobriety.

His upbringing was of the best. His father, though but a freedman who had received his name, Horatius, either because he had been the property of some member of the patrician family of Horatii, or because his birthplace, Venusia, was part of their vast estates in Apulia, was sanely ambitious for his promising young son. He took him to Rome to be educated—an extravagance he could ill afford—provided for him liberally, and watched over him with care. We hear nothing of the mother, so presumably she was dead. Rome was more concerned with the functions of motherhood than was Greece. She could not have endowed the world with her two great gifts, the sanctity of the family and the majesty of the law, she could not have given to it, as she did, a life morally worth the living, if she had not looked sharply after her women, emphasizing their duties rather than their privileges. But she was far from being a matriarchy like the United States. She was not a nation of husbands, but a nation of men. The foundation of the family was the father. He had undisputed authority, unshared responsibility, and often unlimited devotion.

Certain it is that Horace pays a tribute of gratitude to the father who begrudged him nothing that it was in his power to give. He permitted the boy to be freely flogged by his severe master, Orbilius, having the male parent's insensitiveness in this regard; but he protected him alike from folly and from misdoing. "He kept me chaste," wrote Horace in after years, "free from shameful deeds, and from the breath of dishonor."

His Roman schooling over, young Horace was sent to Athens, still the thrice superb teacher of the world; and there, free from his father's restraining hand, he did what all young men of spirit have

done since the beginning of time—he went to the wars. The profit-
less murder of Julius Caesar had brought Brutus to Greece. Horace,
being twenty-two, an age singularly sensitive to oratory, joined the
republican army, and was given the post of military tribune—a circumstance usually mentioned as proof of his talent, but which seems
rather to indicate a shortage of trained soldiers. If we may trust to
his recollections, as embodied in his lines to Pompeius Varus, his
military experiences were not altogether unpleasant. There were
hours of relaxation to compensate for hours of peril:

> Full oft we sped the lingering day,
> Quaffing bright wine as in our tents we lay,
> With Syrian spikenard on our glistening hair.

It is an agreeable picture of campaigning; but the curtain fell on
the desolate field of Philippi. Brutus and Cassius died by their own
hands; and Horace, convinced that his was not a military genius,
profited by the general amnesty to return to Rome.

It was a hard home-coming. His father was dead, his small
estate in Venusia had been confiscated—which was to have been
expected—and he himself was under suspicion as a pardoned
enemy of the state. He had much to live down, and he had much to
build up. He secured his daily bread by working as a scribe in the
quaestor's office, and he began his career as poet. Naturally he began
it by writing satires. What else should a brilliant and bitterly disappointed young man have written? And just as naturally he regretted
many of these satires when time had brought him reason.

We all remember how Byron strove to blot out of existence his
outbreak of ill-temper, "English Bards and Scotch Reviewers," and
how he found out that as soon as English readers discovered they
could no longer get that particular poem they were all possessed
by a desire to have it. Horace would have liked to blot out his early
satires. They were not his métier. The concentrated anger of Juvenal
or of Swift was utterly foreign to his nature. Swift was a great and
powerful humorist, and Juvenal was esteemed a wit; but in their
two souls "rage accumulated like water behind a dam," and burst
into devastating floods. Horace had not even the tenacity of wrath

which made an indifferent poet like Lucilius a fairly great satirist; but in its place he had a gift which was slowly maturing—a balanced and delicate irony, playful but with a rapier's point. The charming picture of country life, simple, serene and self-respecting, which the moneylender, Alfius, contemplates with unction but decides not to live, is a perfect example of the ironical, of the laughter that is so low-pitched it seems—for one mistaken moment—to be kindly. As admirable in its more worldly way is his epistle to the young Tiberius, heir to the throne, introducing a persistent acquaintance who will not be set aside. This is the ninth epistle of the first book. As there are few of us who have not suffered a somewhat similar experience, its study cannot fail to be of service.

In the fifth epode we find the first direful picture of the witch, Canidia, a singularly disgusting person. It is at once the most tragic and the most dramatic poem that Horace ever wrote. Curiously dramatic, for it opens with the outbreak of terrified anger from the patrician child who has been trapped into the witches' den, there to die in slow torment for the better making of a love philter; and it closes with the curse which the doomed boy hurls at his destroyers. Fear has left him, and fury has taken its place. He bids the hags remember that no magic can alter right and wrong, or avert retribution. He, dying at their hands, will pursue them to their shameful deaths. The rabble will pelt them with heavy stones, and fling their unblessed bodies to the wolves:

> This shall my parents see,
> Alas! surviving me.

Horace was always concerned with witches and sorcerers; but the trend of his mind was skeptical. He reached the sane conclusion that they were malignant but impotent.

All this time he was making friends of an agreeable order. The reign of the great Augustus, even the consulship of the great Octavius, was singularly favorable to brilliant young men. Rome was extravagant and immoral; but it was full of artistic and intellectual fervor. Horace's personality was charming, his attainments were remarkable. Virgil, whose own estate had been confiscated and restored, was his intimate companion; and it was Virgil who presented him to Maecenas, the minister and confidential adviser of Octavius. From this introduction and the friendship that followed sprang one of the most perfect interchanges of gifts the world has ever known. Maecenas gave Horace a farm in the Sabine hills, and the very modest independence he desired. Horace gave Maecenas an immortality that can never be disassociated from his own. The more we think about it, the more sure we are that the fates—kindly for once—put these two men in the same place at the same time for the perfecting of their lives.

Augustus would have taken the accomplished young poet for one of his own secretaries, and would in all likelihood have treated him with the generosity he lavished upon Virgil; but Horace, lacking ambition, was not of the stuff out of which good courtiers are made. His political views had undergone a sobering change. He began to understand the mighty mission of Rome; the need of her to hold the western world together; her policy of conciliating and amalgamating conquered nations; her "thrice-hammered hardihood" which nothing human could resist. No pride of citizenship ever equaled hers; and even her politicians still retained some measure of disinterested patriotism. Her monumental achievement, her lasting gift to the world she ruled, as law.

In the strengthening of imperial Rome, Maecenas played an important role. He was of Etruscan descent and a very great gentleman, scholarly, hospitable, public minded. Where the superb basilica of Santa Maria Maggiore now stands, there stood his villa. Thither Augustus when ill had himself carried, to recover in purer air and more spacious quarters than his own palace, simple and plain, afforded him. The self-indulgence of the Roman emperors had no example in him. Since the lamentable Ides of March which saw the murder of Caesar, Maecenas had guided, supported, and restrained Caesar's nephew and heir. Many are the stories told of him, the most characteristic being that of his prompt action in the Forum when Octavius in an unrelenting mood was sentencing one political offender after another to death. Unable to approach the tribune on account of the crowd that surged about it, Maecenas wrote on his tablets, *Surge tandem Carnifex!* ("Butcher, break off!") and flung them straight into the ruler's lap. Octavius read the words, rose silently, and quitted the judgment seat which he had been pronounced unworthy to fill.

Under the protection of Maecenas, Horace lived his life serenely, and his talents ripened to perfection. His lovely odes gave the same delight then that they give now; his Roman soul venerated what was admirable, and strove for what was attainable. He spent the best months of the year in the country, where, unhurried by engagements and unharassed by acquaintances, he wrote with delight and deliberation. Like Marcus Aurelius, he was able to be alone; but he was far too wise to make of himself that lopsided thing called a recluse. He felt with Montaigne the rare delight of dividing his life between the solace afforded him by nature and the stimulus afforded him by men.

It must be admitted that he had uncommon luck in his dealings with both. Most of us could live in stable harmony with nature if our meeting place were a beautiful and fertile corner of Italy. What did Horace know of the malignant nature that rules supreme over wilderness and jungle, desert and swamp? What of disastrous nature hurling tornadoes and dust storms at her helpless children? What of relentless nature that hates a farmer, and sends sodden floods, or blighting droughts, or armies of pestiferous insects, to ruin him? The casual fashion in which the poet alludes to unfavorable weather conditions proves how small a part they played in his life. Not for nothing has Italy been called the sweetheart of the world. Horace's farm was small, thirteen hundred feet above the sea, and surrounded by beautiful woods. It produced corn, olives and vines, though he thought poorly of the wine made from its grapes. It was managed by a bailiff, and cultivated by five families of freedmen. All its owner had to do was to eat and drink its products. He had also eight slaves to wait upon him, and, like most Roman slaves, they had uncommonly little to do. Even his modest meals of pancakes, lentils, and peas were served to him by three young slaves, smiling boys with whom he occasionally conversed. It was what was then called the simple life; but, as compared with the crude and elemental thing which goes by that name in this our land today, it is recognizable as the austere luxury of a very cultivated poet.

Rome, too, had its simplicities as well as its grandeurs. The citizen who stepped from his silken litter into a Roman street might be tripped into the gutter by one of the pigs that, like the happy Plantagenet pigs of London (at a later date), enjoyed unmolested the freedom of the city. Horace preferred on the whole the free and roving pig to the free and roving dog. The pig was at least sane. The dog might be rabid, and snap at him as it ran by. His satires, which grew at once keener and kinder as he approached his thirty-sixth birthday (they were given to the world collectively in 29 B.C.), describe for us the follies and extravagances of Rome; and, as unmitigated seriousness is always out of place in human affairs, these follies and extravagances amuse us as they amused the satirist two thousand years ago, as they must always amuse as well as instruct the student of human nature. It was from Horace that Thackeray learned how to people the canvas of "Vanity Fair." "To Thackeray," says Sir Theodore Martin, "Horace was a breviary."

"Out of Plato," says Emerson, "come all things that are still written or debated among men of thought." And if this be true, we may add one word more. Out of Horace come most things that are still enjoyed and respected by men of feeling. The clear-sighted do not rule the world, but they sustain and console it. It is not in human nature to be led by intelligence. An intelligent world would not be what it is today; it would never have been what it has been in every epoch of which we have any knowledge. Horace had no illusions on this score. He did not pass his life in ignorance of the ills about him. Men lived on their elemental instincts then as now. They wanted to keep what they had, or they wanted to get what their neighbors had, just as they do today. Horace knew this, and he invented no fancy phrases to decorate a bald fact. To understand life was, indeed, a classic form of consolation, a mental austerity which Pope failed to take into account when he wrote:

> Horace still charms with graceful negligence,
> And, without method, talks us into sense.

Yet the little Queen Anne man had a deep admiration for the poet who distilled philosophy from life, and whose counsel of perfection is based upon the feasibility of performance. There was none of Goethe's "negative and skeptical neutrality" about Horace. He knew that Rome was the best possible means for ordering a large fraction of humanity. He knew that discipline at home and invulnerability abroad were necessary for this end. He loved with a passionate intensity of devotion the greatness of Roman traditions, and the memory of the mighty dead. Two notes of admonition he struck. One is in the tenth ode of the second book, where he warns Licinius, and through him all Romans, of the unwisdom of plotting against the state: "Reef your sails while there is yet time." The other is the third ode of the third book, one of the great Alcaics on which the fame of the poet securely rests. In it Juno herself sings the praises and the triumphs of Rome—Rome destined to unite the severed countries of the world, provided only that she paid no heed to her own rabble (Horace and Shakespeare held the same opinion as to the intelligence of mobs), and curbed her own cupidity:

> Riches the hardy soldiers must despise,
>> And look on gold with undesiring eyes.

It is not clear why this ode is held by most commentators to refer to the hidden treasure of Darius (which, by the way, still awaits discovery). It seems to allude merely to the gold which all men knew to be buried deep in mines, and which wise men believed had much better be left there.

"The understanding sadness of Horace," says Edith Hamilton, "tempers the gaiety of his verse into something infinitely endearing." The sobering truth which he bore ever in mind he expressed with customary terseness:

> We may be wise, or rich, or great,
>> But never can be blest.

Therefore he sang unceasingly the praises of sweet content which springs from "those deep regions of self where the issues of character are decided." This tenderness combined with disillusion has made him a helpmate for two thousand years. Cheerfulness and

melancholy can be, and usually are, equally odious; but a sad heart
and a gay temper hold us in thrall. Even the amatory odes, which are
so perfect and so unweighted by passion, have in them an undertone
of regret. Commentators, always immersed in sentiment, have concluded that Cinara was to Horace what Lucy was to Wordsworth—a
lost love and a lasting memory. But all we know is that she died
young, and that Horace regretted with tempered sadness her early
loss:

> I am not the man I was under the reign of Cinara.

Lucy has no rival in the field. Cinara shares the canvas with shy
Chloe, and false Neaera, and forward Glycera, and heartless Barine,
and that accomplished flirt, Pyrrha,

> "Plain in her neatness"

and Lydia, the lady of an ode as fragile and as flawless as a butterfly,
which has been entitled in English "The Reconciliation." It has been
translated by many lovers of Horace, never better perhaps than by
Ben Jonson, though its sentiment is far from the direct and powerful emotions of the Elizabethans and of their immediate successors. It accords with the grace of the cavaliers, the playtime of the
Restoration. Sir Charles Sedley should have translated it. Lovelace
might have written it. Horace opens the dialogue. He is reproachful, but far from downcast, as he reminds Lydia that once he was her
chosen lover. Lydia replies with spirit that when she reigned in his
heart and in his song she asked no happier fate; but that she is not
prepared to play second fiddle to Chloe. Horace admits the impelling
power of Chloe, her sweetness, and her skill with the lyre. Of course
his heart is hers. Lydia, not to be outdone in inconstancy, avows her
love for Calais, Calais the son of Ornytus, a youth so engaging she
would gladly die for him. Horace, an old hand at the game of love,
asks what would happen should he discard bright Chloe, and return
a suppliant to his earlier love. Lydia, in a suspiciously sudden surrender, responds with a cry of joy: though Calais be fairer than a star,
and Horace inconstant and rough as the sea,

> "Yet should I wish to love, live, die with thee."

Horace, like Virgil, remained contentedly unmarried. He had the uneasy married lives of Augustus and of Maecenas by way of warning. His interest in women was an undertone. The stifling problem (it is called a problem) of sex which excites half the world to frenzy, and bores the other half to extinction, resolves itself in his hands into its simplest elements. His great emotions lay elsewhere, and he held even his great emotions in control. The supreme Roman virtue was patriotism—to serve the state and to die for it. Yet in what temperate language Horace clothes his maxims, the very triteness of which proves them immortal. *Dulce et decorum est pro patria mori.* Not a flourish! Not a gesture! Yet life becomes a thing of value and of sweetness because men can renounce it with dignity. And there is nothing in the written history of the world to outstrip Horace's description, in the fifth ode of the third book, of Regulus returning to Carthage: "'Tis said he put away his chaste wife's kisses and his little children, as one bereft of civil rights, and bent his gaze upon the ground till he should strengthen the Senate's wavering purpose by advice never before given, and turn his steps to exile."

Next to the unswerving loyalty to Rome came the love which Horace bore his friends, and, above and beyond all other friends, to Maecenas, whose bread he ate, and whose heart he held in his keeping. "Remember," said the dying Maecenas to the Emperor Augustus, who stood sorrowing by his bedside, "remember Flaccus as you would remember me."

There was no need for this entreaty. In three weeks Horace followed his friend, and was buried by his side on the Esquiline Hill. This was as he had always foretold. "When the blow falls it will crush us both; and to whatever bourne you lead the way, I shall follow." Fifty-seven years the poet had lived, enjoying the ripeness of middle age, and escaping the frosts that ensue. He had achieved the utmost renown that Rome could give. A great lyric poet; a philosopher whose epistles embody all pagan wisdom and a perfect understanding of humanity. The writer of the Secular Hymn had become the arbiter of taste, the spokesman of the Emperor, the persuasive exponent of a reasonable life, the clear, sad thinker who led no man astray. His death was so sudden that he had no time to summon a scribe and dictate a will. Therefore he made it orally, bequeathing his modest estate to the Emperor. Such wills held good in Roman law, where many simplicities survived; but, in view of the uncertainties attendant upon men's recollections, it was wise to leave all to the throne. If ever an oral will was sure to be remembered rightly, it was when Augustus was the heir.

Horace not only reverenced his gods, but he believed that he had been kindly treated by them. He was disposed to see something above and beyond nature in the protection afforded him. When he was a little lost child in the forest, and the leaves drifted upon him as he slept, he felt sure that the birds had covered him, as in later years they covered the hapless Babes in the Wood. The falling tree that grazed but did not harm him, the wolf that turned from his path when he was wandering in the Sabine hills, composing an ode to Lalage—these things did not happen by chance. Maecenas, too, had in his day been snatched from danger; but mighty Jove conceived it his duty to look after Maecenas; whereas

> Pan, who keeps watch
> O'er easy souls like mine,

had turned smiling to the aid of Horace. Therefore it behooves Maecenas to build a shrine and offer tribute; but Horace will sacrifice a young lamb to the sylvan god.

The poet was the most hospitable of men. He dearly loved the companionship of friends; and, having a perfectly correct sense of values, he saw no reason why Maecenas should not leave his stately home, which so far exceeded in splendor the Emperor's palace, and spend his birthday by the Sabine fireside, where Virgil had been content to sit. The preparations for his coming were of a joyous rusticity. Horace does not appear to have had the furniture polished, as when the advocate, Torquatus, came to visit him; but the silver vessels were burnished brightly, garlands were gathered, the altar wreathed with sacred leafage, the kitchen fires roared hospitably, and a jar of Alban wine, nine years old, was waiting to be unsealed. Horace had the poorest possible opinion of water drinkers, and was convinced that not one of them ever wrote a song that lived.

It behooved the poet to be out of the way a goodly portion of his time, because he was too much wanted in Rome. Maecenas wanted him and the Emperor wanted him; and these two august and powerful men thought it right that they should have what they desired. Horace thought otherwise. He clung tenaciously to his liberty, and he achieved it because he stood ready to sacrifice, if need be, all luxuries, comforts, and pleasures for its sake. He would not write his verse and he would not live his life to order. In a very determined and very delicate fashion he makes this known to Maecenas in the seventh epistle of the first book. He has left Rome for a week and he has stayed away a month—greatly to his friend's displeasure. After all, the month was August, and August is a season when anyone would be well advised to stay away from Rome. Horace says so plainly. It is the season, he writes, when the first figs and the mounting sun keep the undertaker busy. His health requires the cooler air, and, what is more important, his soul requires the freedom to make its own choice. "Every man must measure himself by his own rule and standard."

With Augustus the task was more difficult. The Emperor wanted to be sung, and he wanted to be sung in an intimate and homely strain. Horace wrote his most noble odes to celebrate the triumphs of Rome. He wrote charming songs to celebrate the peace and plenty which Augustus ensured to the Romans: "The ox roams the pastures in safety, Ceres makes plentiful the crops, the sea is calm, the shrines are sacred, the home is unpolluted." He also wrote the Secular Hymn at the instigation of the ruler. But that was as far as he would go. He never lessened the distance between the Emperor and the subject. He never affected an easy intimacy with the throne, though Augustus had asked him mockingly if he were ashamed of such a friendship. We cannot conceive him addressing the Caesar as the courtiers of Charles the Second addressed their easygoing monarch. And in all this he was more than worldly-wise. He was safeguarding his own self-respect, and preserving a fine and delicate standard of personal honor.

Of the poet's second home at Tibur we know little save that he loved it, and that it was surpassingly beautiful. The villa probably belonged to Maecenas, who slept more sweetly to the sound of falling waters, and Horace lived in it, off and on, for nineteen years. The Franciscan monks, with that unerring eye for beauty which all the religious orders have displayed, built the monastery of San Antonio on the site of his villa. It stood on the borderland between the Sabine country and the Campagna. Catullus, who lived near by, was wont to say that if his friends wished to mock at him as a rustic, they called him a Sabine. If they wished to imply that he was a gentleman, they called him a Tiburtine.

For Tibur, now Tivoli, is an older city than Rome, and was once its equal. In its earlier phase it was a city of smiths who fashioned and sharpened swords for the perpetual warfare of the day. The surrounding soil is more fertile than in the hill country. It grows better vines and more abundant crops. If Horace missed the Fountain of Bandusia, that leaping cascade which he was wont to climb so far to see, and to whose guardian deity he sacrificed a flower-decked kid, he had in its stead the falling waters of the Anio; the Cascata Grande, not then the torrent it is now, and the lovely Cascatelle streaming down the hillside in broken threads of silver. The orchards of Tibur were wet with spray, and the Tiburtine Sibyl delivered her oracles to the sound of many waters. Even Italy had nothing better to give. Small wonder that Horace wrote with a sigh of content, "May Tibur, founded by Argive wanderers, be the home of my old age and my final goal."

The scholars of the last century believed firmly that the classics offer us both a training for life and a help in living it. This is the hold that Horace has had on humanity, and his fashion of speech is such that educated youth gladly accepts his spokesmanship. We are told that a hundred years ago most public-school boys in England, and almost all Etonians, knew their Horace if they knew nothing else. It was not unusual for a lad of intelligence to have most of the odes by heart. The twentieth century has many new voices (some of them very insistent), but no one of them speaks to us with the accent of Horace. Hugh Macnaghten, for many years a master at Eton, and a translator of the classics, tells us a pleasant story in this regard. In the second year of the World War he had a letter from a former student, Henry Evelyn Platt, then fighting in France. It requested—of all things in the world—a copy of Horace, a small book, "with perhaps a crib for the hard words," and it gave the reason why. Young Platt was one of three Etonians in that line of trenches, and they had recently been joined by a Harrovian who was always quoting Horace. The Etonians were not so preoccupied with the deadly details of their lives as to be indifferent to this challenge. Come what might, they would reread their Horace for their own satisfaction, and for the honor of Eton.

Surely the soul of Horace, wherever it is located, was made glad by that letter. It was just what he had foretold. Death for the pagan was a dismal thing. The bright gods dwelt on Olympus; but they shared their bliss with none, and the realm of Pluto was but a poor exchange for Athens or for Rome. But Horace knew that he would triumph over death. *Non omnis moriar* ("Not all of me shall die"). He spoke as prophets speak, piercing the future. While Rome lived, he would live. "As long as the Pontiff climbs the Capitol with the silent Vestal by his side, I shall be famed, and beyond the boundaries of Rome I shall travel far."

Barbarians unborn my name shall know.

We know it and are glad.

Biographical Sketches

19

The Masterful Puritan*

When William Chillingworth, preaching at Oxford in the first year of England's Civil War, defined the Cavaliers as publicans and sinners, and the Puritans as Scribes and Pharisees, he expressed the reasonable irritation of a scholar who had no taste or aptitude for polemics, yet who had been blown about all his life by every wind of doctrine. Those were uneasy years for men who loved moderation in everything, and who found it in nothing. It is not from such that we can hope for insight into emotions from which they were exempt, and purposes to which they held no clue.

In our day it is generously conceded that the Puritans made admirable ancestors. We pay them this handsome compliment in after-dinner speeches at all commemorative meetings. Just what they would have thought of their descendants is an unprofitable speculation. Three hundred years divide us from those stern enthusiasts who, coveting lofty things, found no price too high to pay for them. "It is not with us as with men whom small matters can discourage, or small discontentments cause to wish themselves at home again," wrote William Brewster, when one half of the Mayflower Pilgrims had died in the first terrible year, and no gleam of hope shone on the survivors. To perish of hunger and cold is not what we should now

* From *Under Dispute*, 1924.

call a "small discontentment." To most of us it would seem a good and sufficient reason for abandoning any enterprise whatsoever. Perhaps if we would fix our attention upon a single detail—the fact that for four years the Plymouth colonists did not own a cow—we should better understand what life was like in that harsh wilderness, where children who could not get along without milk had but one other alternative—to die.

Men as strong as were the Puritan pioneers ask for no apologies at our hands. Their conduct was shaped by principles and convictions which would be insupportable to us, but which are none the less worthy of regard. Matthew Arnold summed up our modern disparagement of their standards when he pictured Virgil and Shakespeare crossing on the Mayflower, and finding the Pilgrim fathers "intolerable company." I am not sure that this would have been the case. Neither Virgil nor Shakespeare could have survived Plymouth. That much is plain. But three months on the Mayflower might not have been so "intolerable" as Mr. Arnold fancied. The Roman and the Elizabethan were strong-stomached observers of humanity. They knew a man when they saw one, and they measured his qualities largely.

Even if we make haste to admit that two great humanizers of society, art and letters, played but a sorry part in the Puritan colonies, we know they were less missed than if these colonies had been worldly ventures, established solely in the interest of agriculture or of trade. Sir Andrew Macphail tersely reminds us that the colonists possessed ideals of their own, "which so far transcended the things of this world that art and literature were not worth bothering about in comparison with them." Men who believe that, through some exceptional grace or good fortune, they have found God, feel little need of culture. If they believe that they share God with all races, all nations, and all ages, culture comes in the wake of religion. But the Puritan's God was a somewhat exclusive possession. "Christ died for a select company that was known to Him, by name, from eternity," wrote the Reverend Samuel Willard, pastor of the South Church, Boston, and author of that famous theological folio, "A Compleat Body of Divinity." "The bulk of mankind is reserved for burning," said Jonathan Edwards genially; and his Northampton congregation took his word for it. That these gentlemen knew no more about Hell and its inmates than did Dante is a circumstance which does not seem to have occurred to any one. A preacher has some advantages over a poet.

If the Puritans never succeeded in welding together Church and State, which was the desire of their hearts, they had human nature to thank for their failure. There is nothing so abhorrent—or so perilous—to the soul of man as to be ruled in temporal things by clerical authority. Yet inasmuch as the colony of Massachusetts Bay had for its purpose the establishment of a state in which all citizens should be of the same faith, and church membership should be essential to freemen, it was inevitable that the preacher and the elder should for a time dominate public counsels. "Are you, sir, the person who serves here?" asked a stranger of a minister whom he met in the streets of Rowley. "I am, sir, the person who rules here," was the swift and apt response.

Men whose position was thus firmly established resented the unauthorized intrusion of malcontents. Being reformers themselves, they naturally did not want to be reformed. Alone among New England colonists, the Pilgrims of Plymouth, who were Separatists or Independents, mistrusted the blending of civil and religious functions, and this mistrust had deepened during the sojourn of their leaders in Holland. Moreover, unlike their Boston neighbors, the Pilgrims were plain, simple people; "not acquainted," wrote Governor Bradford, "with trades nor traffique, but used to a countrie life, and the innocente trade of husbandry." They even tried the experiment of farming their land on a communal system, and, as a result, came perilously close to starvation. Only when each man cultivated his own lot, that is, when individualism supplanted socialism, did they wring from the reluctant soil food enough to keep them alive.

To the courage and intelligence of the Pilgrim and Puritan leaders, Governor Bradford and Governor Winthrop, the settlers owed their safety and survival. The instinct of self-government was strong in these men, their measures were practical measures, their wisdom the wisdom of the world. If Bradford had not made friends with the great sachem, Massasoit, and clinched the friendship by sending Edward Winslow to doctor him with "a confection of many comfortable conserves" when he was ill, the Plymouth colonists would have lost the trade with the Indians which tided them over the first crucial years. If Winthrop had not by force of argument and persuasion obtained the lifting of duties from goods sent to England, and induced the British creditors to grant favorable terms, the Boston colony would have been bankrupt. The keen desire of both Plymouth and Boston to pay their debts is pleasant to record, and contrasts curiously with the reluctance of wealthy States to accept the Constitution in 1789, lest it should involve a similar course of integrity.

It is hardly worth while to censure communities which were establishing, or seeking to establish, "a strong religious state" because they were intolerant. Tolerance is not, and never has been, compatible with strong religious states. The Puritans of New England did not endeavor to force their convictions upon unwilling Christendom. They asked only to be left in peaceful possession of a singularly unprolific corner of the earth, which they were civilizing after a formula of their own. Settlers to whom this formula was antipathetic were asked to go elsewhere. If they did not go, they were sent, and sometimes whipped into the bargain—which was harsh, but not unreasonable.

Moreover, the "persecution" of Quakers and Antinomians was not primarily religious. Few persecutions recorded in history have been. For most of them theology has merely afforded a pious excuse. Whatever motives may have underlain the persistent persecution of the Jews, hostility to their ancient creed has had little or nothing to do with it. To us it seems well-nigh incredible that Puritan Boston should have vexed its soul because Anne Hutchinson maintained that those who were in the covenant of grace were freed from the covenant of works—which sounds like a cinch. But when we remember that she preached against the preachers, affirming on her own authority that they had not the "seal of the Spirit"; and that she "gave vent to revelations," prophesying evil for the harassed and anxious colonists, we can understand their eagerness to be rid of her. She was an able and intelligent woman, and her opponents were not always able and intelligent men. When the turmoil which followed in her wake destroyed the peace of the community, Governor Winthrop banished her from Boston. "It was," says John Fiske, "an odious act of persecution."

A vast deal of sympathy has been lavished upon the Puritan settlers because of the rigors of their religion, the austerity of their lives, their lack of intellectual stimulus, the comprehensive absence of anything like amusement. It has been even said that their sexual infirmities were due to the dearth of pastimes; a point of view which is in entire accord with modern sentiment, even if it falls short of the facts. Impartial historians might be disposed to think that the vices of the Puritans are apparent to us because they were so industriously dragged to light. When all moral offences are civil offences, and when every man is under the close scrutiny of his neighbors, the "find" in sin is bound to be heavy. Captain Kemble, a Boston citizen of some weight and fortune, sat two hours in the stocks on a wintry afternoon, 1656, doing penance for "lewd and unseemly behavior"; which behavior consisted in kissing his wife "publiquely" at his own front door on the Lord's day. The fact that he had just returned from a long voyage, and was moved to the deed by some excess of emotion, failed to win him pardon. Neighbors were not lightly flouted in a virtuous community.

That there were souls unfit to bear the weight of Puritanism, and unable to escape from it, is a tragic truth. People have been born out of time and out of place since the Garden of Eden ceased to be a human habitation. When Judge Sewall read to his household a sermon on the text, "Ye shall seek me and shall not find me," the household doubtless protected itself by inattention, that refuge from admonition which is Nature's kindliest gift. But there was one listener, a terrified child of ten, who had no such bulwark, and who brooded over her unforgiven sins until her heart was bursting. Then suddenly, when the rest of the family had forgotten all about the sermon, she broke into "an amazing cry," sobbing out her agonized dread of Hell. And the pitiful part of the tale is that neither father nor mother could comfort her, having themselves no assurance of her safety. "I answered her Fears as well as I could," wrote Judge Sewall in his diary, "and prayed with many Tears on either part. Hope God heard us."

The incident was not altogether uncommon. A woman of Boston, driven to desperation by the uncertainty of salvation, settled the point for herself by drowning her baby in a well, thus ensuring damnation, and freeing her mind of doubts. Methodism, though gentler than Calvinism, accomplished similar results. In Wesley's journal there is an account of William Taverner, a boy of fourteen, who was a fellow passenger on the voyage to Georgia; and who, between heavy weather and continuous exhortation, went mad with fear, and saw an indescribable horror at the foot of his bed, "which looked at him all the time unless he was saying his prayers."

Our sympathy for a suffering minority need not, however, blind us to the fact that the vast majority of men hold on to a creed because it suits them, and because their souls are strengthened by its ministrations. "It is sweet to believe even in Hell," says that archmocker, Anatole France; and to no article of faith have believers clung more tenaciously. Frederick Locker tells us the engaging story of a dignitary of the Greek Church who ventured, in the early years of faith, to question this popular tenet; whereupon "his congregation, justly incensed, tore their bishop to pieces."

No Puritan divine stood in danger of suffering this particular form of martyrdom. The religion preached in New England was a cruel religion, from which the figure of Christ, living mercifully with men, was eliminated. John Evelyn noted down in his diary that he heard the Puritan magistrates of London "speak spiteful things of our Lord's Nativity." William Brewster was proud to record that in Plymouth "no man rested" on the first Christmas day. As with Bethlehem, so with Calvary. Governor Endicott slashed with his sword the red cross of Saint George from the banner of England. The emblem of Christianity was anathema to these Christians, as was the Mother who bore Christ, and who saw Him die. The children whom He blessed became to Jonathan Edwards "young vipers, and infinitely more hateful than vipers." The sweetness of religion, which had solaced a suffering world, was wiped out. "The Puritans," wrote Henry Adams pithily, "abandoned the New Testament and the Virgin in order to go back to the beginning, and renew the quarrel with Eve."

It took strong men to live and thrive under such a ministration, wrestling with a sullen earth for subsistence, and with an angry heaven for salvation. Braced to endurance by the long frozen winters, plainly fed and plainly clad, in peril, like Saint Paul, of sea and wilderness, narrow of vision but steadfast to principles, they fronted life resolutely, honoring and illustrating the supreme worth of freedom.

That they had compensations, other than religious, is apparent to all but the most superficial observer. The languid indifference to our neighbor's moral and spiritual welfare, which we dignify by the name of tolerance, has curtailed our interest in life. There must have been something invigorating in the iron determination that neighbors should walk a straight path, that they should be watched at every step, and punished for every fall. The Puritan who said, "I will not. Thou shalt not!" enjoyed his authority to the uttermost. The prohibitionist who repeats his words today is probably the only man who is having a thoroughly good time in our fretful land and century. It is hard, I know, to reconcile "I will not. Thou shalt not!" with freedom. But the early settlers of New England were controlled by the weight of popular opinion. A strong majority forced a wavering minority along the road of rectitude. Standards were then as clearly defined as were boundaries, and the uncompromising individualism of the day permitted no juggling with responsibility.

It is not possible to read the second chapter of *The Scarlet Letter*, and fail to perceive one animating principle of the Puritan's life. The townspeople who watch Hester Prynne stand in the pillory are moved by no common emotions. They savor the spectacle, as churchgoers of an earlier age savored the spectacle of a penitent in sackcloth at the portal; but they have also a sense of personal participation in the dragging of frailty to light. Hawthorne endeavors to make this clear, when, in answer to Roger Chillingworth's questions, a bystander congratulates him upon the timeliness of his arrival on the scene. "It must gladden your heart, after your troubles and sojourn in the wilderness, to find yourself at length in a land where iniquity is searched out, and punished in the sight of rulers and people." An unfortunate speech to make to the husband of the culprit (Hawthorne is seldom so ironic), but a cordial admission of content.

There was a picturesque quality about the laws of New England, and a nicety of administration, which made them a source of genuine pleasure to all who were not being judged. A lie, like an oath, was an offense to be punished; but all lies were not equally punishable. Alice Morse Earle quotes three penalties, imposed for three falsehoods, which show how much pains a magistrate took to discriminate. George Crispe's wife who "told a lie, not a pernicious lie, but unadvisedly," was simply admonished. Will Randall who told a "plain lie" was fined ten shillings. Ralph Smith who "lied about seeing a whale," was fined twenty shillings and excommunicated—which must have rejoiced his suffering neighbors' souls.

The rank of a gentleman, being a recognized attribute in those days, was liable to be forfeited for a disgraceful deed. In 1631, Josias Plastowe of Boston was fined five pounds for stealing corn from the Indians; and it was likewise ordered by the Court that he should be called in the future plain Josias, and not Mr. Plastowe as formerly. Here was a chance for the community to take a hand in punishing a somewhat contemptible malefactor. It would have been more or less than human if it had not enjoyed the privilege.

By far the neatest instance of making the punishment fit the crime is recorded in Governor Bradford's *Diary of Occurrences*. The carpenter employed to construct the stocks for the Plymouth colonists thought fit to charge an excessive rate for the job; whereupon he was speedily clapped into his own instrument, "being the first to suffer this penalty." And *we* profess to pity the Puritans for the hardness and dullness of their lives! Why, if we could but see a single profiteer sitting in the stocks, one man out of the thousands who impudently oppress the public punished in this admirable and satisfactory manner, we should be willing to listen to sermons two hours long for the rest of our earthly days.

And the Puritans relished their sermons, which were masterful like themselves. Dogma and denunciation were dear to their souls, and they could bear an intolerable deal of both. An hourglass stood on the preacher's desk, and youthful eyes strayed wistfully to the slender thread of sand. But if the discourse continued after the last grain had run out, a tithingman who sat by the desk turned the glass, and the congregation settled down for a fresh hearing. A three-hour sermon was a possibility in those iron days, while an eloquent parson, like Samuel Torrey of Weymouth, could and did pray for two hours at a stretch. The Reverend John Cotton, grandfather of the redoubtable Cotton Mather, and the only minister in Boston who was acknowledged by Anne Hutchinson to possess the mysterious "seal of the Spirit," had a reprehensible habit of preaching for two hours on Sunday in the meetinghouse (his family and servants of course attending), and at night, after supper, repeating this sermon to the sleepy household who had heard it in the morning.

For a hundred and fifty years the New England churches were unheated, and every effort to erect stoves was vigorously opposed. This at least could not have been a reaction against Popery, inasmuch as the churches of Catholic Christendom were at that time equally cold. That the descendants of men who tore the noble old organs out of English cathedrals, and sold them for scrap metal, should have been chary of accepting even a "pitch-pipe" to start their unmelodious singing was natural enough; but stoves played no part in the service. The congregations must have been either impervious to discomfort, or very much afraid of fires. The South Church of Boston was first heated in the winter of 1783. There was much criticism of such indulgence, and the "Evening Post," January 25th, burst into denunciatory verse:

Extinct the sacred fires of love,
   Our zeal grown cold and dead;
In the house of God we fix a stove
   To warm us in their stead.

Three blots on the Puritans' escutcheon (they were men, not seraphs) have been dealt with waveringly by historians. Witchcraft, slavery and Indian warfare gloom darkly against a shining background of righteousness. Much has been made of the fleeting phase, and little of the more permanent conditions—which proves the historic value of the picturesque. That Salem should today sell witch spoons and trinkets, trafficking upon memories she might be reasonably supposed to regret, is a triumph of commercialism. The brief and dire obsession of witchcraft was in strict accord with times and circumstances. It bred fear, horror, and a tense excitement which lifted from Massachusetts all reproach of dullness. The walls between the known and the unknown world were battered savagely, and the men and women who thronged from house to house to see the "Afflicted Children" writhe in convulsions had a fearful appreciation of the spectacle. That terrible child, Ann Putnam, who at twelve years of age was instrumental in bringing to the scaffold some of the most respected citizens of Salem, is a unique figure in history. The apprehensive interest she inspired in her townspeople may be readily conceived. It brought her to ignominy in the end.

The Plymouth colonists kept on good terms with their Indian neighbors for half a century. The Bay colonists had more aggressive neighbors, and dealt with them accordingly. It was an unequal combat. The malignancy of the red men lacked concentration and thoroughness. They were only savages, and accustomed to episodic warfare. The white men knew the value of finality. When Massachusetts planned with Connecticut to exterminate the Pequots, less than a dozen men escaped extermination. It was a very complete killing, and no settler slept less soundly for having had a hand in it. Mr. Fiske says that the measures employed in King Philip's War "did not lack harshness," which is a euphemism. The flinging of the child Astyanax over the walls of Troy was less barbarous than the selling of King Philip's little son into slavery. Hundreds of adult captives were sent at the same time to Barbados. It would have been more merciful, though less profitable, to have butchered them at home.

The New England settlers were not indifferent to the Indian's souls. They forbade them, when they could, to hunt or fish on the Lord's day. John Eliot, Jonathan Edwards, and other famous divines preached to them earnestly, and gave them a fair chance of salvation. But, like all savages, they had a trick of melting into the forest just when their conversion seemed at hand. Cotton Mather, in his

Magnalia, speculates ruthlessly upon their condition and prospects. "We know not," he writes, "when or how these Indians first became inhabitants of this mighty continent; yet we may guess that probably the Devil decoyed these miserable savages hither, in hopes that the Gospel of the Lord would never come to destroy or disturb his absolute Empire over them."

Naturally, no one felt well disposed towards a race which was under the dominion of Satan. Just as the Celt and the Latin have small compunction in ill-treating animals, because they have no souls, so the Puritan had small compunction in ill-treating heathens, because their souls were lost.

Slavery struck no deep roots in New England soil, perhaps because the nobler half of the New England conscience never condoned it, perhaps because circumstances were unfavorable to its development. The negroes died of the climate, the Indians of bondage. But traders, in whom conscience was not uppermost, trafficked in slaves as in any other class of merchandise, and stoutly refused to abandon a profitable line of business. Moreover, the deep discordance between slavery as an institution and Puritanism as an institution made such slave-holding more than ordinarily odious. Agnes Edwards, in an engaging little volume on Cape Cod, quotes a clause from the will of John Bacon of Barnstable, who bequeathed to his wife for her lifetime the "use and improvement" of a slavewoman, Dinah. "If, at the death of my wife, Dinah be still living, I desire my executors to sell her, and to use and improve the money for which she is sold in the purchase of Bibles, and distribute them equally among my said wife's and my grandchildren."

There are fashions in goodness and badness as in all things else; but the selling of a worn-out woman for Bibles goes a step beyond Mrs. Stowe's most vivid imaginings.

These are heavy indictments to bring against the stern forbears whom we are wont to praise and patronize. But Pilgrim and Puritan can bear the weight of their misdeeds as well as the glory of their achievements. Of their good old English birthright, "truth, pitie, freedom and hardiness," they cherished all but pitie. No price was too high for them to pay for the dignity of their manhood, or for the supreme privilege of dwelling on their own soil. They scorned the line of least resistance. Their religion was never a cloak for avarice, and labor was not with them another name for idleness and greed. Eight hours a day they held to be long enough for an artisan to work; but the principle of giving little and getting much, which rules our industrial world today, they deemed unworthy of freemen. No swollen fortunes corrupted their communities; no base envy of wealth turned them into prowling wolves. If they slew hostile Indians without compunction, they permitted none to rob those who were friendly and weak. If they endeavored to exclude immigrants of alien creeds, they would have thought shame to bar them out because they were harder workers or better farmers than themselves. On the whole, a comparison between their methods and our own leaves us little room for self-congratulation.

From that great mother country which sends her roving sons over land and sea, the settlers of New England brought undimmed the sacred fire of liberty. If they were not akin to Shakespeare, they shared the inspiration of Milton. "No nobler heroism than theirs," says Carlyle, "ever transacted itself on this earth." Their laws were made for the strong, and commanded respect and obedience. In Plymouth, few public employments carried any salary; but no man might refuse office when it was tendered to him. The Pilgrim, like the Roman, was expected to serve the state, not batten on it. What wonder that a few drops of his blood carries with it even now some measure of devotion and restraint. These were men who understood that life is neither a pleasure nor a calamity. "It is a grave affair with which we are charged, and which we must conduct and terminate with honor."

20

On the Banishing of Tea from the English Colonies of America Being a Digression[*]

"**D**etested tea!" That is what an obstinate king, a stupid cabinet, and an angry populace had made of this blameless and beneficent herb. Its long service, the friendly intercourse it had promoted, were forgotten. It had become a tool in the hands of the oppressor, who had chosen it because of the esteem in which it had been rightly held.

The colonists on the Atlantic seaboard were tea drinkers like their English forbears. They were also tea-smugglers like their English forbears. The taxed East India article was an expensive luxury, and the Dutch stood ever ready to undersell it in the American market. Trevelyan says that Thomas Hancock, uncle of John Hancock and a staunch Tory, made a fair fortune by importing smuggled tea from Holland, and supplying it to the mess tables of the British army and navy. He is also our authority for the excessive use of tea in the colonies prior to 1773. "The most portable, as well as the most easily prepared of beverages, it was drunk in the backwoods of America as it is drunk today in the Australian bush. In more settled districts, the quantity absorbed on all occasions of ceremony is incredible to a generation which has ceased to mourn in large companies and at great cost. Whatever the gentlemen, who rode or drove into a

---

[*] From *To Think of TEA!*, 1932.

funeral from thirty miles around, were in the habit of drinking, the ladies drank tea. The very Indians, in default of something stronger, drank it twice a day."

It had its enemies—it has never lacked them; and stout advocates of beer and cider found little in it to commend. What need had John Adams, who drank a tankard of hard cider every morning, for an infusion of China leaves! It was denounced as a "base exotick," as "rank poison, far-fetched and dear bought." But "tea-tables" came into use as early as 1712, the "long table" being held too formal for such an intimate form of entertainment. Judge Sewell, to whom few things to eat or drink came amiss, was a lover of tea; and he observed with pleasure that Madame Winthrop served it in her house after a lecture, a combination than which nothing could be more modern. In New York, where the water supply was notoriously bad, there was a famous "Tea-water Pump," the outpourings of which were sold by the barrel to people rich enough to be fastidious. In Albany everybody drank tea for breakfast when the Swedish naturalist, Kalm, visited that town in 1749. Coffee was rare, "chuchaletto" was rarer, and the poor contented themselves with beer, which he feelingly characterizes as "very small."

This was the right and happy state of affairs when there entered into the mind of Lord North and his colleagues the unholy design of cajoling the colonies into paying a three-pence duty on tea by taking off the heavy British tax, and so making it cheaper, as well as better, than the smuggled tea from Holland. "They have no idea," wrote Franklin, "that any people can act from any other principle but that of interest; and they believe that three-pence on a pound of tea, of which one does not perhaps drink ten pounds in a year" (a generous allowance) "is sufficient to overcome the patriotism of an American."

"They" were mistaken. That trumpery three-pence was the match which ignited the revolutionary fire. It was as dear to the king's heart as it was abhorrent to the hearts of the colonists. It was in itself of no value to the British treasury, and it represented no appreciable loss to American tea drinkers. Only as representing a cause, it assumed an enormous importance to both sides; and it dragged into the con-

flict the harmless, necessary tea, which, with the harmless, necessary cat, made up the sweet content of the domestic hearth.

This is evidenced by the language employed in patriotic protests.
Tea had become that "worst of plagues," and was denounced accordingly. Thomas Hutchinson tells us that prior to the Revolution some
of the most determined "friends of liberty" were importers of tea
from England; but they stood ready to sacrifice their interests in the
cause of freedom. It was of absolute importance that women should
be induced to forego their wonted indulgence, and they responded
nobly to the call. In Boston three hundred "Mistresses of Families"
pledged themselves to banish tea from their own tables, and to refuse
to drink it when it was offered at the tables of their acquaintances.
One lady, with a turn for *vers libre*, printed a farewell to her

> Cups and saucers, cream jug, sugar tongs,
> And pretty tea-chest also.

One hundred young girls promised to follow the example set by
the matrons. Even children, who drank nothing but milk, engaged
joyously to give up tea as soon as they were old enough to have
a voice in the matter. Students of Harvard College—or a goodly
number of them—resolved to use no more of the "pernicious herb"
(pernicious herb!) until the tax was lifted.

The *Boston Evening Post* gave loud praise to these patriotic
pledges. "The wise and virtuous part of the Fair Sex in Boston and
other Towns," it said proudly, "are sensible that by the consump-
tion of Teas they are supporting the Commissioners and other Tools
of Power. They have voluntarily agreed not to give or receive any
further Entertainments of that Kind until such Creatures, together
with the Boston Standing Army, are removed, and the Revenue Acts
repealed."

From the South came protests as emphatic as those voiced by
the North. There were, for example, the fifty-one ladies of Edenton,
North Carolina, who, under the leadership of Mrs. Penelope Barker,
three times married and three times widowed, bound themselves
solemnly to refuse "to Conform to the Pernicious Custom of Drinking Tea, until such time that all Acts which tend to enslave our

Native Country shall be repealed." Their lead was followed by other Southern towns; and the movement became so strong that we find Mercy Warren, wife of James Warren of Massachusetts, and author of a *History of the American Revolution*, sending to John Winthrop some satiric lines in which she strives to make clear to him how hard it was for women to sacrifice their tea:

> For if 'twould save the nation from the curse
> Of standing troops—or name a plague still worse,
> Few can this choice, delicious draught give up,
> Though all Medea's poison fill the cup.

They did give it up with abrupt completeness, and they helped to set the scene for the great drama that was shortly to be played. When word came over the sea that ships were bringing the taxed tea to four American ports, New York, Boston, Philadelphia, and Charleston, steps were promptly taken to prevent its landing. The first meeting was held in Philadelphia, when resolutions were adopted asking the consignees to refuse to accept the tea, and furthermore declaring that any man who should assist in unloading or receiving it was to be ranked as an enemy to his country. That settled the matter so far as Philadelphia was concerned. The consignees were reasonable men who knew a stone wall when they saw one. The ships came and the ships went; the good tea was spared to be "some man's delight"; and King George and Lord North were so far thwarted in their fell design.

New York and Charleston had little more trouble. Indeed, kind winds blew some of the ships off the coast, and made New York's resistance easier. In Charleston the tea was unloaded, but never received. It was left to rot in a damp vault—a regrettable circumstance. Only in Boston were the consignees—two of them sons of Governor Hutchinson—sufficiently stiff-necked, or stout-hearted, to refuse compliance with the people's will. They were ready to promise that the tea should not be sold without the consent of the governor and council; but that was as far as they would go. Honor and honesty, they said, compelled them to receive and to store it.

It was a time tense with excitement. The letters of Anne Hulton, sister of Henry Hulton, Commissioner of Customs in Boston, give us an agitated account of life in the throes of rebellion. The lady was loyalist to the core, and deeply outraged by the violent demonstrations of the mob. On the 25th of November she writes to an English friend:

> The Ships Laden with Tea from the East India House are hourly expected. The people will not suffer it to be landed in Boston. They demand the Consignees to promise to send it back. Mr. Clark resolutely refuses to comply, and will submit to no other terms than to put it into a warehouse till he can hear from England. They threaten to tear him into pieces if it Lands. He says he will be tore to pieces before he will desert the Trust reposed in him by the Consigners. His Son, who is just arrived from England, and all the family were got together the first night, rejoicing at his Arrival, when the Mob surrounded the House, attacked it with stones and clubs, and did great damage to the windows and furniture. Young Clark spoke to them, and told them if they did not desist, he should certainly fire at them; which he did, and wounded one of them, it is supposed, for they retreated, carrying off a man. A great number of stones, each one so large as to have killed any person it had hit, were thrown about the Table where the family were at supper; but Providence directed them so that they did not fall on anyone. All the avenues to the House were guarded by armed Men to prevent Mr. Clark escaping. This was beyond anything of the kind since we came here.

It was bad enough, but worse in words than in deeds. The mob used an ugly threat, and Mr. Clark was oratorically defiant; but such a crime as that which forever shames the Hague was happily impossible in Boston. The crisis was met and settled in a fashion serious and decisive, yet of a sportiveness which makes it pleasant reading for young Americans today. The fifty men who rushed the wharf where the three tea ships lay side by side were well disguised. Hutchinson describes them as "covered with blankets, and making the appearance of Indians." John Andrews says that they were "cloathed in Blankets, with their heads muffled, and copper-color'd countenances, being each armed with a hatchet or axe, and a pair of pistols." Protected by a large and friendly crowd, they went to work with a will; and, in less than three hours, three hundred and forty-two chests of good tea, valued at ten thousand pounds, had been lifted from the holds, and their contents emptied into the incurious sea. Great secrecy was observed. Friends and relatives, employers and employed, worked side by side with no more words than were needed; and when their task was done they went quietly to their homes, without making or receiving confidences. Many of them were well known, but by common consent there was no naming of names.

What followed needs no telling. Boston port was closed, the charter of Massachusetts was annulled, war was on, and Americans drank no tea. On this score at least there is little call for commiseration. They continued to speak of it with anger as though it had taxed itself for their discomfiture. John Andrews called it "the baneful herb," and nobody saw anything illogical in this designation. It is on record that John Adams, being for once in no mood for cider, asked at a tavern: "Is it lawful for a weary traveller to refresh himself with a dish of tea, provided it has been honestly smuggled, and has paid no duty?" To which the landlord's daughter made stern reply: "No sir! We have renounced tea under this roof. But, if you desire it, I will make you some coffee."

The only people who wanted their tea were the loyalists, and its loss was but a small part of their growing discomfiture. Miss Hulton, whose letters are informative, wrote that after the sinking of the chests, Boston quieted down, though the unfortunate consignees remained under the protection of the military at the castle, and were not allowed to return to their homes. She was naturally divided between her sentiments of loyalty to king and crown and her interests which were endangered by England's wrathful reprisals. The closing of Boston port she considered would "probably end in the total ruin of the Town and the Individuals." Trade was already paralyzed, and ruin stared merchants in the face. The thing to be feared, however, beyond all else was the ultimate triumph of the American arms; and her reasons for fearing it had the peculiar irrelevancy of an electioneering address today. "If we now submit," she wrote feelingly, "our lands will be taxed, Popery introduced, and we shall be slaves forever. My Brother says the ways of Heaven are dark and intricate."

Trevelyan is of the opinion that the spirited rejection of tea before and during the American Revolution must be held responsible for its inferior position in the United States today, coffee having so far supplanted it in public favor. But other causes brought about its downfall. When the descendants of the English tea-drinkers were overwhelmed by heavy tides of emigration, and dwindled to so pitiful a minority that, as an immigrant author tauntingly observed, they could not swing an election, the drink of their forefathers dwindled with them. For years the Irish kept it going; but the Irish failed to hold what they had gained, and America became the great melting-pot of the world. What was the delicate distinction of tea to these massed invaders, for whom it held no significance, no pleasant memories, and no delight. Anybody can drink and love coffee. It is a generous and thoroughly democratic little bean. If, as Pope avers,

it makes the politician wise, And see through all things with his half-shut eyes,

it also starts the laborer on his day's work, is drunk by the gallon in modest eating places throughout the day, and is given to the unhappy poor who are compelled to ask for charity.

Perhaps, indeed, the imitation teas, which were drunk with pretended enthusiasm during the struggle for liberty, gave to real tea a bad name which was not lightly shaken off. It is pathetic to read the list of substitutes which were highly praised in patriotic journals, and timidly dispensed at patriotic tables. There was Liberty Tea, made from the four-leaved loosestrife, which was sold for sixpence a pound, and which seems to have been held in a sort of abhorred esteem. There was Hyperion or Labrador Tea, described in highly imaginative advertisements as having been first brewed by the Indians, borrowed from them by the Canadians, and now triumphantly established in favor "among people of all ranks." There was Balm Tea, the name of which was enough to condemn it, and teas made of ribwort, currant leaves and sage. There were in fact so many accommodating plants pressed into service that we begin to understand George Meredith's story of the old man who was seen gathering weeds on the outskirts of Brussels, and who, being asked what he was picking, answered simply, "Tea for the English."

All this time the loyalists drank China tea when they could get it. Ruinously dear, and sold secretly under the disguise of snuff or tobacco, it grew more precious year by year, as representing a sentiment and an indulgence, both hidden from the world. Miss Hulton alludes casually to drinking it with a friend in 1776. Alice Morse Earle quotes Abbé Robin as saying that the "Revolutionary soldiers" were able to endure military flogging because of their use of tea. But apart from the painfulness of the association and the doubtfulness of the result, one fails to see where, when, or how the Revolutionary soldiers got tea. They would have been the last men in America to achieve a forbidden luxury; and it is sheerly impossible to imagine them braced and fortified by raspberry leaves.

From Mrs. Earle we get proof positive that when the United States became the United States, tea drinking was already on the wane. The "baneful herb" was no longer consumed by the gallon at public gatherings. An election dinner was of course a strictly masculine and confessedly jovial event. Guests were expected to drink themselves into maudlin enthusiasm, and this could not be done on tea. But Mrs. Earle gives us the tavern-keeper's bill for a presumably austere festival—the ordination of the Reverend Joseph McKean in Beverly, Massachusetts, 1785. It appears to have been an all-day affair, including a light luncheon and a dinner. There were eighty guests in the morning, and sixty-eight in the afternoon. The eighty luncheon guests, assisted, let us hope, by a few outsiders, consumed thirty bowls of punch and ten bottles of wine "before they went to meeting." The dinner guests, sixty-eight valiant souls out of the original eighty, consumed, "while at table," forty-four bowls of punch, eight bowls of brandy, eighteen bottles of wine, and one shilling's worth of cherry rum. At the bottom of this formidable bill appears the modest item: "Six people drank tea—9d." Falstaff's half-pennyworth of bread looms large and lordly by its side.

21

The End of an Era*

If the destruction of the California missions was swiftly accomplished, it had been long impending. Two things bring ecclesiastical institutions into disfavor. If they are poor, they become a burden
and a grievance. If they are rich, they incite cupidity. According to
the simple standards of the time and place, the missions were rich;
not rich like the English monasteries looted so lustily by Henry VIII,
but fat and prosperous. The Pious Fund, though nibbled at from
year to year by hungry officials, was still big enough to be eyed with
envy. After the independence of Mexico had been established, Governor José María de Echeandía proposed that the fund should bear
the cost of secularizing the missions, a sublimely ironical suggestion. In 1842 the Mexican Congress, at the request of General Santa
Anna, confiscated all the money that was left and all the property,
and ordered it to be transferred to the national treasury "as a loan."
Which rang the curtain down.

An impelling motive in modern revolutions is confiscation. It
is not prattled about on platforms, but it is understood and deeply
appreciated. Not only land, not only buildings, not only securities and bank accounts, but every kind of "portable property" is
snatched at by revolutionaries. Have we not seen the loot of a pal-

---

* From *Junípero Serra: Pioneer Colonist of California*, 1933.

ace, secured by a singularly callous murder, exposed for sale in the capitals of Europe?

The Mexican insurgents would have been strangely unlike their kind if they had not coveted the mission lands. The California insurgents, who in turn declared themselves free of Mexico, were largely stirred by the same animating purpose; but they were late in the field. Both parties had a perfectly good and reasonable case to present to the world. The Indians were to be released from bondage. A modicum of land, with the necessary equipment, was to be assigned to each and all. They were to raise their own crops, live their own lives, and be free and self-respecting citizens. Here and there churches were to be open for their service. Something—very vaguely stated—was to be done for the maintenance of such friars as remained at their posts; perhaps a field or so reserved for their use (nine acres, for example, out of two thousand at San Carlos); but the livestock, the stored grain, the mills, the warehouses, everything that was remunerative outside the church walls was sold to fill the yawning pockets of patriots.

What happened was inevitable; but it came to pass more quickly than even the least sanguine observer had anticipated. Perhaps the missionaries' system was ill adapted to the training of citizens. Perhaps nobody really expected that the Indians would respond to the incentive of independence, and become industrious, sober, and frugal. Idleness was in their blood; irresponsibility had been fostered by their training. The Franciscans, while enforcing systematic labor, had been careful never to overwork their wards, and to give them recreation and holidays. Now it became imperative for them to extract a living out of their land, and to do this with one wife apiece, which was manifestly absurd. Their forefathers had had all the land they wanted, and wives enough to do the necessary work; they themselves had always been sure of their dinners; but in this comfortless freedom, which they had never sought or desired, nothing was secure. There was neither help nor direction.

Then came the discovery that liberty was more than a name. They were free to sell their few acres for a few dollars. Gamblers and spendthrifts (but not as a rule drunkards until after the American occupation), those few dollars yielded a brief delight, followed by the direst want. The friars had no place to shelter them, no food to give them. Other friends they had none. The amazing thing is the speed with which they died. They had always been a delicate race. That toughness of fiber which made the five Iroquois tribes a lasting wonder to the French *habitants* had no counterpart among the California Indians. Even in the missions the death rate was high, which accounts for the crowded churchyards. Under the new conditions they wandered away or fell by the roadside, and no one mourned their going. Of the thirty thousand natives, sober, temperate, and reasonably industrious, who filled the missions in 1810, hardly three thousand were left by the middle of the century. The survivors were the least fortunate of their race.

Here and there groups of Indians held together and made a pathetic effort to live. In the Temecula valley, which had belonged to San Luis Rey, two hundred of them farmed the fertile land. The valley was part of a Mexican grant, and in it there was the vaguely worded clause "without injury to the natives," which was supposed to protect them from molestation. It did protect them until 1869, when the property was sold to American purchasers who insisted upon their withdrawal. It was a repetition on a small scale of the story of the Cherokee Indians in Georgia. The Temecula farmers had no such gallant defender as John Marshall; but an effort was made to save them from eviction. It was as useless as Marshall's effort to save the Cherokees. The American claim was based on grants made by Governor Micheltorena in 1844. The clause in the old grant offered no defense. The Indians were told to go, and advised to go quietly. They built a refugee village three miles away, in a spot so bare and waterless that no white man would live there. The industry of the women, who wove baskets and made the Mexican drawnwork which had been taught them in the mission, earned a scanty subsistence. The word "temecula" became in the Indian speech a synonym for grief.

A few words about the missions in general are essential to an understanding of this historic episode. They were founded in the spirit of faith and charity. They were carried on with unremitting zeal and unexampled success. They held within themselves the seeds of decay because they represented a fixed period in a changing world. A benevolent despotism was an anomaly in the eighteenth century; it was inconceivable in the nineteenth. America was to tolerate slavery for another half-century, but only as an economic necessity. Benevolence was a side issue.

That the missions ran less smoothly in their later years may be conceded. How could they fail to do so when their existence was perpetually threatened? From the time that the Mexican republic was established, it never ceased its efforts at secularization. Two things only stood in its way: the amazing but none the less undeniable reluctance of the Indians to be emancipated, and the oft-repeated fact that seven eighths of the country's produce was raised in the missions. Their dissolution would mean the collapse of industry and trade.

The friars, recognizing the insecurity of their position, were the readiest taxpayers known to history. They had long been generous purveyors. Between 1801 and 1810, the missions furnished the *presidios* with food and supplies valued at eighteen thousand dollars. Later on they met endless exactions with equanimity. They supported the troops kept originally for their defense. They paid a per-capita tax on every Indian they harbored. By 1820 the outstanding drafts amounted to four hundred thousand dollars. All this should have made them reasonably safe; but we know that the original goose that laid the golden egg never failed of its duty until the farmer cut it open to reach the accumulated store.

The nineteenth century brought many travelers to the hitherto unvisited California, and we have the testimony of all of them concerning the practical utility of the missions, and of the spirit of kindness that prevailed. The most valuable commendation, because the most reluctantly spoken, is that of Alexander Forbes, who spent the greater part of the year 1832 on the Pacific coast, and whose *History of Upper and Lower California* was written in 1835. Forbes disapproved on principle of priests and priest-craft. His dislike of American Protestant missionaries, about whom he seems to have known very little, was more intense than his dislike of the Franciscan friars about whom he came to know a great deal. Of their system he speaks with disfavor; of its results with a sort of stupefied admiration. Men, and especially priests, who have undue authority ought to grow tyrannical. These priests did not. Men who are held in subjection ought to grow dissatisfied. These Indians did not. Theoretically, everything was wrong; practically, everything came right. Forbes cannot account for this irregularity, and he is not to be cajoled for a minute into thinking that singing hymns before an image of the Virgin Mary is true religion. Nevertheless, he bears witness to what his eyes have seen:

> Considering the absolute and irresponsible authority possessed by the missionaries, their conduct has been marked by a degree of humanity, moderation, and benevolence unexampled in any other situation. There are few instances to be found where men, enjoying such unlimited confidence and power, have not abused them. Yet the missionaries of California neither betray their trust nor show themselves unworthy of confidence. On the contrary, there are many proofs of their zeal, industry, and philanthropy. Since the country has been opened up, strangers have found in their missions disinterested hospitality and kindness.

As for the Indians—simple creatures whom the friars have snatched from the enjoyment of freedom, and have turned into "superstitious, pusillanimous slaves," they showed nothing but gratitude for the wrong that had been done them.

> Their mode of life accords too well with the native indolence of their character, and with their total lack of independent spirit. Their labor is light, and they have leisure to waste in their beloved inaction, or in the pastimes of their aboriginal state. They venerate their masters with an affectionate fervor approaching to adoration. When, as has recently happened, priests have been removed for political reasons, the distress of the Indians at parting with them has been extreme. They have entreated with tears and lamentations to be allowed to follow them in their exile. There never was a more perfect resemblance between a pastor and his disciples and a shepherd and his flock.

Other travelers, a trifle less serious and a good deal less polemical than Forbes, have emphasized the wise management of the missions and their enviable prosperity. Alfred Robinson, an American
who came to California in 1829 and remained there several years,
witnessed the first secularization and was greatly disgusted thereby;
partly because he deemed it "a policy of plundering and permitting plunder," and partly because he had enjoyed the hospitality of
the friars. The orchards of San Buenaventura had yielded him good
fruit; the monastery of San Luis Rey, then under the guardianship
of Fray Antonio Peyri, whom all wayfarers praised, had afforded
him pleasant quarters. The sudden increase of prices under the new
conditions deepened his dissatisfaction. It was naturally annoying
to a Yankee to be charged forty dollars for the rent of horses which
the liberal missionaries had let him have for six.

Robinson considered the Indians to be clever workmen and poor
dancers. He had the good fortune to see a Nativity play on Christmas
Day at San Diego, and was somewhat scandalized at its being given
in the church. It was of course acted by Indians, six of whom represented shepherds, and a seventh the angel Gabriel, who announced
to them the birth of Christ and bade them hasten to seek him. Then
came Lucifer, who strove with specious arguments to hold them back;
while the comic relief (faithful to the tradition of such dramas) was
supplied by a lazy vagabond who sought nothing but his own comfort. Gabriel, as discursive as Raphael in *Paradise Lost,* but a good
deal less melodious, routed Lucifer, and sent the simple shepherds
singing a Christmas hymn to the "courtly stable" of Bethlehem.

Americans were not California's only visitors. Von Langsdorff,
scholar and diplomat, who accompanied Rezanoff to San Francisco,
and who, speaking no Spanish, was obliged to converse with the
friars in Latin, had praise for everything but the wine. That he considered to be thin. But he warmly commended the thrift and intelligence everywhere evidenced, the great herds of cattle (hides were
an important source of revenue), and the open-handed welcome
accorded to strangers. He thought the Indian women more industrious and intelligent than the men, who danced better than they
ploughed; but all alike were docile and content.

The French *voyageur,* Duflet de Mofra, who saw the missions when they had but a few more years of life, has left us a minute account of their domestic economy and of their flourishing commerce: "When the hides, tallow, grain, and oil are sold to traders, the friars distribute cloth, tobacco, handkerchiefs, cutlery, and trinkets among the Indians. The surplus they devote to the replenishing of farms and the embellishment of churches. Like good husbandmen, they are careful to keep a part of the harvest in the granaries to provide for a bad season."

It is always the same story. Even young Richard Dana, who spent most of his "Two Years Before the Mast" sailing along the Pacific coast, has added a word of evidence. He was well fed at the missions, he was badly fed elsewhere. The best of the hides which it was his business to collect, and which he calls "California's banknotes," came from San Juan Capistrano. Indians had them in charge, and helped him with the transportation. The beauty of the spot so impressed the Massachusetts lad, familiar with Newport and Nahant, that he declared it to be the loneliest and loveliest site that he had ever seen.

If its loneliness and its loveliness availed it little, if darkness was closing down over the California missions, and ruin and death awaited their neophytes, who shall say that the work was done in vain? Man has only the present in which to live his life, and he must make what use of it he can. Junípero Serra, pioneer and missionary, loaded every rift with ore, witnessed the rich reward of his labor, and left the development—necessarily—to fate. We have a curiously distinct picture of him at each and every step of his progress. Serra joyfully abandoning the old world for the new. Serra defying his lameness and reaching San Diego in triumph. Serra praying all night by the sea, and holding back Portolá's flight by sheer determination. Serra pleading before the *Junta* for justice to his missions. Serra planting the cross nine times in the wilderness. Serra profoundly spiritual and undeviatingly practical. Serra humblest and stubbornest of men. Serra consumed by a desire to save souls for heaven, but always mindful of man's bodily needs. Serra living under the shadow of the cross, and holding in his heart the maxim of Saint Theresa:

Tout passe;
Dieu seul.

22

The Silencing of Laughter*

If illiteracy be sufficient to ensure cheerfulness, then Elizabeth's England has a right to be called, as it always is called, "merry." When people say "merry England," they refer, as a rule, to her great and glorious reign. They have Spenser's warrant for so doing:

Saint George of merry England, the sign of victoree.

When Sir Edward German wrote a gay little opera which has been successfully revived, and called it *Merrie England*, the audience expected to see, and did see, the court of the Virgin Queen. It was not a merry court (merry courts have been few and far between), and the land it dominated was not a merry land; but reading and writing cannot be held responsible for its uneasiness. We have Sir Thomas More's word for it that in his day one half of England's inhabitants were unacquainted with their letters; and the disturbing march of education had gone but a little way in the succeeding half century. If Judith Shakespeare could not sign her name, we have no reason to suppose that universal book learning—unkindly deprecated by Mr. Lang—was sowing the seeds of unrest.

We are so dazzled by the glory of Elizabeth's England that we never look beyond the row of glittering names. We rightly consider that a country that had Shakespeare had enough. The greatest pos-

* From *In Pursuit of Laughter*, 1936.

session in the world was hers, and hers to keep. She had also the most perfect possession in the world, Sir Philip Sidney. She had a battered little ship called the *Golden Hind,* which was the first English vessel to circumnavigate the world, and which was carefully preserved as a monument to the greatest mariner in the world, Sir Francis Drake. She had statesmen as astute and as unscrupulous as any on earth; and she had gentlemen adventurers more brave and more unscrupulous than any on the seas. She had the first public theater ever built in London, and she had great plays acted on its boards. She had natural loveliness unsurpassed and unpolluted—"the garden of God," said John Speed. She had even the precious boon, tobacco, though she did not fully understand the value of the gift. She had much that was better worth having than laughter; but she did not laugh spontaneously, and she had already begun the serious cultivation of mirth. The *Hundred Merry Tales,* dull enough for the most part, represent an earnest endeavor to promote that hilarity which the Middle Ages had vainly striven to suppress.

There was peace in the land. Or, at least, there was no war to sap the country's strength. "We Englishmen live in security," wrote Walsingham, "grounding our quietness on others' harms." But this quietness was shot through with tragic happenings (the loss of young Marlowe in a tavern brawl, the sadness of Spenser's deathbed), and with a bitter current of discontent. Barnabe Rich said that the poor were too poor, and that no one cared "for such as were in want." His words were borne out by Nicholas Breton, a cheerful soul not given to repining, but none the less a close observer of his day. It was his opinion that poverty, once esteemed as the child of Heaven, was wearing the garments of disgrace, and that "the honest poor man" was having a hard time of it. "He is a stranger in the world, for no man craves his acquaintance, and his funeral is without ceremony when there is no mourning for the miss of him." Thomas Nash observed the growing ill-will between the classes. "The courtier disdaineth the citizen, the citizen the countryman, the shoemaker the cobbler." England was growing rich on wool; but the sheep were grazing on what had once been arable land, and the ploughman paid the price of prosperity. So did the petty consumer.

> The more sheep, the dearer is the corn,
> The more sheep, the fewer eggs to the penny,

expressed his view of the situation.

Above all, there was an ever-darkening quarrel over creeds, an ever-deepening distrust of neighbor for neighbor. "Reineche Fuchs" was to be had in its English text by all disposed to laughter; but it was not so popular as "The Hunter of the Romish Fox," the title of which sufficiently indicated the bellicose nature of its contents. "The Bailiff's Daughter of Islington" was a popular, cheerful, and not too sensible ballad; but by its side might be seen "The Lamentation of a Damned Soul," which sounds like an advance guard of Wesleyan literature. England did not waste her strength on civil wars and call them religious, as did France; or expend on polemical disputes the energy which should have gone into colonization, as did Germany; but she fussed and fumed, passed savage laws, and saw them defied by her worthiest sons. The Jesuit priest went to his hideous death, protesting his loyalty to the Crown. The Puritan whose right hand had been chopped off raised his bleeding stump, and cried, "God save the Queen!" But the priest had a successor ready to take up his work, and the Puritan went his way, protesting when he felt it his duty to protest. Both were unconquerable, and neither was provocative of laughter.

The dissolution of the guilds, which went hand in hand with the dissolution of the monasteries, was responsible for the extreme poverty of the people. The monasteries themselves were sorely missed. No one pretends that the greedy courtiers who got possession of the Church estates made as good landlords as the monks had made. And with the monasteries went the rural "hospitals," most of which were simply almshouses, harboring the maimed and helpless. Their inmates were turned into the roads, to beg, or steal, or die. From one such shelter a hundred blind men were cast out with no provision for their future. The artisan and the laborer were not much better off than was the beggar, for the loss of their guilds—"stripped," says Augustus Jessopp, "of their last farthing, their last rag and cup and platter"—meant the loss of all that had ensured them the reward of labor.

Dr. James Walsh corroborates Mr. Jessopp's statement that there were no less than thirty thousand of these guilds in pre-Reformation England. They had reached their highest development in that golden age of craftsmanship, the thirteenth century; and they represented democracy in its best and sanest aspect. Beginning as beneficial societies, they showed what could be done by self help and organization; and they became the great educators in every field of work. It was the guilds that ruled the important and turbulent world of apprenticeship; the guilds that lent money, settled disputes, ensured against fire and other calamities, regulated hours of labor (seven, eight, or nine hours a day for artisans), and gave every year great feasts, "designed to promote love and amity and good communication for the several weal of the fraternity." Tankards of ale were given to the poor on these occasions, and as much as thirty pence was paid to the minstrels who made music for the banqueters. The guilds did for the workmen of the thirteenth century all that the trade-unions do for the workmen of the twentieth century, and a great deal more, for they fostered the best possible production, the highest personal achievement. The medieval craftsman who spent long and loving weeks over the lock, key, and hinges of a sacristy chest was sure of his wages and of intelligent understanding. There was room in his life for pride as well as for bodily comfort.

Mr. Jessopp, who looked back upon the lost guilds with the deep regard of an antiquarian, mourned for them as if he had been a sixteenth-century priest rather than a nineteenth-century parson. He did not even take comfort in the thought that a few powerful companies like the merchant tailors, the goldsmiths, and the stationers survived the Reformation by pleading their purely secular character. Nine tenths of the guilds were too closely associated with the Church and with the monasteries to escape destruction when they had funds and property worth seizing; and this universal confiscation reduced to uttermost poverty thousands of English workingmen. The increase of destitution paved the way for the Tudor poor-laws, first of their kind, which at their best may be described as codes for badgering the indigent, and at their worst as statutes for the persecution of the unhappy. An act passed in the reign of Edward VI has been described as written in letters of blood. It aimed at sweeping out of sight all the unfortunates who had been beggared in his father's reign, as well as the less miserable creatures who had never owned anything to lose. Both classes were set down as vagabonds. If they were rude handicraftsmen, they were forbidden to work. If they were petty tradesmen, they were forbidden to sell. "Tynkers, pedlars, and such like vagrant personnes are more hurtfull than necessarie to the Common Wealth of this realme," said the act, and this was doubtless true. But the tinker and the pedlar were trying to live, because there had come down to them from happier ages a belief that life was good.

The statutes of Elizabeth's day went much further than any which had preceded them. An "Acte for the punishment of vagabonds" would have driven Autolycus into hiding. Not only "all pedlars, tynkers, and petye chapmen," but "all scollers of the Universities of Oxford or Cambridge who goe about begginge"; not only "ydle personnes fayninge to have knowledge of phisnomye and palmestrye," but "jugglers, fencers, bearwardes, common players in interludes, and minstrels not belonging to any baron of this realme," were classed together as rogues and vagabonds, and handed over to the courts, thereby extinguishing much laughter in England.

The law was doubtless disobeyed. Any law forbidding Englishmen to roam was disobeyed. They could not be kept in one spot when they wanted to move on. Rural records in Tudor days present a monotonous narrative of wayfarers apprehended, whipped, and returned to their own parishes, which did not welcome them, and where they would not stay. There was no taint of serfdom in their blood. The earth beneath their feet and the cloud-flecked sky overhead were their inheritance. They would go where they listed. They would be "masterless men," subject as such to harsh penalties, but part and parcel of the age-old revolt against despotism—a revolt which had the wandering tinker at one end of the line, and the barons of Runnymede at the other.

There were kind Christians and worthy citizens in Elizabeth's day, as there were before and after; but they could do little to stem the general distress. The hospital at Greenwich was rebuilt by that "goodly good gentleman," William Lambarde. The almshouses founded by Lord Burleigh at Stamford still stand. They sheltered thirteen poor men, and the almshouses erected at Aldenham by the brewer, Richard Platt, held the same number. Thomas Cuttell left a fund to provide one good dinner a year for the prisoners at Newgate, which was a kindly deed. Sir Martin Bowes, a London alderman, left money for the repairing of the city's neglected conduits. Elizabeth Gavener of Devon bequeathed her manor of Shalcombe to be sold, and the proceeds devoted to the repairing of the equally neglected highways.

All this was work well done, and historians have made much of it. But thirteen paupers sitting down to their daily dinners meant nothing to the hordes of dinnerless men who skulked and hid and stole and died, unhindered and unhelped. Beg they dared not, for even licensed beggars who wore a badge to proclaim their privilege were permitted to solicit alms in their own parishes and no other. They no longer went "light-heart and gay" wherever their fancy led them. Fletcher, indeed, wrote a play called *The Beggar's Bush* which had a cheerful beggars song; but he discreetly located it in the Netherlands, where, for all he knew, these "children of idleness whose lives are a resolution of ease" might go singing and whistling on the highways.

A less merry sight met the eyes of Lord Howard, admiral of the Queen's fleet, when he beheld his seamen sick, penniless, and starving in the streets of Margate. Elizabeth could not be induced to pay or feed her soldiers and sailors. "It was not that the commissariat broke down," says Gordon Goodwin. "There was no commissariat." She honestly believed and said that if her subjects were loyal to her, they should be ready to defend her "at their own charges"; a point of view intelligible in a Highland chieftain who gathers his clan about him, but not in the sovereign of a great nation. "When England was thrilling with its triumph over the Armada," says the historian, Green, "the Queen was grumbling at the cost, and making her profit out of the spoiled provisions she had ordered for the fleet that saved her."

Miserliness is the one vice that grows stronger with increasing years. It yields its sordid pleasures to the end. What had been thrift

23

The Merry Monarch[*]

A merry monarch, scandalous and poor. —Earl of Rochester

That was the courtier's point of view, and it became as firmly fixed in men's minds as was the "merrie England" of Elizabeth. The casual reader has regarded Charles II as a witty libertine. The casual critic—with some vague recollections of Macaulay—as a blot on Britain's scutcheon. John Leech, wishing to draw a comprehensive portrait, conceived of him as a satyr, goat-legged and very drunk. That his face was singularly sad, that his mind was singularly acute, are circumstances which have not been suffered to interfere with popular opinion. Yet features are an index to character; and intelligence, while essential to an understanding of the comic spirit, does not lend itself to goatish revelry.

The keynote of the Restoration was a pursuit of pleasure. Not a glad acceptance of pleasure as part of life's experience, but a furious pursuit calculated to defeat its own ends. Just as the unrealities of pacifism—peace congresses, and prizes, and processions, and bands of bewildered young men who solemnly pledge themselves never to bear arms for their country—just as these things are the natural reaction from four years of war, so the unhealthy absorption in pleasure which characterized the Restoration was the natural reaction from eleven years of Puritan rule.

* From *In Pursuit of Laughter*, 1936.

in Elizabeth's middle age became an overmastering passion before she died. Her soldiers for foreign service were taken from the prisons, and picked up by press gangs. "Loose and runaway men" were gathered in and jailed until they could be shipped to the Low Countries. Easter Sunday offered a magnificent chance for stratagem, for on that day everyone was legally bound to take the sacrament. The press gangs surrounded the parish churches, and seized the younger men. Unless they were handsomely redeemed they were sent across the sea to be shot, or die of fever, or be returned wasted with disease. The system was not always so economical as it seemed. In the spring of 1563 there were dispatched to Havre "cut-purses, horse-stealers, and highwaymen," with a sprinkling of old soldiers to leaven the mass. It mattered little of what material these troops were made, for the plague was waiting for them, and by midsummer was taking a toll of sixty men a day. Havre was surrendered, and a remnant of its garrison returned to Portsmouth in August. There was no quarantine and no provision made for their reception. They scattered to their homes, carrying disease with them. Where hundreds had died in France, thousands died in England; and London, which had deemed itself safe, suffered the heaviest loss.

Twenty-five years later the destruction of the Armada was the burden of exultant song and story; but there were those who took little pride in the part that England played. Every one knows about Drake and his game of bowls; but how many of us hear Leicester testify that the four thousand recruits who assembled at Tilbury found not so much as a loaf of bread or a draught of beer on which to break their fast? How many hear Howard's appeal: "For the love of God send us powder and shot!" or his sad admission that, while the ships dispatched by cities and citizens were well fitted out, those sent at the expense of the crown lacked "the barest necessities"? Above all, how many hear Walsingham's heartbroken cry: "The Queen's parsimony at home hath bereaved us of the famousest victory that ever our nation had at sea." It was a great and glorious reign, but merry it was not. Compared to the penniless seamen of Margate, the medieval herbalists led a pleasant life. Compared to the "begging poor" who were permitted to ask for alms, and the "vagabond" poor who were expected to starve in silence, the medieval "toth-drawers" and needle-sellers were free and happy men. When we are listening for laughter, it is not on the Queen's highways that we may hope to hear it.

Yet her subjects were never without their simple pleasures. They had the Cotswold games. They had their May queen as of yore, and at Christmas time their Lord of Misrule, who made no trouble because he no longer ruled. He was merely carried into church when the service was over and carried out again. They had bears to bait. Every township kept a bear for this laudable purpose. We are told that one petty borough which had the misfortune to lose its bear sold the church Bible to buy another. Villages too poor to afford a bear were perforce content with humbler sports. A cat hung up in a leather bag as a target for crossbows, or a cock in an earthenware vessel to be stoned, or a few doves to be "sealed" (blinded) for the sake of their strange, disordered flight.

Now and then a witch was done to death by a too strenuous mob; but this was a diversion hard to come by, and receiving no encouragement from authority. Elizabeth's firm intelligence was well-nigh superstition-proof. Her successor acquired fame as a foe to witchcraft; but he had been bred in Scotland, and the English witches were poor feckless things compared to their terrible Scottish sisters. It is true that in 1560 Bishop Jewel, freshly appointed to the see of Salisbury, besought the Queen to enforce the laws against witchcraft, which had fallen into disuse. He drew an agitated picture of the evils which had resulted from her leniency, of a hapless people unprotected from the power that works in darkness. "Your Grace's subjects pine away even unto death. Their color fadeth, their flesh rotteth, their speech is benumbed, their senses are bereft."

This was good measure on Satan's part; but the recountal carried no conviction to Elizabeth, though she was ready to take mild measures of precaution. When a waxen figure was picked up in Lincoln's Inn-fields, and pronounced to be her own image and likeness, she sent for her astrologer, Dr. John Dee, and bade him counteract its malice. She made the same use of the learned gentleman when she had the toothache, being actuated in both cases by a desire to get all the good she could out of a salaried official. She no more feared injury to English constitutions from witchcraft than she feared injury to English ethics from playing cards. Henry VIII, who had a tender regard for the morality of his subjects, restricted the sale of cards; but his daughter was less austere. She held them to be a commendable amusement for such as bad weather kept indoors.

In all this there was much sense, but little mirth. Where the medieval observers had laughed, the Elizabethans too often berated. The shrewishness of wives, the willfulness of women, were no laughing matter to John Stubbs, who said that they beggared their husbands by their extravagance, and cared not who paid for their finery. It was no laughing matter to Thomas Dekker, who conceived that English husbands were ill-treated by their wives, and whose satire has an angry edge. To be ruined by wastefulness was no worse than to be mastered by ill-temper; and the folly of women who "diet their faces," and "ensparkle their eyes with spiritualized distillations," incited him to loud contempt. Only Nicholas Breton reproduced the medieval atmosphere in his story of the wife who devoured the great eel which her husband was fattening as a gift for his landlord. The serving maid, "who had wit enough to make a fool of a tame goose," adroitly suggests to the angry man that her mistress is perhaps breeding, which would account for her inordinate appetite; and that she may bear him a fine boy worth many bushels of eels. The poor simpleton looks at his gluttonous helpmate sitting heavily in her chair, and his heart is softened. Gently he approaches her, patiently he listens to the "home complaints" which she has all ready for him, and gratefully he accepts the next morning a small portion of what is left of the eel pie. It is a perfect picture of domestic life, undisturbed by any hint of reprobation.

The curious thing about the situation was the defenselessness of women under the law. An Antwerp merchant who visited England in 1579, and who pronounced it to be "the female Paradise," was amazed and amused by the fact that English wives were "entirely in the power of their husbands, life only excepted." A man might not kill his wife or sell her. He occasionally did one or the other, but the act was illegal. For the rest she belonged to him as did his dog or his horse; but she was far from emulating the submissiveness of these useful animals. She lorded it over her household at home, and was treated with deference abroad. "At all banquets and feasts she is shown the greatest honor, is placed at the upper end of the table and is served first." Women of the well-to-do class led an easy life, "visiting their gossips and being diverted thereby." Women of the lower class forgathered in taverns and pothouses to tipple. This had been their reprehensible custom before Elizabeth's day; and—to their shame be it spoken—they paid their score, if need be, with their yokemates' belongings:

> One bringeth her husband's hood,
> Because the ale is good;
> Another bringeth his cap
> To offer to the ale tap.

Skelton was disposed to lay the blame for women's outrageous behavior upon Chaucer, inasmuch as the Wife of Bath had taught them that the one thing desirable was sovereignty over their husbands, and that in this sovereignty alone lay all chance of marital content. But Chaucer counteracted the Wife's tale with the Clerk's tale of Griselda the patient. In Elizabeth's day patience, or at least obedience, was out of date. A popular song hawked about the streets had for a title "God Send Me a Wife that Will Do as I Say!" and another exalted the carefree life of the bachelor:

> Married men may sit and groan;
> He is content and letteth well alone.

The Queen herself was not safe from reproach, being of a most willful and changeable disposition, and wholly lacking in the royal virtue of punctuality. A pleasant tale is told of her removal from Windsor to London. The wagon train (she was weightily burdened with luggage) was ordered to be in readiness. Three days running it waited for its rich loads, and three days running she postponed her departure. When on the third day the master carter was informed of this fact, he swore lustily. "Now I know," he said, "that the Queen is just such another as my wife." From an open window overhead came an angry laugh. Then a messenger brought him a gold angel.

Her Majesty had overheard, and had sent it to stop his mouth. The Tudors were never deficient in humor.

Elizabeth's progresses throughout her kingdom awakened enthusiasm when her reign was young, and became a grievous tax upon her subjects when she had outworn her welcome at their doors. She liked being entertained at their expense, and she liked it better and better as they grew more unwilling, or perhaps more unable, to entertain her. Her second visit to Oxford in 1592 occasioned as little merriment as the memorable visit of George the Third in 1786. Her court, once brilliant, always dignified, but never gay, grew insufferably tedious as the years went by. Men were men then as before and since. Some of them wanted mistresses, many of them wanted wives. They gratified both inclinations, but at the risk of losing the royal favor. They were ambitious then as before and since. Even in the matter of wedlock, ambition played its part. They sought well-dowered brides, or, better still, influential fathers-in-law. Sully was not the only courtier in Europe who expressed his profound conviction that the really important element in marriage was a father-in-law.

Married or single, they grew reasonably tired of pretending that the mere presence of the Queen was enough to satisfy all ardent emotions, and dispel all mutinous desires. When there was hope in a great lord's heart that she would marry a subject, and that he might be her choice, ambition flared high. As that hope faded, there was nothing to replace it. For years they watched her amorous antics with the Due d'Alençon, and derived what entertainment they could from that mockery of courtship. For years they saw their strong-stomached sovereign fondle and caress the hideous little creature for whom she professed a tender regard, and to whom she wrote amorous letters which failed to deceive his clear-sighted, cold-hearted mother. Not being in the habit of truth-telling, Catherine de Médicis was never at the mercy of a lie.

The hope of enrichment at Elizabeth's hands was as futile as the hope of marriage. Her purse-strings were drawn tight, her grants were few and far between. Leicester was the sole recipient of her bounty; and when he died, she seized upon his estate and sold it to repay his debts to the exchequer. Burleigh, her faithful minister, and twelve times her host, never grew rich; Walsingham and Hatton died insolvent. It was understood that the Queen did not give money, she received it. A purse filled with gold pieces was an acceptable offering from any gentleman of her court. On New Year's Day, 1578, she took in—to her vast pleasure and contentment—the sum of nine hundred and ninety-three pounds and thirteen shillings. It was customary for the bishops to send her from ten to twenty pounds, which was as little as they could do, seeing that if they died their incomes went to the Crown until their successors were appointed. Elizabeth's devotion to the Church of which she was the head may be measured by the fact that Wells did without a bishop for ten years, Ely for eighteen years, and Oxford for forty-one. The famous remark of a devout but profane Episcopalian, "Who in Hell will confirm us?" would have been appropriate to this singular situation.

Thirty-three years ago Mr. Owen Seaman wrote some characteristic verses in praise of Queen Elizabeth's England. He said nothing about its greatness and glory, matters with which his readers were conversant; and nothing about its merriment which he apparently failed to observe; but a great deal about the one aspect which won his heart—its very convenient spaciousness. The nations of the world were not then their brothers' keepers, and it took them a long time to find out what their brothers were about:

> Large-hearted age of cakes and ale!
>   When, undeterred by nice conditions,
> Good master Drake would lightly sail
>   On little privateer commissions;
> Careening round with sword and flame,
>   And no pretence of polished manners,
> He Planted out in England's name
>   A most refreshing lot of banners.
>
> No Ministry would care a rap
>   For theoretic arbitration;

They simply modified the map
　To meet the latest annexation;
And so without appeal to law,
　Or other needless waste of tissue,
The lion where he put his paw,
　Remained and propagated issue.

Credit where credit is due. England sent her roving sons over a world in which she was to build a mighty empire. She had the qualities that befit a pioneer. "The nature of our nation is free, stout, haughty, prodigal of life and blood," wrote Sir Thomas Smith in 1621. She had also qualities of discretion—reasonableness of outlook, a wise concession to things as they are, and an unfailing grasp on the feasibility of performance. "The leadership of the world," says Edward Martin, who evidently believes in such a thing, "will go to, or remain with, the country that produces the best thinkers and the highest courage." The leadership of the world would be a sorry task, considering what there is to be led; but steadiness of purpose, coupled with moderation of aim, keeps civilized men from reeling off the track. Elizabeth's England, steady and moderate, was stirred with high hopes and ambitions; but she was short of laughter, and was beginning to want to laugh. That is why clowns overdid their parts, greatly to Hamlet's—or Shakespeare's—annoyance. What the thirteenth century had striven to subdue, the sixteenth century strove robustly to encourage. The pursuit of silenced laughter had begun.

England had never liked this rule. She knew that she was respected abroad, but she also knew that she was uncomfortable at home. She hated the efficiency of military despotism, preferring her inefficient Parliaments which represented constitutional liberty. She hated a life of enforced dullness, wishing to be dull in her own way and at her own discretion. She hated the suppression of holidays and the heavier taxation. John Evelyn said his estate in Essex was so eaten up by taxes that he could not hold on to it. She was depressed by the increase of poverty. The bitter jest of the day was that men no longer gave to beggars because the farthing had disappeared from the currency, and a farthing represented the widest range of almsgiving. Cromwell was strong enough to maintain his government against all discontent and all opposition; but he knew that he had not founded it on the acceptance of the nation, and that it had taken no root.

In London the discontent was deepened by trivial annoyances. Her citizens who had ridden or driven in Hyde Park all their lives resented a tax of sixpence on the horse if they rode, or a shilling on the coach if they drove. It was bad enough to have their theaters, and often their churches, closed; but when it came to their park, they were ripe for the Restoration. The overpowering delight with which that *coup d'état* was received may be measured by the fact that the prayer of thanksgiving which was ordered to be said in the London churches every twenty-ninth of May (the day Charles entered his capital) continued to be recited until 1849. England had in the meantime ridded herself of the Stewarts, worried along under the Hanoverians, and was twelve years deep in Victoria's glorious reign before she stopped thanking God that Charles II had come into his own.

"Had this king but loved business as well as he understood it," said that loyal gentleman, Sir Richard Bulstrode, "he would have been the greatest prince in Europe." He would, in fact, have been one of the greatest rulers that England ever had. None more intelligent had filled her throne. But what a fight must have ensued, what a struggle against forces ranged solidly against him—Parliament, Puritanism, bigotry, distrust and credulity walking hand in hand,

and the sour withholding of supplies. Even for the fleet, his one kingly pride and joy, Charles could win no support. Disillusioned with monarchy, he surrendered its obligations one by one in favor of its indulgences, and found them an unsatisfactory substitute. For the blood of princes ran in his veins, and the love of England burned in his heart. All of England's kings, good or bad, loved her until she brought over the bored and indifferent Hanoverians. How could the son of Charles I, and the great-great-grandson of James V—tragic rulers of England and Scotland—have ever been indifferent?

It is the story of lost leadership. Charles II, disappointed in every noble design, thwarted in every rational ambition, turned deliberately to the things he could command. "So far as it goes," he said, "I am the King." He delighted in wit, and was besotted over women. He knew the worst of both—of wit that was profane and indecent, of women who were gross and greedy. The brief entries in Evelyn's diary are comprehensive and instructive. "A lewd play," is his summary of Wycherley's *Country Wife*. "A very profane wit," is all he has to say about Rochester. "This day se'nnight I saw the king sitting and toying with his concubines," epitomizes his gentlemanly distaste for open immorality. Perhaps it is only fair to state that when these last condemnatory lines were written, all three of the concubines had reached middle age, and that one of them, the mother of grown sons and daughters, had long past the toying and amatory stage. Another, the Duchess of Portsmouth, divined the wishes of the dying king, and had the courage to persuade Barrillon to prompt the Duke of York to bring Father Huddleston into the royal chamber.

"We know the degree of refinement in men," says George Meredith, "by the matter they laugh at and by the ring of the laugh." But a society bent on restoring laughter to a grim world loses nicety and balance. The Commonwealth had made short work of the theaters. An edict of 1649 called for their complete demolition. There was no finical discrimination between the most accomplished tragedian on the boards and the strolling mummer of the countryside. All were classed together as "rogues according to the law," and all disappeared—if they were wise—from the eyes of a hostile government. The Restoration opened the theaters wide, freed them from the taxation which the humblest home had to bear, and crowded them in a noisy disorderly fashion. It was at this period that the sober middle-class of London, which had heartily supported the Elizabethan playhouse, withdrew from all participation in an amusement which grew more licentious every year. Sir Richard Garnett says that decent women did go to see the tragedies, but eschewed the comedies, or, if they went, wore masks. As the London harlots also went masked, this compromise was not remarkably protective.

Charles loved the theater. He was wont to protest against the custom of making all the villains as black-visaged as he was himself, but this represented a personal grievance. Nature and education had fitted him to enjoy the comedy of manners which reached its zenith with Congreve under the chilling eye of William III. Burnet, paying tribute to his critical qualities, says that while he had no great acquaintance with literature, he had, thanks to his training in France, a correct taste in style, liking what was "clear, plain, and short," and preferring lucidity to all other merits. If, as we are bidden to believe, the Restoration saw the birth of modern English prose, and Dryden was its noble sponsor, the King had a good deal to do with its safe delivery. It took, under his approving eye, the form that pleased him best. Wit and taste he possessed in a supreme degree; the deeper emotions he banished as mutinous and trouble-making; and from poetic vision he was free. That belonged to the Elizabethan world.

We know that Lamb and Hazlitt, living in an age of complacent virtue and pretentious mediocrity, were wont to sigh over the lost drama of the Restoration, and over the lost libertinism which made such drama acceptable. Perhaps an evening spent with *The Inflexible Captive* or *The Fatal Falsehood* was calculated to provoke such a sentiment. "Happy thoughtless age," sighed Hazlitt, "when king and nobles led purely ornamental lives; when the utmost stretch of a morning's study went no farther than the choice of a sword-knot, or the adjustment of a side curl; when the soul spoke out in all the pleasing eloquence of dress."

As stout a misconception, as misplaced an envy, as ever were recorded on paper. Charles II kept his throne (that much he had resolved upon from the beginning), and he kept his hold upon the hearts of his people, a circumstance which he found mightily consoling. But what other king of England began his reign with precisely eleven pounds two shillings and tenpence in the national exchequer, to say nothing of a debt of two million pounds bequeathed by the Commonwealth to its successor? What other king of England was called on to face a disastrous war, a disastrous fire, a disastrous plague, a disastrous mock conspiracy, and a disastrous miscarriage of justice which he was powerless to prevent? What other king of England had to defend his wedded wife against the assaults of an English Parliament? What other king of England watched through a goldsmith's window a hostile mob sweep through the streets, insulting his servants and himself? Well might Lord Halifax swear that a wasp's nest was a quieter place to sleep in than London town when Lord Shaftesbury and Titus Oates were sharing its control.

From the violence of factions, from the persecutions of Parliament, from the Act of Uniformity (enough to sour any reign in Christendom), from the inconvenient poverty of a king (rich on paper and poor in coin), and from the defeat of his dearest hopes, Charles turned for refuge to the pleasures which earned for him the epithet "merry." He loved good music and good pictures; but he did not love very good books. He loved, like a true Englishman, horse-racing and all outdoor sports. He loved, as though he had been a true Frenchman, good talk and good plays; not the best of plays (Paris heard *Le Misanthrope* and London *The Plain Dealer*), but comedies like *Marriage à la Mode* and tragedies like *Venice Preserved.* He delighted in the satire of *Hudibras,* which was but natural. He knew that Butler's assumption that all Puritans were knaves fell short of proof; as a matter of fact Marvell was the man he most admired in England; but he also knew from experience that all Puritans were liable to cant. Their power of disapproval, a power from which they drew strange sustenance and delight, was simply miraculous to a man who found so little in life that called for reprobation.

If Charles loved gay and brilliant talk, he gave more generously than he received. He had not peer for keenness or for charm. He was ever and always the most agreeable of companions. The grace of his manner, the beauty of his voice, made his simplest civilities enchanting to their recipients. They said with conviction that he was "so pleasant a monarch that no one could be sorrowful in his reign." He could let pass with a jest the liberty taken by an intoxicated civilian: "He that is drunk is as good as a king." He could sit content by the side of a lady mayoress, "all over scarlet and ermine, and half over diamonds." He could mingle by day with the crowds at Newmarket, and go at night to see plays acted in a barn by very ordinary Bartholomew Fair comedians. Lord Elgin bears witness to the fact that once on board his yacht, he was "all mirth and of a most pleasing conversation." There was in his day great simplicity of essence beneath complexity of manner, and no man was better fitted than Charles for a diffused life of genial enjoyment. His hours of escape heartened him for the hours when he sat grim and silent through the trials of Shaftesbury's victims, or watched Monmouth, his beloved and deeply disloyal son, swaggering in the House of Lords, as though sure of his succession to the throne.

A life of genial enjoyment which means acceptance is vastly different from a life of irrational diversion which means pursuit. The Elizabethans, conscious that laughter was escaping them, encouraged it to stay. The wits of the Restoration, indignant that they had been robbed of laughter for a matter of ten years, set it above price and above codes. "The comedy of manners," says George Meredith, "began as a combative performance, under a license to deride the Puritan, and was here and there Bacchanalian beyond the Aristophanic example; worse, inasmuch as a cynical licentiousness is more abominable than frank filth. The men and women who sat through the acting of Wycherley's *Country Wife* were past blushing." This degradation of the spirit of comedy inevitably affected the whole field of literature, and stood responsible for the stupidities as well as for the grossness of social life.

There is no shadow of doubt that the rakish society of the Restoration began by tolerating indecency for the sake of wit, and ended by tolerating dullness for the sake of indecency. By 1661 women were playing female parts on the London stage. They were held to be, and frequently were, no better than prostitutes. Twenty years later, English audiences were entertained by hearing girl-children recite epilogues and dialogues full of filthy obscenities. There was nothing amusing about these performances except the suggestion they conveyed of precocious corruption.

'Tis now no Jest to hear young girls talk Bawdy!

voiced in 1682 the weary protest of one Londoner who failed to be diverted. Yet the custom lasted. Charles had been dead ten years and William graced the throne when a six-year-old child, Denny Chock, delighted the play-going world by lisping indecent prologues, which, coming from her infant lips, provoked shouts of laughter. The time was ripe for Jeremy Collier's great protest; and the immediate success of his "Short View of the Immorality and Profaneness of the Stage" (a work hated with a fury of hatred by Hazlitt) showed plainly enough that existing conditions were tolerated rather than enjoyed.

For the laxness which had demolished decency had also broken down the barriers of taste. The Elizabethans had done without scenery. They were told that they were in Venice, or Denmark, in a Syracusan mart, or on a plain in Syria, and that sufficed them. But a Restoration tragedy was liable to degenerate into a thing of horror or a thing of absurdity because of its setting. Settle's *Empress of Morocco* had a dungeon scene filled with mutilated bodies impaled on stakes; and in *The Siege of Constantinople* the stage direction shows "a number of men dead or dying in several manners of deaths." The noise and disorder in the theater were so great that only an exceptional actor like Betterton could command a hearing. Pepys bears witness to the fact that a fashionable audience preferred talking to listening, and that, as a consequence, he was unable to hear what was said upon the stage. No wonder that *A Midsummer Night's Dream* seemed a tiresome play, and *Othello* a typically bad one, to the careless courtiers who never heard the magic of the lines.

Charles was wittier than the wittiest of his subjects. In this regard the child was father to the man. Many stories are told of his infancy, but one gives perfect promise of the future. He was nine years old when he was confided to the care of William Cavendish, Earl of

Newcastle, and his first revolt against authority took the form of refusing physic when he was ill. The Earl appealed to the Queen, who promptly enforced obedience. A month later Newcastle went down with a fever, and his little charge wrote him an affectionate letter, laden with a line of counsel: "My Lord, I would not have you take too much physic, for it doth always make me worse, and I think it will do the like by you."

"*La malignité naturelle aux hommes est le principe de la comédie.*" It dictated the letter of the nine-year-old boy, and it prompted the King's flawless jest anent William Penn and his hat; a jest supremely good-tempered which nonetheless mocked the absurdity of a purely formal pietism.

It was natural that Charles should delight in an accomplishment of which he was a perfect exponent, the interchange of humorous and agreeable civilities. In him, said Chesterton, may be sought and found "the magnanimous politeness, the dramatic delicacy, which lie on the dim borderland between morality and art." His friends understood this perfect tone, and strove to imitate it. As a consequence they were liable to rise at times above the level of wit and rottenness which was their habitual *métier*. Even Buckingham,

A man so various that he seemed to be
   Not one, but all mankind's epitome,

had his occasional flight. Even Sir Charles Sedley, who managed— Heaven knows how!—to produce a play so indecent that it was forbidden the boards, made what amends he could by writing "Phillis is my only Joy," a song which has given wise and innocent delight to thousands. Even Rochester, utterly bad and ignoble, was not only a poet and a wit but a loyal husband (constant if not faithful) to the bride he had rudely snatched, and to whom he wrote his best poem. His jests were the bywords of the court. When he said, "All men would be cowards if they durst," he merely put into a few words a truism which had hitherto been more expansively voiced; but when he said to a dog which had bitten him, "I wish you were married and living in the country!" he appealed through a laugh to the suffering heart of humanity. Charles Lamb would have loved that bitter word, and so would Alfred de Musset; the first because he detested the country, the second because he detested both the country and dogs.

Wit was the order of the day. Addison observed of Cowley that his only fault—a pardonable one—was "wit in excess." No man won praise which was more worth the winning than did this poet of the Restoration. Dryden said of him, "His authority is sacred to me," and Charles said, "He has left no better man behind him"; flawless epithets both of them, and suited to the reign in which they were spoken. Hazlitt declared that Cowley's "Anacreontiques" brim over with the spirit of wine and joy. "Though lengthened out beyond the originals, it is by fresh impulses of an eager and inexhaustible delight." Yet this exponent of joy describes himself as "the melancholy Cowley"; and he uttered his full complement of complaints against a world that had treated him well, but in which he observed too often the sharpness of injustice which disturbs men's minds.

We do not turn for wit and humor to Bunyan; but they are qualities which, in common with his age, he possessed. When he wrote, he said things as neat as this: "Oaths and obligations in the affairs of the world are like ribbons and knots in dressing. They seem to tie something but do not." When he spoke, his words were swift and illuminating. "Ah, Mr. Bunyan, that was a sweet sermon," said an edified parishioner. "You need not tell me that," was the reply. "The devil whispered it in my ear before I was well out of the pulpit."

But Bunyan was far from being a merry man. He taught too stern a creed, and he was too prone to apply its precepts to his own harmless life. And the merriment of king and court was a mask, a thing of purpose, a weapon with which to smite the Puritan and take pleasure by storm. "Genuine humor and true wit," says Landor, "require a sound and capacious mind, which is always a grave one." The gallants of the Restoration who went for amusement to see the chained maniacs of Bedlam, and the women prisoners flogged at Bridewell, and a stallion baited by dogs, were on as wrong a track as any generation that trod before or after them. The poor laws of Charles's reign, as pitiless as those of the Commonwealth, sent foundling children of seven to work in the mines, dragging loads of coal until they dropped dead in their tracks. There was a lack of imagination as well as a lack of feeling when such things were possible; yet now and then, as in the days of Elizabeth, we come suddenly upon the divineness of pity. When Nell Gwynn, the "unasking" harlot who never was rich, left the sum of twenty pounds a year for the release of some poor debtor or debtors on Christmas Day, she linked her charity to man with the noblest traditions of the Church.

Congreve was but fifteen years of age when Charles II died. In the following fifteen years he wrote his three famous plays, and abandoned the role of dramatist. Supremely fortunate in life and death, the friend of great men, the holder of rich sinecures, he sleeps under a fitting monument in Westminster Abbey, and has been extolled as the wittiest of English playwrights. Hazlitt, who sedulously cherished the unrealities of the stage, dreamed of his day as the sons of Adam might have dreamed of Paradise. He thought and said that Congreve's Millamant was better fitted for comedy than was Shakespeare's Rosalind because she was "more artificial, more theatrical, more meretricious." Lamb voiced a similar conviction with the courage of one who never sought concurrence. "That hag, Duty," having ruled him all his life, his natural reactions were in favor of irresponsibility. He gave his adherence once for all to the form of drama which excludes a moral sense. "The great art of Congreve is especially shown in this, that he has entirely banished from his scenes—some little generosities of Angelica perhaps excepted—any pretensions to goodness or good feeling whatsoever. Whether he did this designedly or instinctively, the effect is as happy as the design (if design) is bold."

The effect *is* happy when produced with skill. "Treasures of sparkling laughter are as wells in our desert," admits George Meredith. But it is open to one objection. It does not represent life. We can no more imagine a world without goodness or good feeling than we can imagine a world which is all goodness and good feeling. The comedies of the Restoration made no attempt to reflect the manners and morals of the English people, as they were reflected fifty years later in "Tom Jones"; but only the manners and morals of a small section of the English people, to which, let us hope, they were unjust.

Apart from the songs occasionally introduced, they depended upon Dryden for poetic value. Sir Richard Garnett has pointed out that the Elizabethan drama is steeped in poetry. Consequently it will always be read even if it is not acted, and will always be a living force in English literature. The Restoration drama, though it has been occasionally revived (with careful chiseling), is a thing indefinably remote. It deals with types rather than with nature or nationality, and Bunyan was the only man in England who could breathe the breath of life into his types.

Yet hardly had this brilliant and brittle thing passed into the twilight of neglect, when we find the nineteenth century loudly lamenting its loss. It is inevitable that every generation should regret the silenced laughter of its predecessor, and that the echo of these lamentations should come down to us today. Mr. Allardyce Nicoll, who has written a severely critical study of the Restoration drama, forgets his censures when faced with this sense of deprivation. "Cibber and Farquhar and Vanbrugh," he says, "each in his own way, kept the spirit of humor alive for a time, as did later Fielding and Moore and Sheridan and Goldsmith. But the free expression of pure laughter, untouched by thought or by conscience, has passed away for ever."

So speaks the modern world; but Charles was still on his throne, and England was still rejoicing over the fact, when Dryden penned these lines:

> Then our age was in its prime,
> Free from rage and free from crime,
> A very merry, dancing, drinking,
> Laughing, quaffing and unthinking time.

It sounds—the two last lines certainly sound—like a perfect picture of the Restoration. But the fact is that Dryden placed his blissful period in classic days; and Diana (who must have lived abstemiously to be such a good markswoman) is the divinity in whose praise the jovial chorus is sung. It sweeps us into acquiescence, as a good chorus should always do; and then the poet, clear-eyed and disillusioned, rejects our sympathy, and rejects the claims of the pagan world to permanent delight:

All, all of a piece throughout;
The chase had a beast in view;
The wars brought nothing about;
The lovers were all untrue;
'Tis well an old age is out,
And time to begin a new.

24

"Hum'rous Hogart"*

How singular has been the history of the decline of humor. Is
there any profound psychological truth to be gathered from consideration of the fact that it has gone out with cruelty? A hundred years ago—nay fifty years ago—we were a cruel but also a
humorous people. We had bull-baitings, and badger-drawings,
and hustings, and prize-fights, and cock-fights; we went to see
men hanged. With all this we had a broad-blown comic sense. We
had Hogarth, and Bunbury, and George Cruikshank, and Gill-
ray. We had the Shepherd of the "Noctes," and we had Dickens.
—Andrew Lang

This is only a renewal of a timeworn complaint. The interesting thing to note is that the list of "broad-blown" humorists
is headed by Hogarth—Hogarth, who preached as consistently as
did Bunyan, and whose sermons—as sound as Bunyan's—were, we
are asked to believe, regarded by his own generation as comic. Mr.
Edmund Blunden tells us authoritatively that Charles Lamb wrote
the first study of this great painter in which his genius was ana-
lyzed as being "far above mere burlesque"; and that in so doing the
writer was well aware that his point of view was unpopular, inasmuch as England preferred the joke to the sermon. Lamb's attitude
was firmly fixed when, as a child, he gazed day after day upon the

---

* From *In Pursuit of Laughter*, 1936.

prints of *The Rake's Progress* and *The Harlot's Progress* which hung on the walls of Blakesware. Children are impervious to satire, and these pictures are not satiric. They tell their story with violence, but violence restrained within the limits of accuracy. "Other prints we look at," said Lamb, "these we read"; and few adults can peruse paintbrush fiction with the deep attention, the lasting memory, of a child. Compare Hazlitt "bursting his sides" over an artist "whose pictures are a jest-book from one end to the other" with Lamb's seriousness, and his prim commentary in a letter to Thomas Manning: "In my best room is a choice collection of the works of Hogarth, an English painter of some humor."

"Some humor" has a chilling sound; but Lamb's delight in the chimney sweeper who stands grinning in the *March to Finchley* is a tribute to mirth "snatched out of desolation." Sweeps were dear to Hogarth as to Lamb because they were part and parcel of "London with-the-many-sins." Hogarth painted the London streets as other artists painted hills and meadows; and that "prodigious abundance of human knowledge," which is our wonder and delight, was the gift of the great city to her favorite son. Lamb loved these crowded canvases with not a "furniture face" in the crowd. He loved the littered rooms. Not a cat or a kitten, not a broken pipe or a picture on the wall escaped his close attention. If he wondered a little why so many depraved characters were noseless, he granted to the delineator the right to deal with features as he felt inclined.

It was a strong-stomached generation. Nothing was coarse enough to sicken it. It was an outspoken generation which called things by their biblical names. Hogarth had the good fortune to belong to his own time as distinctively as he belonged to his own race and to his own birthplace. "He was a moralist after the fashion of eighteenth-century morality," says Mr. Austin Dobson; "not savage like Swift, nor ironical like Fielding, nor tender like Goldsmith; but unrelenting, uncompromising, uncompassionate; peopling his canvas with vivid types of that cynical and sensual, brave and boastful, corrupt and patriotic age."

What is perfectly plain to Mr. Dobson is Hogarth's careful exclusion of humor from scenes where it might have softened the moral he meant to convey. The *Election Prints* are triumphantly comic. They deal with a subject which has provoked laughter for generations, and which, in our own time, George Birmingham has made as absurd and as diverting as ever. There is no subtlety in Hogarth's treatment of this familiar theme. He did not know the meaning of the word. His *Canvassing for Votes* has the simple candor of *Pickwick*. It was a great help to the painter to know that a vote could be bought like any other piece of merchandise in the open market, and that nobody paid more than it was worth. Our modern system of polling presents no such compensatory features.

Hogarth *was* uncompassionate. So presumably was Rhadamanthus, and there is something Rhadamantine in Hogarth's administration of justice. Thackeray in an unregenerate moment confessed to a sentiment of pity for Tom Idle, the apprentice whose name damned him from the start. He said he was glad that the Toms of his day had a better chance than when Hogarth painted and Fielding hanged them. But then Thackeray also confessed to a downright affection for the Artful Dodger and Charley Bates, an affection which Dickens (who did not hesitate to make his young thieves amusing) would have condoned, but which Hogarth would have thought indefensible. *Industry and Idleness* is a sermon undisguised, with every circumstance fitted neatly into place, which is the privilege of the preacher. But to one who has known it from early childhood, as Lamb knew his *Harlot* and his *Rake*, and has believed in it with the credulity of innocence, the prints are charming, especially the one in which the correct young couple are singing out of the same hymn book in church. And the antiquarian cannot fail to be pleased when the industrious apprentice marries his master's daughter, and the butchers in the street play manfully on the "hymenaean," that combination of marrowbone and cleaver which when properly struck produced, so we are assured, "no despicable clang."

This is cheerful if not laughable. Hogarth had then no more thought of diverting his public than had Solomon when he said, "Go to the ant, thou sluggard." No more than when he painted *Gin Lane* and *Beer Street* to show that destitution and disease followed the drinking of imported Hollands (which entered England with

William the Third), and that health and prosperity blessed all good topers who drank home-brewed beer:

—warming each English generous heart
With liberty and love.

It was, as Mr. Dobson has noted, a patriotic age, and Hogarth was nothing if not a patriot. Foreigners to him meant Frenchmen (he had been to France and did not like it), and the most despicable thing about them was their leanness. Pampered priests might be swollen with food, but the rest of the people were starvelings. The curious notion that the nation, as a nation, lived on frogs was prevalent, and was considered comical. Even Garrick, who knew better, made merry over the idea that such a diet could nourish soldiers:

Beef and beer give heavier blows
Than soup and toasted frogs.

A century later the same thought found expression in an Ingoldsby Legend which pictured "a cold sirloin big enough to frighten a Frenchman."

Hogarth's antipathy to France was more than a distaste. It was a sound, all-embracing disapproval which included every circumstance of life. "Poverty, slavery, and innate insolence covered with an affectation of politeness, give you a true picture of the manners of the whole nation," he wrote with that pleasing self-assurance which the civilized man occasionally shares with the savage.

Holland was less iniquitous (being unvisited) than France; but its intoxicant was so deadly that it made the very houses in Gin Lane totter to their fall. Lamb, who compared this terrible picture to Poussin's *Plague at Athens*, gave it precedence as being more imaginative and more replete with strange images of death. "Every thing contributes to bewilder and stupefy. The houses tumbling about in various directions seem drunk"—whereas the Athenian dwellings remain untouched by disease. It certainly did not occur to this sympathetic critic to see anything humorous in the scene, or he would not have made his comparison (no one is expected to laugh at the plague); but he is the only commentator who does not draw our attention to the fact that the single evidence of prosperity in Gin Lane is given by the pawnbroker's shop, whereas the same business in Beer Street languishes for lack of custom. Times had changed since the days of Skelton when a workman's wife would pawn her husband's cap and hood

Because the ale is good.

Hogarth's enmity toward all things foreign extended itself to those Continental artists who were popularly spoken of as the "old masters." Rembrandt was his particular detestation (he had never seen the *Night Watch*), and Correggio ran a close second. Having painted his *Sigismonda* to show that he could "rival the ancients on their own ground," he refused to sell the picture for less than four hundred pounds, that being the sum for which a presumed Correggio (really a Furini) had been recently bought in London. Possible purchasers being unable to see the compelling force of this argument, *Sigismonda* remained unsold; and the painter, nailing his colors to the mast, forbade his wife, or widow, to part with it for less than the original price. After her death it was bought by the Boydells for fifty-six guineas, and now hangs in the National Gallery. The best thing that critics have found to say about it is that it is in excellent preservation.

Hogarth's portraits had better fortune, the most immediately successful being that of Garrick as Richard III, for which, as he proudly tells us, he was paid two hundred pounds; "more than any English artist ever received for a portrait, and that too by the sanction of several painters who had previously been consulted about the price, which was not given without mature consideration." Garrick was a difficult subject to paint because, though he could assume at will any expression he chose, he could not, or did not, keep that expression long. The Richard III look passed into something less tense while Hogarth was striving to convey it to the canvas. On the other hand, it is said that the actor was of help to the artist when the latter was endeavoring to paint a portrait of the dead Fielding. Garrick did not in the least resemble Fielding; but he could mould his features into something which was like a resemblance because it conveyed characteristics. The gay little sketch of Mrs. Garrick taking the pen from her husband's hands passed eventually into the possession of George IV, who, unlike his predecessors, knew a good thing when he saw it.

The friendship between Hogarth and Garrick was firm and lasting. "He is a great and original Genius," wrote the player to Churchill. "I love him as a Man and reverence him as an Artist. I would not for all the Politicks and Politicians in the universe that you two should have the least cause of ill-will toward each other." In his prologue to *The Clandestine Marriage* he gave spirited praise to "matchless Hogarth," to the artist "who pictured Morals and Mankind, and whose object in so doing was to make mankind more moral." On that point, at least, there was never any doubt.

Walpole, who considered that "as a painter Hogarth had but slender merit," patronized him timidly, and invited him to dine with the poet Gray—a not very successful dinner. Host and guest had but little in common save an intense aversion to cruelty, especially cruelty to animals, in which regard they were, as Mr. Lang avers, far in advance of their time. Yet Walpole said one word—and said it with his customary precision—that would have given more pleasure to Hogarth than all the praise that has ever been lavished upon him: "He observes the true end of comedy—reformation."

Dr. Johnson and Hogarth first met at the home of Richardson. Hogarth, a warm Hanoverian, was expressing his amazement that George II, whom he considered a clement man, should have refused a pardon to Dr. Cameron—as guiltless a rebel as ever graced a scaffold. Johnson, who had been standing somewhat apart looking out of a window, came forward suddenly and burst into a torrent of words, accusing the King of harshness and heartlessness. Hogarth, unacquainted with the speaker, was petrified with wonderment at his manner, which was agitated to the verge of violence, and at his arguments, which were persuasive and convincing. He reached the justifiable conclusion that the stranger was certainly mad, and that his madness was certainly inspired.

The two men were eminently fitted to appreciate each other's merits. Hogarth said to Boswell that Johnson's conversation was as far above the talk of other men as Titian's portraits were above those of Thomas Hudson; a comparison which proves that there was at least one old master whose greatness the British painter reverently admired. Dr. Johnson's emendation of Garrick's epitaph on Hogarth is certainly an improvement on the original. The two lines,

Here Death has closed the curious eyes
That saw the manners in the face,

show what can be done with a simple phrase, "the curious eyes," when it chances to be the right one.

The jovial parson who is ladling out punch in the *Modern Midnight Conversation* was a relative of Dr. Johnson's, a gentleman named Ford. As the print hung on the walls of the dining-room at Streatham, the doctor had every opportunity of identifying his kinsman. He does not seem to have taken umbrage at the discredit done the cloth, being the most lenient as well as the staunchiest of churchmen; ready to forgive a laggard for not attending the service on Sunday, provided he doffed his hat when he passed the sacred edifice on week-days. His comment on Ford was brief and calm: "I have been told he was a man of good parts; profligate but not impious."

Among the points of resemblance between Hogarth and Dr. Johnson may be reckoned a strong distaste for Papists and dissenters. Methodists appear to have affected Hogarth as Puritans affected *Hudibras*. The confused medley entitled *Credulity, Superstition, and Fanaticism* is supposed to be directed against Methodism, though no member of that church, nor of any other, would ever know it. It is true that Whitefield's "Journal" is placed prominently on a hassock under the reading desk, a hassock which in the first impression was occupied by a dog wearing a collar inscribed G. Whitefield. But as that far-travelled preacher was as much of a Calvinist as a Methodist, and as all forms of religion outside the English Establishment are impartially insulted in both prints, honors are easy. Hogarth painting allegory is as lost as Fielding would have been writing a symbolic Maeterlinckian drama. His passion for detail traps him into strewing his canvas with an assortment of mysterious odds and ends, every one of which means something that it isn't.

The respect accorded to such work as *Credulity, Superstition, and Fanaticism,* and the obscure *Bathos,* was due to the firmly established belief that, as Hogarth was primarily a moralist, every picture preached. Walpole, indeed, observed that "for useful and deep satire the print on the Methodist is the most sublime"; but Walpole's dislike for this particular brand of dissenters was as strong as Hogarth's, or as Dr. Johnson's, or as Sydney Smith's. Anything that could be construed into an attack upon them would have seemed to him sublime. *The Bathos* was designed as a travesty on the unforgiven "old masters"; but it would have answered just as well as a satire on ambition, or covetousness, on war, or peace, on ignorance, or learning. The main thing was to make sure of a moral which, like the Application of Aesop's Fables, took up much time and attention. If there was a slackening on the painter's part, he was promptly reminded of his duty. One admirer wrote to warn him that he had rivals in art, but that no one had ever attempted to equal him in the moral walk. Another besought him, as a moralist, to protest against the cruelty and cupidity of the cockpit, which he did after a fashion so lusty that his contemporaries may not have recognized the very popular print as a remonstrance.

It is hard to believe with Mr. Blunden that Charles Lamb was the first writer to raise the genius of Hogarth "far above mere burlesque," when we read the kind of things which were written during the painter's lifetime and immediately after his death. His prints were used as texts for sermons, and were commented upon with that sincere regard for the obvious which is the most popular characteristic of the pulpit. A volume entitled *Hogarth Moralized* was published in 1768 by John Trusler, a gentleman who did not hesitate to paint the lily, and whose kindly purpose it was to assist people to see what they could not possibly miss. Thus the *Harlot's Progress* teaches us that "a deviation from virtue is a departure from happiness"; and *Marriage à la Mode* enables us to "form a just estimate of the value of riches and high life when abused by prodigality or degraded by vice." Commenting on *Industry and Idleness*, Mr. Trusler calls our attention to the happy crowds that turn out to see the industrious apprentice made Lord Mayor of London, and to the no less happy crowds that turn out to see the idle apprentice hanged, and observes with sprightly intelligence: "After this it would be unnecessary to say which is the more eligible path to tread." Even the portrait of Garrick as Richard III, which, being but a portrait, would seem innocent of texts, conveys its lesson to the world. Mr. Trusler goes back of Hogarth, back of Shakespeare, and landing safely in history, 1485, is able to authoritatively inform us that "naught is productive of solid happiness but inward peace and serenity of mind."

And this was the generation which we are bidden to believe regarded Hogarth's prints as a giant jest-book. This was the England envied by Mr. Lang for it's "broad-blown comic sense." This was the artist, whom Lamb rescued from the ranks of "mere burlesque," and over whose pictures Hazlitt burst his sides with laughter. Who would venture to say that Hogarth's mirth is "heart-easing"? Better than any man that ever lived he knew how the grotesque elbows the terrible. The wise child, Charles Lamb, recognized this alliance. He felt it in the last scene of *The Rake's Progress*, where two finely dressed, simpering ladies have come to be entertained by the tragic absurdities of Bedlam.

The Four Stages of Cruelty are as definitely removed from the field of humour as from the field of art. So Hogarth meant them to be. He took little pains with the designs, and did not consider that careful engraving was necessary. He wanted them to be as cheap as possible so as to be within the means of the class he hoped to reach. They were intended for one purpose only, and he said that if they achieved this purpose he would be more proud of them than if he had painted Raphael's cartoons; a remark which proves that he did not undervalue the beauty of the cartoons.

Whether the depraved and vicious were made good and kind by these dreadful pictures we shall never know; but people who were already good and kind wrote lengthy homilies in praise of goodness and kindness. They even dropped into verse to make their words persuasive, and this verse was printed as an accompanying text for the illustrations. In the first and most hideous of the series a little lad pleads for the tortured dog, an incident which is thus described by the poet:

> Behold! a youth of gentler heart,
> To spare the creature pain,
> "O take," he cries, "take all my tart!"
> But tears and tart are vain.

The appeal is pleasantly reminiscent of a still more generous child in the ballad of the "Cruel Step-Mother":

> Then outspake the scullery lad,
> In a loud voice spake he:
> "Oh spare her life, good master cook,
> And make your pies of me."

Horace Walpole was so deeply impressed by the *Four Stages of Cruelty* that he read into the fourth (which is really an anticlimax, being only a dissection room with nobody cruel in it) a moral which he proclaimed solemnity to his world: "How delicate and superior is Hogarth's satire when he intimidates in the College of Physicians and Surgeons that preside at the dissection, how the legal habitude of viewing shocking scenes hardens the human mind, and renders it unfeeling. The president maintains the dignity of insensibility over an executed corpse, and considers it but as the object of a lecture." How else could he have considered it, we naturally ask; but it is only fair to say that Tom Nero's corpse, being of Walpole's mind, appears to be protesting gruesomely against the liberties taken with it—liberties which are loathsome without a suggestion of purpose. What, one wonders, did the travelled Walpole think of the serene and serious Tulip discoursing to his seven associates in Rembrandt's *Lesson in Anatomy*? A certain horror emanates from that great canvas, but it is an awe-inspiring horror; it has the dignity of science and the seemliness of art.

There is no shadow of doubt that Hogarth's contemporaries regarded the *Enraged Musician* as purely comic, and were by way

of thinking that *Distrest Poet* diverting. The musician is plainly a
foreigner, and it serves him right to be deafened by the racket of
a London street. Today, when noise is one of the recognized evils
of the world, our sympathy for the poor fiddler is modified by the
thought that he lived and died before the advent of the radio. The
din that torments him is, after all, transient. The bawling woman,
the pipe-playing Jew, the child with a drum will pass on, they are
only human; the radio alone has the infernal permanence of mech-
anism.

The details of the *Distrest Poet* are made as absurd as possible to
lessen the painfulness of the subject. A poverty-stricken poet is as
tragic as a poverty-stricken knife-grinder (Chatterton was a poet);
but Hogarth desired the picture to be humorous, which, in a fashion, it is. Possibly he also desire *A Modern Midnight Conversation* to
be as amusing as satire could make it. English critics were disposed
to think it a temperance tract of tremendous force and vigour; but
in Germany, where the plate was very popular, its moral lesson
played a minor rôle. It may be found painted on German porcelain
pipes, and engraved on snuff boxes. If the drinker who is vomiting
his liquor, and the drinker who tumbles headlong and wigless to
the floor, illustrate the tract, the drinker who is trying to light his
pipe with a candle, and lights his sleeve instead, is felicitously and
flawlessly funny.

Hogarth himself was a man of temperate habits and of cheerful
conversation; easily offended, needlessly quarrelsome, and staunchly
loyal to his friends. He had the reputation of being parsimonious,
for no apparent reason save that he paid his debts, which seems to
have been considered a miserly thing to do. He did not believe that
the poor were more virtuous than the rich, but he loved fair play.
Had he been a sportsman, he would have been best pleased when a
wise and wary hare eluded the dogs. He gave the chimney-sweeps
whom he sketched in *Chairing the Member* a half-crown apiece, and
he would not permit his servants to take fees from clients who came
to have their portraits painted. Like all self-made men, he under-
valued the things he did not know. He was more insular than Hannah More, and his "clamorous rudeness" in France expressed his
annoyance that even such an inferior country should be peopled

by Frenchmen. His friends loved and honored him, and told pleasant stories of his candour, simplicity, and absentmindedness. He went once to visit Beckford, then Lord Mayor of London, driving sedately in his new coach decorated with a highly emblematic crest; and, coming out into the pouring rain, forgot all about the waiting vehicle, and walked home drenched and unconcerned as in his apprentice days.

A coach indicates extravagance, but Hogarth had little chance to be extravagant. His paintings sold badly because of his absurd insistence on auctioning them. The six masterpieces which make up *Marriage à la Mode* were timidly purchased in 1750 for a hundred and twenty-six pounds. In less than fifty years they were resold for fourteen hundred pounds, and now they are worth any conceivable sum. The admirable and highly comic *Election* series were bought by the wise Garrick for two hundred guineas, and became the most precious possession of his life. *The March to Finchley*, a picture of irresistible and irreclaimable disorder, was first dedicated to George the Second, who having, as Walpole expresses it, "little propensity to refined pleasures," considered it an insult to his Foot Guards, and expressed such Hanoverian wrath that the dedication was transferred to the King of Prussia, as "an encourager of Arts and Sciences." That redoubtable monarch, who tolerated no disorder, but to whom no flattery came amiss, made a handsome acknowledgment of the compliment. The painting was sold by lottery, and Hogarth gave the unpurchased tickets to the Foundling Asylum, which became the owner of this rather incongruous prize. A few years later the artist presented to the same institution his *Moses Brought to Pharoah's Daughter*, a perfectly suitable subject, but a bad picture, and therefore no prize at all.

If Hogarth was unfortunate in the sale of his paintings, the prints brought him steady income. They never lacked subscribers, and some of them, like *Industry and Idleness*, enjoyed years of unbroken popularity. Always at Christmastime there was a demand for these admonitory pictures, which we have reason to fear were given, like adminitory books, by uncles and godparents to imperfect youth. The most dramatic success was that accorded to the print of Lord

Lovat. When this unregenerate rebel was brought from Scotland to London, Hogarth met him at St. Albans, and made a rapid, masterly sketch of the eighty-year-old Jacobite for whom the scaffold was waiting. The trial, the execution, and the grim humour with which the condemned met his well-merited death, aroused so tense an interest that a London bookseller actually offered its weight in gold (which sounds like the prodigal East) for the copper plate on which the drawing was engraved. The offer was wisely refused. The prints were in such demand that the rolling presses worked day and night to supply them. They sold for a shilling each, and Hogarth made twelve pounds a day as long as the excitement lasted. He had also the pleasant recollection that the old lord was so glad to see him at St. Albans that he stopped midway in shaving to kiss his welcome visitor, and transferred the lather to his cheek.

In all this there is little to suggest the uproarious mirth which so delighted Hazlitt. The academic *Pool of Bethesda* and the *Good Samaritan* are decorous mural paintings presented by the artist to St. Bartholomew's Hospital. The spirited *Shrimp Girl* in the National Gallery expresses nothing but its own comeliness and bloom. The treatise on the *The Analysis of Beauty* amused unfriendly critics when it was published; but all that is left of it today is a serpentine line drawn on the palatte of Hogarth's best and most familiar self-portrait—the one with his dog, Trump, and what Leigh Hunt describes as "a sort of knowing jockey look." He was undoubtedly, as Hazlitt says, "one of the greatest comic geniuses that ever lived"; but—Mr. Lang to the contrary—it was not as a humourist that he valued himself and was valued by his contemporaries. He was actuated by a sincere desire to benefit and improve mankind, to leave the world better than he found it. "I have invariably endeavoured to make those about me tolerably happy," he wrote with enviable assurance, "and my greatest enemy cannot say I ever did an intentional injury; though without ostentation I could produce many instances of men that have been essentially benefited by me."

The rising fame of Sir Joshua Reynolds partially eclipsed Hogarth's renown. The amazing distinction of Reynolds's portraits, which seemed to convey to the beholder a revelation of what was essentially distinguished in English character, gave to his art a supreme and noble significance. For an understanding of his work no one could do better than read Santayana's *Soliloquies in England*. But Hogarth's fame rests on a sure foundation, and he has never lacked the affectionate regard of artists. Whistler, for example, praised him in season and out of season; but with Whistler, as with Lamb, it was a question of sympathetic recollection rather than of criticism. A little sick boy with a blistered chest tucked into an arm chair with a great volume of Hogarth's prints propped securely on the bed, near enough for him to turn the pages. It is as perfect a setting as that of the child, Charles Lamb, wandering solitary and content through the halls of Blakesware. He had only the *Harlot's Progress* and the *Rake's Progress* to delight him, whereas little James McNeill Whistler had the whole rich array spread out before his ravished eyes. "From this time until his death," said Mrs. Pennell, "he always believed Hogarth to be the greatest English artist who ever lived, and he seldom lost an opportunity of saying so."

The three words "from this time" give the situation away. For all of us there are memories which take the place of judgment. And moreover it was possible that Whistler hoped someone would disagree with him. Joseph Pennell gave an amusing account of Mr. Harper Pennington, who had been told that Hogarth was a caricaturist, and who thought, not unnaturally, that it had been left for his eyes to discover the artist. He looked long and closely at the superb collection in the National Gallery, and then said with emphasis to the amused Whistler, "Hogarth was a great painter." "Sh—sh!— yes—I know it," was the answer. "But don't you tell 'em."

If Reynolds portrayed the quality of distinction which is an attribute of the few, Hogarth portrayed the recognizable qualities of the many. Better than any artist, and as well as any author that ever lived, he understood and expressed British temperament in the bulk, "from the battle of Blenheim to the loss of the American colonies." It was this clear understanding which won for him the admiration of a very great man who likewise knew humanity in the bulk, and served it loyally. The last gratifying episode of Hogarth's life was the receipt of "an agreeable letter from the American, Dr. Franklin."

The painter was ill when this letter came; but it roused him from the apathy of weakness, and he scribbled a few lines meant to be the rough draft of an answer. Two hours later he was dead.

25

The Stage and the Pulpit*

There they stand, side by side, comments worth considering. Reading them, two thoughts penetrate into our puzzled minds. Had Sheridan remained faithful to his muse, he might have had a merry instead of a tragic old age. Had Sydney Smith lived up to his own severe dictum, he would certainly have died a bishop.

Hazlitt was but one year old when the first representation of *The School for Scandal* crowned Sheridan, not with roses only, but with unfading laurels. His words of praise are fraught with that desire to hear lost laughter which is the burden of every century's lament. He lived in a day of mediocrity. Lamb said of him that he was the only man in London whose conversation was worth listening to; and he might have said the same of Lamb, save that there was Theodore Hook flashing meteor-like through the social world, and there was Coleridge, who, if listened to long enough, was sure to say something memorable. Hazlitt, who had a passion for the stage, never disassociated Sheridan from his early triumphs, and probably never thought of him save as portrayed by Byron—as the irresistible talker to whom he (Byron), Rogers, and Moore had listened from six P.M. until one, without a yawn among them.

Yet Sheridan could be monumentally dull; witness his epilogue to Voltaire's *Sémiramis*. The play, as adapted by Captain Ayscough,

* From *In Pursuit of Laughter*, 1936.

had reduced a good-natured audience to the verge of despair; and before they could escape and forget it, the epilogue caught them, and preached them a sermon which they were in no mood to hear. It assumed that they had been deeply moved by the tragedy, and bade them turn this emotion to good account:

> Thou child of sympathy, whoe'er thou art,
> Who with Assyria's Queen has wept thy part,
> Go, search where keener woes demand relief,
> Go, while thy heart still beats with fancied grief,
> Thy lips still conscious of the recent sigh,
> The graceful tear still lingering in thine eye,
> Go, and on real misery bestow
> The blessed effusion of fictitious woe.

And this untimely discourse, this pretentious elegance (the "graceful tear" is worthy of the Swan of Litchfield), came from the pen of Sheridan, whose incomparable wit held friends by his side and creditors at bay, who could charm a bailiff and soften the heart of an attorney. "There has been nothing like it," said Byron, "since the days of Orpheus."

For some unfathomable reason Lord Hertford delayed to license *The School for Scandal* until a few hours before its first performance— a nerve-racking experience for everyone concerned. Its brilliant success ("a marvellous resurrection of the stage," said Horace Walpole) should have brought contentment even to Sheridan, who never was contented, and who had pronounced its predecessor, *The Rivals,* to be the worst play in the English language—which he knew very well it wasn't. A mysterious story concerning the origin of *The School for Scandal* attracted the attention of that large body of people who are ready to believe that anyone except the author wrote a book, or a play, or a poem. It was whispered that this masterpiece was the work of a nameless young lady in ill health who offered it to Sheridan for production, and who died immediately and conveniently at Bath, thus enabling the manager of Drury Lane to appropriate it as his own.

Why did a dramatist who was the first in his field abandon that field so lightly? Why, having written *The School for Scandal, The*

Critic, and *The Duenna,* thus easily outdistancing all rivals, did he turn his back upon the Muse, "crowned with roses and vine leaves," and take the dusty path of politics? It is true that the management of Drury Lane overwhelmed him with debt, and its destruction by fire in 1809 ruined him. But Sheridan would have been overwhelmed with debt in Utopia, and financially ruined in the Garden of Paradise. It was his appointed fate. Garrick could make the great theater pay its way, pay its company, and pay himself liberally; but Sheridan could do none of these things. Yet he had abundant energy, and was industrious, his only labor-saving device being to leave his letters unopened. For this no humane man will blame him; but it is an expedient which eventually leads to confusion. Another pardonable weakness was a disregard of time. "Sheridan's days are weeks," observed his sister-in-law, Mrs. Tickell, with the inflexible accuracy of relationship.

Byron is largely responsible for the popular view of Sheridan—a man always witty, often drunk, and never possessed of a shilling. On the last point he dwells with all the persistency of error. He says that Sheridan told him once, "I have never had a shilling of my own"— "though to be sure," mused the poet, "he contrived to extract a good many of other people's." In 1818 Byron wrote to Moore a letter full of good advice and good feeling: "Remember that Sheridan never had a shilling, and was thrown, with great powers and passions, into the thick of the world, and placed upon the pinnacle of success, with no external means to support him in his elevation."

But we know that as manager of Drury Lane he could count for some years on an income of several thousand pounds, and that after the production of *The School for Scandal* and *The Critic,* this income was temporarily increased. His first wife, the incomparable Miss Linley, "half muse, half angel," kept the accounts, and probably kept them badly—accounts not coming within the province of either angel or muse. That he had property is proved by the fact that he left it unencumbered to his second wife, and that she lived on it and on her own dowry until she died. It was insufficient to support him when he entered Parliament, and became "a splendid drudge without permanent pay." A brilliant and aggressive member of a brilliant and aggressive Opposition is not presumed to be on the road to wealth. He did, however, receive from his patron, the Prince of Wales, the sinecure of the Receivership of the Duchy of Cornwall, which carried a salary of eight hundred pounds. Altogether, he had a number of shillings of his own, and spent them with enjoyment.

Again it seems to have been Byron's ill or good fortune to have found Sheridan in a state of perpetual intoxication. "He got drunk very thoroughly and very soon." It was to Byron that he told the tale of his being locked up by a watchman who encountered him, tipsy and bellicose, in the London streets on the opening night of *The School for Scandal.* It was Byron who, after a convivial evening, conducted him carefully down "a damned corkscrew staircase, built before the time of spirituous liquors." It was Byron who disentangled the intricacies of a forgotten engagement with Rogers, and wrote the best explanation he could to the disappointed host: "Sheridan was yesterday at first too sober to remember your invitation; but in the dregs of a third bottle he fished up his memory, and found that he had a party at home."

The friendly relation between dramatist and poet was never broken. Sheridan told Byron that he cared little for poetry in general, and not at all for his, a verdict which Byron received with perfect good temper. He was not exacting on this point. To him we owe a truer knowledge of Sheridan than any biographers have given us. Byron delighted in his friend's wit, "always saturnine and sometimes savage"; insisted that his drunkenness was Bacchic, never reaching the Selinus stage; cherished an ardent admiration for his genius, and wrote a sincerely felt, but somewhat thunderous, monody on his death.

It was Sheridan's opinion that Byron would have made a good orator. He founded his view on the denunciations of "English Bards and Scotch Reviewers," having apparently no conception of an oration which should be otherwise than denunciatory. In the days of Burke and Fox the Opposition was a magnificent field for invective. George III was enough to drive any sane man into it; but the Prince of Wales was more than enough to drive any sane man out again. Sheridan boasted that the Prince gave him "his entire and unqualified confi-

dence." He said in the House of Commons: "The protecting friendship with which his Royal Highness has condescended to honor me
for so many years has formed the just pride of my life." The "entire and
unqualified confidence" meant that when the Prince had authorized
Fox to deny in the House his marriage to Mrs. Fitzherbert, and had
then frankly admitted it, he selected Sheridan as the man best fitted to
straighten things out with the lady. The "protecting friendship" meant
that, after summoning his friend night after night to Carlton House,
to talk over his affairs until four A.M., "not supping or with a drop of
wine," he did not, after Sheridan's death, send so much as a line of
condolence to his widow. It was left for the Duke of Wellington to
come forward with generous sympathy and offers of assistance. That
the Prince's all-embracing vanity was not lost on his loyal follower is
proven by Sheridan's careless remark: "What his Royal Highness particularly prides himself upon is the late excellent harvest."

Sheridan the legislator lost the sound of laughter which had
echoed through the life of Sheridan the dramatist and manager, and
the world has shared his loss. There was compensation, doubtless, in
the thrilled attention with which his fellow members of Parliament
listened to speeches three and four days long. The wonder to us now
is not so much the continuity of the speaker as the endurance of
the audience. Sheridan, like Gladstone, stood ready to reform the
solar system. Unhappily reformation, which is a profitable line of
business today, was a dead loss in 1788, when Warren Hastings was
impeached on charges of corruption and cruelty. The eloquence let
loose during that remarkable trial flooded the country, and we hear
faint washings of the tide today. Burke's fame rose to its highest pinnacle, Sheridan's was little less brilliant—and Hastings was acquit-
ted. So great was the enthusiasm aroused by Sheridan's first speech
in behalf of the begums of Oudh (even the dispassionate Sir Gilbert
Elliot pronounced it a masterpiece) that when the following year he
addressed the High Court of Parliament, men paid fifty pounds for
a seat. What is more remarkable, they blocked the entrance to Westminster Hall at six A.M., although the Court did not sit until noon.

It was a great opportunity, and Sheridan made the most of it. He
probably knew that the begums were rich and rapacious old ladies

playing a close game; but was there ever an Irishman who could not make a heartbreaking appeal in behalf of defenseless womanhood, and was there ever an Englishman who could remain unmoved by it? In the present instance, the Irishman appealed and the Englishmen listened for three days. On the third, when the impassioned utterances had reached their climax, Sheridan gasped out, "My Lords, I have done" (words they must have been glad to hear), and sank exhausted into the arms of Burke, who stood waiting to receive him. Only a few fragments of this oratory have been left to us—a circumstance not to be regretted. Burke always said that a speech which read well was a damned bad speech, and what he did not know on the subject was hardly worth the knowing.

The death of Burke and of Fox left the Opposition without leaders. The Prince of Wales, elevated to the Regency, found his former friends to be undesirable acquaintances. Sheridan, sad, infirm, hard pressed by creditors (whose natural desire to be paid has always been harshly criticized), was nevertheless surrounded by care and comfort. A sheriff's officer was domiciled in the house where he lay dying; but three of London's leading physicians came every day to help him die, and the very eminent Bishop Howley came every few days with the same laudable purpose. The sick man had never been indifferent to the pomp and glory of the grave ("There is snug lying in Westminster Abbey," he said); and thither after death he was borne in more state, and with a much longer procession, than had fallen to the lot of Fox, or even Pitt. It is said that he desired to be buried by the side of Fox, and that the "Poets' Corner" where he was laid held no attraction for him. But the Muse whom he had flouted in life triumphed in death, and has gone on triumphing ever since. We read about his speeches, but we see—when we can—his plays. If Mrs. Malaprop has grown wearisome, the Absolutes, father and son, still live. If the scandal-mongering of Snake and Lady Sneerwell becomes unbearably monotonous, the auction of the family portraits is good comedy. It illustrates to perfection Hazlitt's analysis of the play, "which professes a faith in the natural goodness as well as in the habitual depravity of human nature."

The playgoer laments to this day that Sheridan, aged thirty-one, turned his back upon the stage in favor of Parliament and speech making; but there is no shadow of doubt that he chose the life he loved. He did not want to walk with silver slippers in the sunshine; he wanted the stress and strain of battle. It may be remembered that Miss Jane Addams, the mouthpiece of American sensibility, said twenty years ago that "dullness will no longer be a necessary attribute of public life when gracious and grey-haired women become part of it." It would have been hard for Sheridan to grasp the lady's meaning. He lived and died in an age when men had a healthy preference for young and handsome rather than for gracious and gray-haired women (*vide* Burke on Marie Antoinette); but not even the youngest and handsomest could have sharpened the keenness of political strife. The begums were doubtless gray-haired if not gracious; but they were comfortably remote, and belonged to the world of abstractions like an after-dinner toast. The dramatist who held up to scorn "an old maid verging on the desperation of six-and-thirty" had no use for mature charms save when associated with affectionate and capable wifehood. Sheridan married twice. He was fairly fortunate in both ventures.

In the year 1794, when the great three days' speech before the High Court of Parliament enthralled Londoners, a fellow of New College, Oxford, named Sydney Smith, took orders because it was the only means of livelihood open to him. Sheridan, the wit, left the field in which he stood unrivalled to follow the flame of his ambition. Sydney Smith, the wit, left the field of law, which he coveted, and accepted work which was alien to his spirit. He made the best— a very shining best—of it all his life.

What more can a man do? Sydney's tastes were as extravagant as Sheridan's. He loved the pleasant things of life as well as did Sheridan. "My idea of Heaven," he said in an imprudent moment, "is eating *pâtés de foie gras* to the sound of trumpets." Yet poverty failed to cost him his self-respect. He begged from no man, borrowed from no man, owed no man a shilling, and managed—heaven knows how—to pay a debt of thirty pounds, which his brother Courtenay had contracted at Winchester, out of his Fellowship income of one hundred pounds. His exuberant gaiety ("He is the gayest man as well as the greatest wit in England," said Jeffrey), which militated against his weight as a churchman, would have been equally out of place in a barrister. The higher reaches of the law are ponderous. His laugh was infectious, but he laughed too much. "To a dissenter like myself," said Harriet Martineau, "there was something very painful in the tone always taken by Sydney Smith about Church matters." But Miss Martineau's immense seriousness was humor-proof, and she liked to do more than her share of talking. Sydney confessed that his recurrent nightmare was being chained to a rock, and being talked to—or at—by Macaulay and Harriet Martineau.

If dining out had been a profession, Sydney Smith would have stood at the head of it. His arrival at a dinner was hailed with rejoicings. He looked precisely what he was. The admirable canvas by Briggs might have been entitled "Portrait of a *Bon Vivant*." Naturally no prime minister could visualize him as a bishop. Lord Grey knew the soundness of his theology, and the value of his political services; but he also knew the weight of visualization. He offered in place of a bishopric the Residentiary Canonry of Saint Paul's Cathedral ("A snug thing, let me tell you"), which brought to the rector of Combe Florey an additional income of two thousand pounds for doing just what he liked best to do—live for three months of the year in London, and preach now and then a sensible and gentlemanly sermon. Yet the great city offered many pleasures to which he was singularly indifferent. He abhorred music, cared little for art, being just sufficiently interested to prefer a bad picture to a good one, and, strangest loss of all, disliked the drama, which ought to have brought him enjoyment. "I should not care if there were no theater in the world," he said. He learned to read Dickens, observing wisely that the soul of Hogarth had entered into the body of Dickens; but he missed a great deal—the rare perfection of Pecksniff, for example; a character drawn for our true delight, who should, by every ruling of art and nature, have been left secure in the seats of the mighty.

Sydney Smith's common sense was so broad, so deep, so steadfast that it reached the domain of wisdom. He combined the reasonableness and stability of the eighteenth century with the humane aspirations of the nineteenth; and if he were not always consistent, that was because nobody ever is, or ever has been. His aversion to cruelty was as all-embracing as Huxley's; he exempted no form of sport which brought pain to bird or beast; but his sympathy for poachers must have made him forget the pitiless traps in which they snared their prey; and his dream of eating *pâtés de foie gras* to the sound of trumpets ignored the calculated barbarity which produced the food he loved. Saintsbury compared his passion for justice to Voltaire's, giving the palm for simplicity and sincerity to the Englishman who was uncontaminated by personal vanity. "A free altar and an open road to Heaven" was his slogan, and it would have been hard to find a better. His sermons were excellent, but he never expected to hold congregations spellbound. He granted them the privilege of distraction. "A sparrow fluttering about a church is an antagonist which the most profound theologian in Europe is wholly unable to overcome."

There he was wrong. He was always wrong when he dealt offhand with matters beyond his ken. The Tullamore cat, that leaped from the rafters onto a woman's head and ran over the shoulders of the congregation, failed to distract the men and women who were listening to John Wesley. "None of them cried out any more than if it had been a butterfly." Sydney Smith's distaste for Methodists was as strong as his distaste for Quakers. He considered them both unreasonable, and reason and religion were to him synonymous terms. But he could not divine the strength of a current by standing on its brink, and he could not be brought to believe that the leadership of men is seldom the reward of intelligence.

And what of the laughter which was his perquisite as a wit? It trailed him through life, and was too closely associated with his name. How did it happen that Sheridan's laugh was rare and sardonic, and Sydney's frequent and jovial? Sheridan had to desert the drama and enter Parliament to be as condemnatory as he chose. Sydney, who had a pulpit from which to safely censure, and Swift before him as a model, felt no inclination for the task. The sense of comedy in life was too strong for him. He saw the world as Vanity

Fair with a background of cruelty and the stake waiting for Faithful, but with absurdities well to the fore. His lightest sayings are the most amusing. He went to see Newton's portrait of Moore, and observed gravely to the artist: "Couldn't you contrive to throw into his face a stronger expression of hostility to the Church establishment?" He fed his pigs on some fermented grain, not wishing to waste it, and was pleased to report them as "happy in their sty, grunting the National Anthem." He said that the attempt to heat Saint Paul's Cathedral was like trying to heat the county of Middlesex. Occasionally there is no visible desire to be funny, only a juxtaposition of ideas which lends humor to a casual remark. "My brother Courtenay," he mused, "has, I am told, a hundred and fifty thousand pounds, and he keeps only a cat." This was the brother whose debt of thirty pounds Sydney paid at Oxford; this was the brother whose death left him a rich man (the cat apparently did not inherit); and this was the brother to whom he said: "We both of us illustrate contradictions in nature. You rise by your weight, and I fall by my levity."

Which proves that the lost bishopric, while never essential to Sydney Smith's happiness of heart, was ever present in his mind. It was the price he paid for laughter.

About the Editor

John Lukacs is the author, most recently, of *Blood, Toil, Tears, and Sweat: The Dire Warning: Churchill's First Speech as Prime Minister.* He taught for many years at Chestnut Hill College in Philadelphia and makes his home in Chester County, Pennsylvania.